The Other Half
of
My Soul

The Other Half of My Soul

A Novel
by
Bahia Abrams

Grateful Steps, Inc.
1091 Hendersonville Road
Asheville, North Carolina
www.gratefulsteps.com

Library of Congress Control Number
2007936277

Abrams, Bahia
The Other Half of My Soul

ISBN 978-0-9789548-3-3 Hard Cover
ISBN 978-0-9789548-4-0 Paperback

First Edition

Cover design © 2007 by: Kirsten Quatela

www.theotherhalfofmysoul.com

To Sarah and Bill

Good friends are priceless.
I could not have done this without you.

ACKNOWLEDGMENTS

I am grateful to the author Marshall Frank, who had once been my teacher. If it were not for his encouragement, I would never have begun this book.

When ideas for a plot began tumbling in my head, I looked for someone, anyone, who would listen. How fortunate for me to find genuine love and interest from my dear friends, Sarah and Bill Seepe. Out of default, they became my first editors. From the initial chapter that I e-mailed to them, all the way through to the final page, their commitment was steadfast and their guidance invaluable.

Dee Weiner-Corets advised me early on in defining the two main characters, and as I got closer to the end, her comments and edits were significant. I treasure her friendship.

From the beginning, my publisher, Micki Cabaniss Eutsler, believed in me and my story. Her patience, support, and counseling went beyond what I could have hoped for in a publisher.

I was privileged to have Dan Cabaniss edit the final manuscript. He provided insight that I could not have found anywhere else.

Moreover, I want to thank my husband for his guidance, and Joan Copperthwaite and Karon Korp for their input. To my close friends Judy Cordover and Rhonda Sachais, and to my children, all of whom I cherish, thank you for providing me with love and moral support while I was writing this book.

AUTHOR'S NOTE

I knew that if I were to write a first novel, it had to be in a style different from what I had been taught in my journalism classes. I approached this narrative by lowering my defenses, exposing my vulnerabilities, and deeply connecting to the thoughts swirling in my brain. Sitting at the computer, I wanted to know the formula for committed love, and to learn of the seeds that fuel hatred. Through tears and smiles, anger and joy, I weaved together a work of fiction, drawing not only from my own life experiences but also from historical events, current happenings, actual places, and life's truths—revealing, all along, the darkness and the light of humanity.

From my son, who worked on the upper floors in the World Trade Center Towers and survived the attacks of 1993 and 2001, I learned so much. I am grateful he is alive. My friend Diana, a native of Bogotá, taught me about the jungles of southern Colombia and the trading of weapons for cocaine. My husband, an avid reader, brought to my attention not only the massacre at Hamah, Syria, but also the lawless region of South America known as the Triple Frontier. Spain, Morocco, New York, New Jersey, Maryland, and Washington, D.C. are places I have lived or visited. My descriptions of Syria and Lebanon were gathered from acquaintances who are native to those countries and who still return for visits. Syrian culture, language, food, and music are what I grew up with. Orthodox Judaism is the source of my beginnings. Additionally, I spent months on research in order to substantiate places and events, which I have intertwined throughout this story.

As vividly as my imagination could travel, there is no journey to equal the prescripts for the human race. Reflecting on reality, I created fictional characters and settings depicting absolute love and loyalty, hatred and intolerance, evil without conscience, and unconditional acceptance. May this story be for you, the reader, a catalyst that permeates the realm of your own visceral world and elevates you to a higher level of inner wisdom.

—Bahia Abrams

The Other Half
of
My Soul

ONE

The life of this world is only idle sport and play, and if you believe and guard against evil He will give you your rewards, and will not ask of you your possessions.—Surah 47:36

August 1996——Aleppo, Syria

Rami Mahmoud's future was planned. He was being given the chance for a new life—an opportunity to raise his status in a country that regarded him as a second-class citizen. Packing his oversized black duffel bag for the trip to America, Rami could barely contain the conflicting feelings of elation and uneasiness. Having excelled in all four of his exams and having attained top honors from his higher secondary school, Rami had stood out impressively with a perfect grade-point average. The ruling Baath Party in Syria and the government-backed terrorist group *al-Shahid* had noted his marked intelligence. They had been observing him from afar for many years.

* * *

Shortly after entering the University of Aleppo, Rami was summoned out of class one afternoon. Inside a small office, two emissaries dressed in military uniform greeted him. One had thinning hair, deep-set eyes, and a noticeable gap between his two front teeth. He was called Muhammad. The other, the one clearly in charge, was a slender man with a Hitler-like moustache. His dark, icy eyes and a long jagged scar prominently etched into his left cheek hardened his appearance. He answered to the name of Yousef.

Commending Rami on his superiority in school, Yousef informed him that in two weeks he would leave for the United States to study Spanish and philosophy at the University of Maryland at its College Park campus located in the suburbs of Washington, D.C. "Arrangements have already been made," Yousef said, stressing the importance of Rami accepting the offer placed before him. "Your tuition and expenses will be paid in full and you will be allowed two yearly trips home to see your family. In four years, you will be accorded the honor of going on *Hajj*, if you so choose."

Rami remained still. Yousef continued, "Following graduation, you will owe us seven years, maybe longer. You will work for the organization that is so generously sponsoring your education abroad."

Knowing better than to refuse his government or to question their motives, Rami silently speculated on the identity of his benevolent sponsor and questioned why Spanish and philosophy were to be the focus of his curriculum. *I am already fluent in Arabic, French, and English. What is the reason for another language? And why philosophy?* Rami had hoped to concentrate his studies on engineering and computers. His thoughts drifted to his best friend, Omar. It was just last winter that Omar had left to study in the United States at the University of Maryland. Politely, Rami smiled and accepted the offer.

"Over the next two weeks, Muhammad will instruct you on the rules and prepare you for your journey to America. Each day, at ten in the morning, he will pick you up by the moat at the Citadel. Muhammad will be driving a black car."

Muhammad looked at Rami and nodded once. Rami waited. When the two men had left and were no longer in sight, he bolted out of the building and toward the *souq* to tell his parents of the news.

* * *

Ibrahim and Salha Mahmoud were hard-working Shi'ite Muslims eking out a living in Aleppo, a city of three million people. They were part of a repressed minority dwelling in a country ruled by the dictatorship of the Assad family—Alawaites of the Baath Party who held all of the seats in government as well as the top positions in the military.

Ibrahim and Salha resided in a small, archaic stone house within the narrow confines of the Babal-Qinnisrine Gate, a neighborhood that still looked much like what it had been when it was the ancient departure point on the old route to Damascus. Their eldest child and only son, Rami, was born August 10, 1978. The ensuing years had brought them four daughters. Struggling to provide for five children, the couple was grateful for their tiny stall in the Aleppo Souq—the largest covered marketplace in all of Syria.

Their large extended family consisted of grandparents, parents, aunts, uncles, sisters, brothers, nieces, nephews, and cousins. Together, they shared celebrations, burdens, laughter, and tears. Firmly interconnected, this religious Shi'ite clan followed the Islamic law of *Sharia*, praised Allah three times a day, observed holidays, and sent their young to *madrasa*, an Islamic school. Enduring inferior Shi'ite status in Syria only intensified their strong bonds.

* * *

Anxious to tell his parents the news, Rami raced toward the souq. The streets of Aleppo were alive with noisy people, blasting car horns, and loud traffic police. Skirting around the congestion, his long legs carried him closer to the vast exterior of stone archways. Rami reached the marketplace and proceeded toward a familiar entrance. His lean, agile body zigzagged through the masses of shoppers and stalls. Arriving out of breath and eager to blurt out the changes about to happen in his life, he found his mother and father swamped with buyers who were haggling over prices for pistachios, dried apricots, candied dates, nut-filled pastries, and round loaves of Syrian bread.

Suppressing what he was bursting to say, Rami struggled with his patience. He hoped that the customers would soon make their purchases and go away. Motioning to his parents, he indicated a need to talk. They, in turn, gestured for his help. Their son's good looks, charming ways, and adept negotiating skills never failed to bring in exceptional prices.

Almost two hours passed. A concentration of shoppers continued to gather around the tiny stall. Then, unexpectedly, Rami's Aunt Zakieh and Uncle Abu appeared. "*Khaltee! Khallee!* We need a break. I need to talk with *Imee* and *Eby*. It is so important." He turned to his parents, "Come, let us go."

"Just a minute," Salha interrupted, taking a moment to embrace her sister Zakieh. "We have been busy all day with no relief. Rami is bursting to tell us some news and we have not had a quiet moment to talk with him."

"What is so important, Rami?" With a twinkle in her eyes, Zakieh clasped her hands in joy. "Is there going to be a wedding? Are you getting married?"

"No, no, I am not getting married, Khaltee. I am much too young for that." Impatiently, Rami began walking, urging both his parents on. "Let us go for coffee."

"Yes, all of you, go for coffee," Abu grinned. "Your khaltee and I will take good care of the business. But you must promise that we will be the first to hear the news after your parents."

* * *

Sipping Turkish coffee in a small, crowded café, Ibrahim asked, "Rami, what is so urgent that it cannot wait until tonight when we are home? And why are you *not* in school?"

Rami gestured for his parents to lean in closer. In a hushed voice so as not to draw attention, he told them about the encounter with the two men in military uniforms. "In two weeks, I will leave for America to attend school in the United States. I will go to the University of Maryland and live in an apartment with Omar."

Salha grabbed hold of her son's arm, "Whaaat?"

"Shhh, Imee, other people do not need to hear our conversation."

"Two weeks? You are leaving in *two weeks*?" A sense of urgency seemed to drive Salha to the brink of imbalance. "I do not want you to go. You will not go!"

"Just a minute, Salha. It seems we do not have a choice." Speaking quietly, Ibrahim tried reasoning with his wife. "Let us try to think clearly and not set ourselves up for big problems. A bad mark against us will make it more difficult to marry off our daughters. And our stall at the souq could be taken from us. We cannot oppose the government." Ibrahim was determined to avoid blemishing his family's reputation. "Remember Faisal? He went to the University of Maryland and is now a professor of civil engineering at Tishreen University. He is highly respected and consults on all kinds of construction projects. And what about Hossam? He also went to the University of Maryland and is now an executive at Syrianair. And Hoda? She studied in America and is now writing for *al-Baath* in Damascus. Maybe getting an education in America will not be so bad. Rami, I think you will do well in America." Inwardly, Ibrahim hoped that Rami would be their ticket to a better life.

* * *

"But Ibrahim, we all know what a bad country America is. Everywhere there is corruption, greed, violence, sex, drugs, liquor, wild parties. We read about it. We see it on television. I know that Rami will not be safe there. I am afraid for him." Salha believed that once Rami left, she would lose him to American influences. "My son, I beg of you not to go. We can hide you somewhere. My brother in Tarsus will welcome you. You will be safe in Turkey."

"Imee, it will be okay. You and Eby have taught me well. And I will be with Omar. In his letters, he writes of a good life in America. Tomorrow, we will go and talk with Omar's parents. I do not want you to worry. I will be fine, really. And I will write often."

Ibrahim said nothing. Salha babbled senselessly, "Maybe I can talk with the two men. I will tell them we need you to help at the souq. That you are a good boy. A good student. Very smart. Never been in trouble. A good son. A good brother. Syria needs you here. It would be wrong to send you to America, to . . . to that horrible country that has so many Jews. Even more Jews than in Israel." Turning her head, she spat twice on the ground to keep away the evil spirits.

Ibrahim reached under the table and touched his wife's hand to quiet her. "Salha. Rami. Let us not continue speaking here. Wait until we are home." He stood. "We must get back to the souq and not take advantage of Zakieh and Abu much longer."

* * *

Festivities and dinners filled Rami's last few days. Relatives and friends threw parties. Aunts, uncles, and grandparents overwhelmed him with gifts, good wishes, and the delicious Syrian food that he so much enjoyed.

Through all the merriment, Salha could not be consoled. She felt sure she would never see her only son again. "Why, Allah, why are you doing this to us?" she wailed over and over.

* * *

Early in the morning on the day Rami was scheduled to leave for America, the family was awakened by pounding on the front door. Salha quickly donned her long black dress and covered her hair with a black *hijab*. Ibrahim scrambled to pull on his trousers. Rami and his four sisters jumped out of their beds, slipped into some clothing, and scurried to the front door.

In the tiny vestibule, the family looked at each other, then at the door, all suspecting the worst. Ibrahim motioned for Rami to open the door. *Let them see my son first*, he reasoned. Cautiously, Rami lifted the heavy latch while everyone held their breaths. Slowly, he cracked the squeaky wooden door. His extended family greeted them with beaming faces and armloads of food. "Surprise!"

"*Yallah! Yallah*! Hurry! All of you go wash and dress," Zakieh directed the family. "We have prepared a big breakfast. And do not worry, Salha, we will clean up everything. The only thing you have to do is get yourself ready and come eat breakfast. And we are all going with you to the airport to see Rami off."

"What a nice surprise." Ibrahim was relieved. He would not have to deal with his wife's hysterics at the airport.

* * *

After breakfast, Rami carried his large duffel bag outside and set it into the trunk of their very old, gray Mercedes. Ibrahim followed his son. A gentle breeze cooled the summer air. "A beautiful day, Eby. I think it is a good omen."

"*Insh'allah*." Ibrahim embraced his son.

"Eby, from you I have learned so much . . . integrity and patience. I will always carry your guidance with me."

"I thank Allah for giving me a son. Your arrival into our lives has been a blessing. I remember when I first saw you. You were crying and scared and . . . " Ibrahim caught himself. "Write often so we do not worry. Keep to Islam, our way. The Shi'ite way. Pray to Allah every day, attend *juma*, observe our holidays, and remain faithful to the month of Ramadan. And Rami . . . keep to our dietary laws. Only *halal* food." With the back of his fingers, he smoothed over his son's cheeks. "Do not get mixed up with American girls.

And keep away from the Jews. Do you understand what I am trying to tell you?"

Perturbed that he had to listen to his father's litany for the twenty-seventh time in two weeks, Rami kept his tongue and respectfully replied, "Yes, I do."

"And always remember that you are Muslim. A Shi'ite. *Allah maak.*"

The exchange was interrupted by the noisy group coming out of the house. "Let's go everybody," yelled Abu, directing them all into six small Suzuki trucks parked just outside the courtyard.

"Am I the only one not driving a Suzuki?" Ibrahim laughed as he climbed into his old Mercedes. There had been times Ibrahim wished for a small Suzuki so he could more easily maneuver the narrow streets. But the old car did run well. He had bought it cheaply from a friend so that he could fit his family of seven inside.

* * *

Leading the caravan out of the Babal-Qinnisrine Gate, Ibrahim steered the old vehicle south onto Highway 5 toward Damascus. For more than two hours, the procession traveled the modern road until they arrived in the capital city. Turning east, they drove parallel to Ash Shabiba Park, passing crowds of people congregated around benches—many were smoking, some read the daily paper, and others engaged in animated conversation. The streets were heavy with honking motorists and noisy traffic police. *Just like Halab*, Rami mused.

The convoy shifted around al-Abbasiyeen Square on al-Hamadani Street, passing more clusters of people and many shops and cafes. When the group veered south onto An

Nasra Street, they caught sight of the signs to International Airport Road. In unison, their horns blasted and they leaned out the open windows cheering vigorously.

Approaching the entrance to the airport, they encountered several checkpoints and were instructed on where to park. Emerging from their vehicles, the large band traipsed across the parking lot toward the British Airways terminal. Security police kept the group at bay while Rami checked in and got his boarding pass.

* * *

With a twinkle in his large brown eyes, Rami flashed his charismatic smile and asked the officers if it would be okay to say goodbye to each of his family members who had come all the way from Halab to see him off. After closely scrutinizing the group, one of the guards stepped back and nodded approvingly.

"Okay everyone, listen, this is as far as you can go." Quickly, Rami bid farewell to each relative. At the end of the line stood his own family. *We never had much money, but there was always an abundance of love to go around.* "I will miss all of you," he said to his sisters. "I plan to come back for each of your weddings. Take care of Imee and Eby. Be strong for them. They will need you." Rami's eyes welled and he swallowed back his sadness.

Reaching out to Salha, Rami already felt a sense of loss. "Allah could not have blessed me with a more special mother. Thank you for loving me and for teaching me how to love." Rami made a gentle fist and lightly tapped at his heart. "Imee, this place is for you. I will not be gone forever. I will be back soon."

With tears running down her cheeks, Salha reached out. "Rami, give me your word. You will keep away from American girls. And be careful of the Jews. America is full of them. Remember who you are. A Muslim. A Shi'ite Muslim. Allah maak."

Rami and his father searched one another's faces. "*Salaam.*"

TWO

I am my beloved's and his desire is for me.—— Solomon: The Song of Songs 7:11

August 1996——Brooklyn, New York

Tomorrow, Rayna Mishan would be moving out. It had been a long struggle. Coming from a Sephardic Jewish home that was steeped in orthodox religion and Syrian culture, it was taboo for a girl to leave home and go away to school.

"If you want to go to college, there are plenty of good schools right here in New York," her parents had argued. "And if you want to pursue journalism, what better school than Columbia University?" It was a point Rayna found hard to dispute. However, she was determined to have her way. Rayna would attend the University of Maryland at College Park, located just outside Washington, D.C.

* * *

Rayna was the youngest child and only daughter of Abe and Sarah Mishan. Abe was known to be overly protective of his daughter. He also showered her with frivolous gifts. Sarah, although not warm and affectionate, kept Rayna dressed in expensive clothes and made sure she had the best that money could buy. Growing up in a home with four older brothers, Rayna was both teased and pampered. The Mishans lived in a richly decorated six-bedroom house in an upscale neighborhood on Ocean Parkway in Brooklyn. It was a perfect location for them because their grandly appointed synagogue, where they were active members and big donors, was just across the wide boulevard.

Anchored in a strongly connected and deeply religious Syrian-Jewish community, the Mishans owned an even grander house at the shore in Deal, New Jersey, where they spent their summers with the other Syrian Jews. Passover holidays were celebrated in the Catskill Mountains with their large extended family.

Abe ran a successful lighting supply business with retail stores in nine states. Additionally, he owned vast amounts of valuable real estate. As Rayna's four brothers each came of age, Abe took them into the firm. Well entrenched in the Syrian community, the wealthy Mishan family was respected and admired for their kindness, generosity, and *tzedakah*.

With a population exceeding fifty thousand, the Syrian Jews made it their concern to know everyone in the community—or at least to know of someone's family, or to know of someone who knew someone. Gossip and judgments made the rounds. The rabbis and the religious and social rules defined their existence. Betrothals were made on the condition of parental approval, and it was taboo to marry outside the group. Sons and daughters lived under their parents' roof until they were wed. Girls were socialized to marry young, choose financially secure husbands, have many children, keep immaculate homes, and be superb cooks.

From kindergarten through twelfth grade, Rayna attended *yeshiva*, a Jewish day school. She was an eager and bright student. Although secular subjects mandated by the state were an integral part of the curriculum, learning Hebrew and religion were paramount.

In tenth grade, Rayna had begun to rebel. "I have my whole life to be married, to cook, and to have children. I want to do other things first. I want to go to college. I want to know the world. I want to have a career in journalism. I want to write. I don't want to have a husband before the age of twenty. And I certainly don't want to be stuck here in Brooklyn."

By eleventh grade, her protests grew stronger. "I hate how money and materialism dominate our way of life. I hate how our strict adherence to religious practices rules us. There are times I feel like I can't breathe, it's so stifling. And I hate how a man is measured by the amount of money he has or doesn't have, and a woman is measured by her beauty or lack of it. We are no better than the rest of the sanctimonious world."

* * *

Infuriated over her daughter's insistence to leave home and go away to college, Sarah tried to reason. "Syrian girls don't do these things. This is not how you were raised. This is not our way. Do you know what this will do to us? Is that what you want, to subject us to harsh disapproval in the community? For God's sake, Rayna, I just don't know where you're getting these crazy ideas. Use your head! You're smart and beautiful. You come from a wealthy, respected family.

You're a good catch. Men are lined up. You can have your pick. What in the world is wrong with you?"

To calm the situation between mother and daughter, Abe offered a compromise. "You can go to any college within daily commuting distance from home. New York City has the finest schools in the country and Columbia University . . ."

"No!" Rayna objected. "We've already been through the Columbia University bit enough times. I'm sick of it. I'm going away . . . somewhere. If you think you can keep me here, it won't work. If you threaten *not* to pay my way, I'll make it on my own." There was nothing her parents could say or do to change Rayna's mind.

"Well, then find a school that's near. No more than four hours away," Abe conceded, much to the dismay of Sarah.

So, after an exhaustive search of colleges within a four-hour radius, Rayna found one that met both her own and her father's approval. The University of Maryland at College Park had a sizable Jewish population, a good journalism school, and a Hillel on campus where Rayna could have her kosher meals and attend weekly *shabbat* services.

Still, her mother remained relentless. "It's not the same. Those Jews are *J-Dubbs*. Ashkenazie Jews. They're not our kind. We're Middle Eastern. They're European. They pray differently. They celebrate differently. They eat differently. And they believe differently. Their history and culture are not ours. They are not Sephardic. Your place is here. I want to see you get married and have children . . . and be with us!" In exasperation, Sarah threw her hands up, trying to control the urge to slap Rayna across the face. "What do you mean you'll go to Hillel for the holidays? My daughter will come home for the holidays."

* * *

The night before departure, Rayna was filled with anxiety and could not sleep. She fretted about the freshman rules requiring all first-year students to live on campus without a car, and she agonized over surviving in a large co-ed dorm. However, Rayna was grateful to her father for the generous donation to the college, which secured her a private room with her own private bath.

* * *

Early the next morning, while her parents leisurely ate breakfast, Rayna paced the large modern kitchen, huffing impatiently and unable to eat. "How much longer? I'm ready whenever you are."

Abe's misgivings surfaced. He smoothed his hand along Rayna's arm in a final effort to dissuade her. "Do you know how much we love you? Do you have any idea what this is doing to us? It's tearing us apart. Is there anything you want that we haven't given to you? Rayna, I beg you to rethink what you're about to do. It's not too late to stop it."

"No, Daddy. Let's not rehash this again. I'm ready to leave whenever you are." Rayna put her arms around her father's neck and kissed his cheek. "I wish you could understand that I'm not doing this to hurt either one of you. You've done nothing wrong. You've been the best parents you know how to be, living in these circumstances."

Visibly fuming, Sarah's voice was at high pitch, "Excuse me young lady. Just what do you mean by 'living in these circumstances'?"

"Mom, would you please let me finish!"

"No! We've heard enough. I never had such heartache from your brothers. I wish I had stopped after them. It would have spared me the aggravation I get from you. I didn't even want a fifth child. It was your father who . . ." Sarah's voice trailed off when Abe gave her a stern look.

Rayna's stomach wrenched. Tears welled and she turned away, not allowing herself to cry. Deep down, she always knew that her mother favored her four brothers over her. "I'm not bad."

With his frustration showing, Abe reached for Rayna's large suitcase. "In this one thing . . . this one big thing, you've gone against our wishes and our ways. But since you're now eighteen, we cannot legally stop you, can we?" Abe let out a long exasperated sigh. "You know, nowhere will you find a community like ours. Nowhere! We take care of our own. Good care! We pull together in hard times. Syrian Jews are good people. Why don't you look at all the positive instead of focusing so much on the negative?"

"Dad, I'm not leaving our community. I'm just going away to study journalism. I . . ."

"What's the use in talking anymore? Come on and help me get your stuff into the car. Your mother made some sandwiches and drinks to take with us. They're in the cooler."

* * *

Rayna climbed into the back seat of the blue Lexus. Sarah sat in the front passenger seat and stewed. Abe backed out of the garage and down the narrow driveway onto Ocean Parkway. Soon, the car crossed the Verrazano Bridge and headed south onto the New Jersey Turnpike. For three hours a deafening silence filled the vehicle.

As they approached Baltimore, Sarah turned around, "Rayna, would you mind getting some sandwiches and drinks out of the cooler?" She glanced at her husband, "Abraham, there's a rest stop in two miles. Let's pull off so we can eat and go to the bathroom." Always, when Sarah was angry, she addressed her husband by his full name—Abraham.

"Mom, we're so close, just another hour. Let's just get there. We can eat in the car. Daddy, do you mind?"

Abe said nothing and drove past the rest stop. In silence, Sarah simmered, furious over Rayna getting her way. At two-thirty, they drove onto the campus of the University of Maryland.

*　*　*

Abe, Sarah, and Rayna unloaded the vehicle, making several trips up to the dorm room. Abe then hooked up Rayna's computer and stereo while Sarah stoically helped her daughter unpack and get settled.

Regretting the past several hours, Rayna made an effort to show her appreciation. With her self-esteem much diminished, she moved closer to Sarah, reaching out to hug the woman. Sarah put her hand up, repulsing Rayna's advance.

*　*　*

By early evening, the three went to Hillel to eat. It was a place where they could keep to their strict kosher dietary laws. "You'll be very careful about eating only kosher food, won't you, Rayna?" Sarah admonished over dinner.

"Yes, Mom. No meat unless it's kosher. No pork. No seafood. No mixing meat and dairy." The tension between mother and daughter heightened. "I've been doing this all my life. For God's sake, Mom, I'm not going off to Mars. I'm going off to get a degree in journalism. I'm not straying from my religion. I'll eat at Hillel. Puhleeze give me some credit for knowing what to do, thank you very much."

After dinner, Abe and Sarah walked Rayna back to her dorm, then checked into the Rossborough Inn on campus.

* * *

In the morning, the three met for breakfast, then strolled around the grounds. The oppressive heat and high humidity of the Washington summer were in full bloom. In contrast, the atmosphere surrounding Rayna and her parents was frigid.

"Well, it certainly appears that Rayna has a full week ahead and we have far better things to do than hang around here. It's best we take off now while we can still avoid the rush-hour traffic of later in the day. Wouldn't you agree, Abraham?"

Subdued, the three walked back to the car. Awkwardly, they faced each other. Abe took his daughter's hand. Sarah remained aloof, standing to the side, almost as a spectator.

"Rayna, your mother and I want some binding promises from you."

Won't they ever quit telling me what to do? "What is it, Daddy?"

"First, promise that you'll remain a virgin until your wedding night."

"I can't believe this."

"Rayna!"

"Yes, Daddy, okay."

"If you must date, he is to be Jewish. Sephardic, like us."

"Can't he just be Jewish? What if he's a religious J-Dubb? Is that okay?"

"Rayna, don't push your luck. And you're not to . . . you know . . . sex . . . you know . . . sleep with any of them. None of them! Do you understand?"

"I understand. Our family has a reputation to uphold." At this point, Rayna could no longer hide the look of disgust on her face.

"You will continue to observe shabbat and come home for the holidays, especially Rosh Hashanah, Yom Kippur, and Passover . . . and get rid of that hateful look on your face."

Rayna clenched her teeth and blew out a full breath from her pursed lips. "I'll do my best."

"That's not good enough. You must promise."

"I'll do my best, Dad. What if I have classes or exams?"

At this point, Sarah let out a shrill sound.

"Okay, okay . . ."

"And keep to your own kind. Remember, you're a Jew. A Syrian Jew."

Rayna kept silent.

"I doubt there are any Syrians here, but if you find one . . . "

"I know, Dad, I know." Rayna frowned. The forced goodbye hugs from her parents made her feel like they were all on their way to a death march. When Abe and Sarah drove off, Rayna breathed a sigh of relief and fought the depression tugging at her.

* * *

In a somber state, Rayna spent the next two days settling in. She registered for classes, purchased books, opened a bank account, and acclimated herself to the surroundings.

Deciding to graduate in three years instead of the normal four, Rayna resolved to cram extra classes into her schedule and attend summer sessions to speed up her ascent to graduation.

At Hillel, Rayna met several Ashkenazie Jewish students from her dorm. They all agreed to walk together, going to and coming from their evening meals. One of the Jewish students was named Jonathan. He lived near her in Brooklyn and eagerly offered to give her rides home.

THREE

Everything on this earth has a purpose, every disease has an herb to cure it, and every person has a mission. This is the Indian theory of existence.—— Mourning Dove (Christine Quintasket)

Rami boarded the British Airways wide-bodied jet to London. After a brief layover at Heathrow Airport, he embarked on the final leg of his journey. From the window seat, he looked out on scattered patches of white, pillowy clouds and the vast Atlantic below. A blinding sun glared in the surrounding blue sky. Daylight was constant as the plane flew west, gaining time. Rami pulled down the shade to block out the light and slept on and off during the remainder of the flight.

* * *

Approaching Washington, the plane circled overhead, waiting for clearance. Bleary-eyed, Rami raised the window cover and peered down on the city. Soon, the jet landed at Dulles International Airport and taxied to a stop. Passengers unbuckled their seatbelts. Some rose and stretched. Others reached into the overheads. Patiently, Rami waited for an opening to step out from his seat. He grabbed his carry-on from above and followed the crowd onto the large jitney that would transport them to the terminal.

* * *

Checking through customs without incident, Rami emerged from the international zone and looked for Omar. He saw no police, no military, and no security. He observed people of all ages moving about freely. From behind, a hand on his back startled him. Spinning around, Rami came face-to-face with his closest friend. "Omar! How good it is to see you. *As-salaam alaykum.*"

"*Wa-alaykum as-salaam.*" The two friends embraced.

Rami held up his carry-on and smiled, "This is filled with Syrian pastries from my mother and your mother. I guarded it with my life."

"Do I dare ask how it got through customs?"

"You do not want to know," Rami laughed. "But a few *ka'ak* and *samboosak* are missing."

* * *

In the car, Rami was full of questions. "What is it like living in America? Do you miss your family? And school? What is that like?"

Smiling, Omar steered the black Camry off the Dulles Toll Road and onto the Washington Beltway. "America first. It is a pill-popping society. Whatever the problem, Americans have a pill to fix it. Drugs, legal and illegal, are abused and overused. Consuming large quantities of alcohol is part of

American culture. At school, there are always parties on Saturday nights. Some drink themselves into a stupor. How they can function is . . . well . . . anyone's guess. In this country, it is easy to buy and own guns. Not like in Syria. Here, there is lots of crime . . . much of it violent. Oh, and sex . . . Americans have a bizarre obsession with it. You should see the skimpy clothes the girls wear. So much skin exposed. It will shock you. This is not Syria. Welcome to America."

Omar's account of America was strangely similar to Salha's description, which added to Rami's already uneasy feeling. Still, he urged Omar to tell him more.

"Life in America . . . you are free, like the wind. It is good to have you here." A long pause followed as Omar concentrated on the road.

"What else, Omar?"

"America does have its good side. You can buy just about everything imaginable, as long as you have the money to pay for it. People are materialistic. Most everyone over eighteen has a car, or hopes to get one. No American can survive without a telephone. And you are free to live and say and do most anything, within limits, of course. No government is watching over your shoulder . . . Rami, are you okay?"

"I am fine." Rami masked his sick feeling. "The long trip and being away from . . ."

"From family, yes? I miss my family very much. My absence has been difficult for them. I worry about my parents."

"I saw your family last week. They are fine, except they do miss you a lot. I have letters for you from all of them." Reaching into his overnight bag, Rami retrieved a cheese-filled pastry and handed it to Omar.

Biting into the Middle Eastern appetizer, pleasure girdled Omar's face. "Mmmmm. This one is from my imee. I know her baking anywhere. Rami, I am so happy you are here."

Rami focused on the surroundings. No horns were honking. No motorists were yelling. No traffic police were shouting. In fact, Rami saw no traffic police anywhere. The heavy congestion of vehicles on the Washington Beltway edged slowly across the Potomac River. Rami noted a sign that read *Welcome to Maryland.*

"We just crossed the Cabin John Bridge. The state of Virginia is behind us."

* * *

Parking the car in an underground garage of the high-rise building, Omar popped the trunk and grabbed Rami's carry-on bag from the back seat. Rami lifted out the large duffel bag filled with his life's belongings. Together, they took the elevator to the top floor.

"Wow! Is this where we will live while we are in school?" Never had Rami envisioned such luxury. The living room had hardwood floors accented by a Persian rug of muted colors. A brown leather sofa and two matching chairs added to the furnishings. On a desk against the far wall sat a computer and printer. Sliding glass doors opened onto a small balcony. Inside a closet off the eat-in kitchen were a washer and dryer. Wide-slatted blinds covered the windows. A dresser, a nightstand, and a matching bed outfitted Rami's bedroom. Rami's eyes could hardly grasp it all.

"And, look," Omar pointed out enthusiastically, "your very own bathroom. You do not have to share it with anyone. Not even me."

A reality check caused Rami to pause. *This is too good to be true.* "Nobody would give us all this without something in exchange. Who is it, Omar? What do they want?"

Omar appeared uncomfortable. "Rami. It has been a long trip for you. Let us go out and get something to eat. When we come back, you can unpack and get a good night's sleep. Perhaps tomorrow you will see things differently." Omar placed his left index finger to his lips and shook his head, signaling for Rami to say no more. He mouthed, "Later, we will talk."

Rami wanted to call his father. He needed to hear Ibrahim's insightful assurance. But Rami's family had no phone. In Syria, only the privileged few had access to telephone service.

FOUR

I have loved you in numberless forms, numberless times, in life after life, in age after age, forever.—Rabindranath Tagore

The smell of fresh coffee awakened Rami. His first full day in America, and he was not sure whether to be exuberant or cautious. He pulled on his jeans and went into the kitchen.

"Good morning, Rami. I did not have the heart to wake you."

"What time is it?"

"Ten-thirty. Come eat breakfast. We have a busy day ahead. First, to the mosque for *juma*. Then a meeting with the imam. And you need to register for classes and buy your books. After that, I want to show you around campus. No more sleeping late after today."

"What do you mean *a meeting with the imam*? What imam? For us, there are only twelve imams . . . the descendants of our Prophet. The twelve imams designated by Allah. That is the Shi'ite way. What imam are you referring to, Omar? A Sunni cleric?"

"Yes, Rami. An imam from the Sunni mosque. It is where . . ."

"Why would a Sunni imam want to meet with us? With Shi'ites? I do not like this."

Omar kicked Rami under the table, shook his head, and again put his finger to his lips.

By now, Rami suspected someone was listening in on everything they said. Quietly, he drank the mug of coffee and ate warm Syrian bread with melted cheese. "Thank you for breakfast."

"Do not get too comfortable with it. From now on, we are responsible for our own meals. Sometimes we will eat together. Sometimes we will eat alone. Depending on our schedules. We will share chores and clean up after ourselves. I will show you how to use the machines to wash and dry your clothes." Omar's tone had changed. From across the kitchen table, he leaned in close to Rami, "Be attentive to your schoolwork, maintain good grades, and do what you are told. Follow the rules."

Rami wrote on the napkin: *I do not like this.*

Omar looked at the napkin, then pushed it aside. "Hurry. You still need to shower and we must get going."

* * *

Arriving at the mosque in time for Friday's noon congregational prayers, the two friends slipped off their shoes and joined the large group of men who were now standing side by side in straight rows facing the *mihrab*, the niche in the wall indicating east toward Mecca. The worshippers raised their hands proclaiming that God is most great, "*Allahu akbar.*" While chanting excerpts from the Quran, they fulfilled the ritual movements of standing, bowing, kneeling, and touching the ground with their foreheads. They then sat upright on the floor and listened to the imam's sermon.

Afterward, the cleric approached Rami and Omar, welcoming them. "There is someone I'd like you to meet. Come into my office." He introduced them to Abdallah, a stocky and intimidating Arab with light-brown skin, an oily pockmarked complexion, and thick black hair that looked like it was matted down with Vaseline. The imam motioned for them to sit at the small conference table.

In a gruff voice, Abdallah acknowledged the two friends, "So, tell me, how do you like your apartment?"

"Fine, sir. Thank you."

"Fine, sir, thank you? Omar, you can do better than that. We set you up in a beautiful place. Show some appreciation. I expect you both to do what you're told. Be attentive in school. Study hard. Get good grades. No parties. No girls. Stay out of trouble. We don't want negative attention focused on us in this foreign land. Do you both understand?" Not waiting for a response, Abdallah pulled out a video from his briefcase and inserted it into the VCR.

Rami already decided that he did not like this man named Abdallah. He did not like being in a Sunni mosque. He did not like the Sunni imam.

The video took only ten minutes. The final message on the screen was clear.

> *We must shrink to nothing those areas where people move freely. We must tear away at the fabric that holds societies together. We*

must remain focused on our mission until
Allah's decree is done. In time, nowhere will
be safe until all the world turns to Islam.

The screen went blank. From his chair, Abdallah scrutinized the two students, then abruptly stood. "Salaam." A sneer tugged wickedly at his lips. He turned and left.

The imam escorted the two friends to the door. "I am here whenever you need to talk."

Silently, Rami and Omar walked out to the car. Omar started the engine. Rami's anger was about to erupt. Omar put up his hand to quiet him, opened the compartment between the two front seats, and took out a pen and small pad. On the paper, he wrote: *I am sure our apartment is bugged. I think this car is also bugged. Write what you want to say.*

* * *

Walking across campus toward the Student Union Building, Omar said, "This was done on purpose. They will be watching to see how we react. The best we can do is *not* react. Be careful what you say in the apartment, in the car, or to anyone."

"Just how long have you known about this, Omar? When were you planning to tell me? Or were you leaving me to find out on my own?"

"Do not be unreasonable, Rami. You have barely been here twenty-four hours . . . and I never saw that tape before. For months I knew nothing. Guessing conjured up my worst images, so I tried not to think. It was only a few days ago that I found out about al-Shahid. We will owe our blood to them, if we do not already."

"Al-Shahid! The martyrs! Those militants! Those lunatics! Is that who is sponsoring our education? Are we doomed to become one of them? If they think I am going to . . ."

"Lower your voice, Rami."

"And the imam? What is his role? I do not trust that man."

"They own him. He gets money to run the mosque. The imam is a good man, but they have his life dangling. He has a wife and seven children and is trying to lead the community the best he can under the situation he has been put into. Do you not see, Rami? The imam has no choice. And we have no choice either."

"So when you said yesterday that in America one is as free as the wind, I take it you did not mean us?"

Omar's eye contact with Rami drifted.

"I will talk with the imam," Rami volunteered.

"You will do no such thing. Only a fool who wants to get killed opens his mouth."

* * *

After eating lunch at the university's food court, Omar led Rami to the big gymnasium where class registration was being held. Stepping into one of the many lines, the two waited their turn. Rami scanned the room, first to the left, then to the right. When he turned around to survey the space behind, the most beautiful female he could ever have imagined stood directly in front of him. A flame ignited and a glorious stream of energy rushed through his blood. Rayna's huge, exotic hazel eyes captured him. He wanted to touch the silky, soft black hair that hung loosely on her shoulders. He wanted to feel the softness of her flawless golden skin. He wanted to kiss her perfectly sensuous mouth. Rayna's sundress, brushed with pink and violet, enhanced her dark beauty and accentuated her small breasts and tiny waist. Never had Rami known his senses to be so aroused. A wordless communication surged between them when she met his gaze.

Omar grabbed Rami's arm and yanked him from the line. "Are you crazy?" he admonished in Syrian. "Get hold of yourself. You have been warned about girls, especially pretty American girls. They are evil temptations. Go to the restroom and cool off. Splash cold water on your face. I will wait for you in another line. Come back and find me."

*　*　*

In bed that night, Rami could not sleep. The young woman had awakened every feeling in his body, every thought in his head. Rami was determined to find her. Wrapping himself around the king-size pillow, he let his fantasies run wild.

FIVE

There is no such thing as chance; and that which seems to us blind accident actually stems from the deepest source of all.—Friedrich Von Schiller

The imam leaned forward in his chair. "Abdallah wants a report. A reaction to the video."

With much uneasiness, Omar mustered the courage to challenge him. "You are supposed to be a religious man. Is terrorizing the world the Muslim way?"

"Omar, we are not here for you to question me. Either I do the asking or Abdallah will. I thought it would be easier for you to talk with me."

Omar glared at the man.

"Well, if you're not going to tell me your reaction, then tell me about Rami."

"Rami can speak for himself."

"Very well. I'm a patient man. We'll wait." Sitting across the desk from each other, the two exchanged a long, uncomfortable silence.

Omar sensed a stifling heaviness in the air. He rubbed his eyes. Confrontation was always difficult for him. "Okay, I will tell you my reaction."

"No, Omar. You will tell me Rami's reaction."

Omar hesitated. His right eye twitched nervously. "Ummm . . . uhhh . . . how did you think he would react?"

Carefully measuring his words, the imam replied. "Omar, listen to me. Allah will not let any Muslim rest until all the world turns to Islam. This is our mission. It is our *jihad*. Our struggle is dictated in the Quran."

Omar's voice quivered noticeably. "Ummm . . . will it be . . . will it be the Islam of Sunnis or the Islam of Shi'ites? After we kill all the infidels . . . then . . . then do you know what we will do? We will kill each other for dominance. Who will be the victors? Who will be the losers?" Circles of perspiration seeped from the underarms of his short-sleeve pullover.

The imam did not answer.

"For most of my life, Rami has been my friend. We have been closer than brothers. He is of good character. Hurting others is not his way. Rami lives his life like a true Muslim. We all would be wise to follow his example." Under a cold sweat, Omar enjoyed his few courageous moments.

The cleric rose from his seat and motioned Omar to the door. "You have given me much to contemplate. Look after Rami. We know he loves his family. Remind him of that whenever you find it necessary to keep him from doing anything foolish. I will give Abdallah a favorable report, and I will protect you both to the extent that I can. But know that my hands are tied. I can only do so much. And Omar, your fears and insecurities . . . they show through. Work on yourself, or you will wind up pulverized by those with greater self-confidence. Goodbye."

* * *

Coming out of the foreign language building after Spanish class, Rami unexpectedly spotted Rayna. His heart pounded wildly and he thought at any moment it would burst from his chest. He followed her to the philosophy lecture hall, the same place where he also had a class scheduled. Holding back, Rami waited until Rayna sat down before scurrying to take the seat next to her.

Students quickly filled the room. Rami's eyes focused only on Rayna. She had an unusual beauty. Vividly, her image flashed before him. That same face had been pervading his dreams for years. Clumsily, Rami attempted conversation. "I saw you come out of the foreign language building. What language are you studying?"

"Spanish. Advanced conversation." She appeared uninterested and turned away.

* * *

Standing on the dais, Professor Quintin Nolan welcomed the class and introduced himself. He boasted about holding two doctorate degrees, one in philosophy and one in chemistry. Over his slight frame, the professor wore a short-sleeve white cotton shirt tucked into baggy gray trousers. His thinning brown hair was combed over to the side to mask his baldness. Sallow skin, large ears, and a protruding Adam's apple gave him a gaunt appearance. Pacing back and forth as he spoke, the educator alternated between pushing back his oversized black-rimmed spectacles and stroking his beardless chin. The teaching assistant handed out the class schedule while Nolan discussed the semester's curriculum. Then the professor began his lecture.

"What if I told you an organism has been discovered that will clean up any oil spill in water or on land, and it will soon be introduced to the world?" He paused, giving the students a chance to absorb his question. "Any comments?"

Several hands went up. "I think a discovery like this would save the world a lot of money, time, and cleanup," said one student.

"This would be an ecological breakthrough," added a tall, lanky boy.

"You say this organism will devour oil? What else will it devour in its path?" Rayna asked.

Nolan continued to pace back and forth while nudging up his glasses and stroking his chin. "Hmmm, I don't know."

"You don't know? What if it devours everything in sight? What if it consumes more than the oil in the water? More than the fuel spill on the road?"

"Good questions. Uhhhh . . . I didn't catch your name."

"Rayna."

"Yes. Good questions, Rayna."

Rami raised his hand. "What kind of an organism is it?"

"Let's call it bacteria."

"Who will have access to these bacteria? Who will own the rights and make the money?"

"Excellent reasoning. Your brains are working. Now, your assignment is to come up with questions and answers. Philosophize. Rationalize. Look at every angle. I want each of you to find a partner and work together on this project. It will be due three weeks from today. Typed, twelve-point Times New Roman, double-spaced, five to seven pages." Professor Nolan looked at his watch. "You have half an hour to find a partner and get started before class ends. And this assignment will be one-third of your grade, so don't take it lightly."

* * *

Rami lifted his eyebrows and smiled. Dare he hope? Rayna returned the smile. Jonathan, who had graciously offered to give Rayna rides back to Brooklyn, tapped her on the shoulder. She turned around. "Want to partner?" he asked.

Rami's faint glimmer of hope faded and he fidgeted in his seat. Rayna hesitated, glanced back at Rami, then looked away. "Thanks Jonathan, but I already have a partner."

"Well, too bad for me. I won't be at Hillel tonight. See you at two tomorrow." He stomped off.

Breathing a sigh of exhilaration, Rami beamed, "I would be honored to work on this assignment with you."

"It's your smile." Rayna's comment was spontaneous.

"My smile?"

"Your smile. It's radiant and sexy. I like it," she blushed.

Rami's face turned crimson.

She extended her hand. "Hi, I'm Rayna."

Feeling the softness of her skin as he gently clasped her tiny hand in his, he knew right then that he would want no one else but her. Ever. "Hi. My name is Rami."

They exchanged telephone numbers and agreed to meet for lunch at eleven the next day in the Student Union.

* * *

Not wanting to be late, Rami left class early. For him, this opportunity was a stroke of good fortune. Scanning the area for Rayna and not seeing her, Rami secured a table before they were all taken by the students streaming in for lunch. Sitting down, he patiently waited and watched. Fifteen minutes. Twenty minutes. Just when he thought she might not show up, Rami saw her glancing around. Excitedly, he stood and waved. Quickly, she made her way toward him.

"Hi." His heart accelerated.

"So sorry I'm late. My journalism teacher was telling us about a summer internship with a very big international magazine. Thanks for getting a table and waiting."

Overjoyed that she really had come, Rami helped Rayna with her books. "I will stay at the table while you get lunch."

"Can I pick up something for you while I'm in line? It will save time." Rayna browsed the room, "God, look at the mob of students already."

Rami reached into his pocket and handed her a ten-dollar bill. "Will this be enough?"

"No, please. Let me get lunch. It's the least I can do for keeping you waiting. What would you like?"

"I insist on paying . . . for both of us." He took her hand and placed the bill in her palm.

Gently, she nudged it back to him. "Next time it will be your treat," she smiled. "Now, tell me what you would like."

He was glad there would be a next time. "Anything but meat. No meat. No pork."

"That makes two of us. Not for me either. Shall I get you whatever I have?"

"I would like that."

As Rayna moved through the line, Rami observed the graceful sway of her hips and the smooth roundness of her bottom. The lavender-colored tank top and snug blue jeans exposed the sensuous curves of her small frame. Rami felt himself stiffen.

When she returned with salads, veggie melts, and two bottles of spring water, Rami thanked her. "Is this your first semester?" he asked, hoping to learn more about her.

"Yes. And you?"

"My first semester, too . . . I did not catch your last name."

"I didn't give it."

"Oh . . ."

"It's Rayna. Rayna Mishan. And yours?"

"Rami Mahmoud. We have the same initials, R. M."

"You're an Arab . . . a Muslim, aren't you?"

"You make it sound like a disease."

"That wasn't my intent. It was just a comment. Where are you from? Your accent . . ."

"Mishan is a Syrian name. Are you from Syria?"

"Well, sort of. Both sets of my grandparents are from Syria. From Halab. Aleppo. But I was born in Brooklyn . . . in New York."

"I am from Halab." Rami was elated to make the connection. "I just arrived last week."

"First time in the United States?"

"Yes." His voice lagged and his gaze upon her deepened.

Rayna forced herself to look away. She grappled for a pen inside her purple-and-pink tote. "We need to get to work. I must leave before two." She opened her notebook. "I've written all of the comments made in class. It's a start."

"That is a nice bag you have. Unusual colors."

"I'm attached to purple and pink," Rayna laughed nervously. "Someday I will grow out of it, I am told."

Rami tucked the information away. "Can I buy a bag like that for my mother?"

"What's your mother's name? You can get her initials like this." She pointed to the *R M* on the outside pocket flap.

"My mother's name is Salha."

"My great grandmother's name was Salha. My mother is named after her but everyone calls her Sarah."

"And your father?"

"My father's name is Abraham. Everyone calls him Abe, except when my Mom's upset with him, then she calls him Abraham. And your father?"

"My father's name is Ibrahim. That is Arabic for Abraham."

Rayna nodded knowingly.

"How old are you? Your birth date?"

"You first."

"August tenth, nineteen seventy-eight. I am eighteen now."

Rayna said nothing.

"Well?" He waited for her to respond.

She stared directly at him. "August tenth, nineteen seventy-eight. I'm also eighteen."

Rami's intuition had been confirmed. *One day, she will be mine.* "Brothers? Sisters?"

"Four older brothers. I'm the youngest and the only girl . . . and you?

"Four younger sisters. I am the oldest and the only boy." He glanced at the food on the table. "You know, neither one of us took meat for lunch. We have the same initials. Our family roots are in Halab. Our parents have almost identical names. We have the same number of siblings and we were born on the same day. This is not a coinci . . ."

"Stop! Please, stop. I don't want to talk about this anymore. I have to leave before two. We better get working on our assignment."

For Rami, the assignment was a wonderful excuse to connect with Rayna. "From the moment I saw you on the registration line, I . . . I . . ."

"Let's talk about the bacteria, or I'm leaving." She stood.

Rami dared to touch her hand. "Please do not go. If I upset you, I apologize. We will work on the assignment." What Rami really wanted was to tell her what he was feeling, to tell her how, over the years, she had filled his dreams. For as long as he could remember, her face had been imprinted in his mind. "If there really were such bacteria and the United States were to get possession, then American businesses would be fighting over the money to be made. Corporate America does not do things for the good of the people. Their actions are profit driven, to fill their own pockets. The more money American executives make, the more they want. It is never enough. I learned that in school in Syria."

"Come on, Rami, I don't want to get into what's right or wrong in America. I could tell you about Syria . . . how the Alawaites enjoy all the privileges, all the jobs, all the money. All at the expense of the Shi'ites and other minorities . . . and some Sunnis, too. So explain to me how the Syrian government does things for the good of the people," she inquired facetiously. "Let's not get into mud-slinging. Stay focused on our assignment."

"Mud-slinging? Is that the term you use here in America? I am not mud-slinging, and you cannot discount my part of this discussion. Now write this down. The oil-eating bacteria ought to be compared with nuclear power, providing a lot of good but disastrous effects if it gets into the wrong hands."

Rayna took notes as Rami spoke. When he stopped, she looked up and gleamed. "Good stuff. I got every word."

Rami liked that Rayna validated his contribution. He also liked her spunkiness and their spirited interaction.

"Hmmm." She arched her brow.

"What?"

"Doctorates in chemistry and philosophy. Isn't that an odd combination for Professor Nolan to have?" Then with a flip of her hand, she added, "Oh, never mind. I'm probably making too much of it. But what a scary thought. If Nolan were offered millions of dollars and he sold it into the wrong hands, God help the world."

"Do you think Nolan may have the bacteria, or is he just giving us some philosophical assignment?"

"There's something strange about him. I can't quite put my finger on it. What do you think, Rami? Philosophical or reality?"

"Reality."

"Me, too." Goosebumps erupted on Rayna's arms. Rami reached out to stroke them away. She drew back. "It's almost two o'clock. I have to leave." Collecting her books, she adjusted her tote over her shoulder.

"What about tomorrow? Can we meet tomorrow?" Rami asked.

"I can't. I'm going home for the holidays. I'll be back Sunday night. I'll call you then."

"Home? Where is home? What holiday?"

"New York. Rosh Hashanah. I have a ride and I can't be late. Bye." She rushed out.

Rosh Hashanah. It hit him like a bolt of lightning. *She is Jewish and has a ride home with that student Jonathan.*

SIX

I offer my hand of five fingers and you offer yours. Together we have a complete ten. This is a handshake. You and I are only fragments of the whole until we come together.—The Rebbe Menachem Mendel Schneerson

The weekend had dragged on far too long and Rayna was upsetting the delicate balance of Rami's world. The more Rami struggled to get his thoughts into some kind of order and erase Rayna from his brain, the stronger she gripped him.

Early on Monday morning, the phone rang. "Yes . . . who is this?" Putting his hand over the mouthpiece, Omar gestured to Rami. "It is for you. She says her name is *Rayna*."

Snatching the phone, Rami knew there would be no privacy with Omar standing over him, so he carefully measured his words. "Hello." Rami cupped the mouthpiece and turned away from Omar.

When he hung up, Omar asked, "Who is Rayna? An American girl? Rami, what are you doing?"

Angrily, Rami shot back. "In the name of Allah, is this how I am to live my life here? With you over my shoulder?

I have a philosophy assignment and the professor paired us off. We are working on a project that is one-third of our grade. Why must you project more into it?"

"She is American."

"Am I not allowed to do schoolwork with an American? Yes, she *is* American! This country is full of Americans. She is also Syrian. Her family is from Halab . . . and why do you have a car and I do not? I, too, should have a car."

The phone rang. Omar picked it up. "Hello." After a brief conversation, Omar put the phone back in the cradle. "The imam expects us at the mosque at seven o'clock this evening. You can ask him about a car then. I do not make those decisions."

* * *

After a delay in sluggish traffic, Omar pulled the car into the mosque's parking lot. He and Rami entered the large vestibule. The imam was waiting. "You're late."

"Traffic was heavy."

"See to it that it doesn't happen again, Omar. Abdallah does not like to be kept waiting." He led the two into his office. As soon as Rami saw Abdallah, the urge to put his fist right through the man's face almost overcame him.

"As-salaam alaykum." Abdallah's heavy hands bore down on Omar's shoulders as he greeted him on both cheeks.

Rami prayed that Abdallah's greasy face would not graze him. His prayer was not answered. As Abdallah approached, Rami was forced to endure the same greeting as Omar had experienced.

The imam motioned for everyone to take seats around the desk. Abdallah asked in his gruff voice, "How was your first week, Rami?"

"Fine."

"Tell me about your classes."

As Rami provided a shallow, one-sentence account of each class, Omar sat quietly.

"I want you to take your Spanish very seriously, Rami. Fluency in the language will seal your future with us." Abdallah grinned, exposing the wide gaps in his teeth.

Brazenly, Rami met Abdallah's focus. "Why is Spanish so important? I am already fluent in Arabic, French, and English . . . and I would like to have a car like Omar."

"Your mission with us will take you to South America. It is important for you to know Spanish." Swiveling his chair, Abdallah turned to face Omar, "Rami can get around on the metro. If he needs use of the car, see to it that you take him wherever he asks . . . within reason, of course."

"It is a very long walk to the mosque," Rami argued.

Abdallah brushed off Rami's comment. "I understand you got a phone call this morning from an American named Rayna. Tell me about her."

"Did Omar tell you this or do you have a habit of listening to private conversations?"

"Where will you meet her?"

"It is a class assignment, Abdallah. And it is none of your business where I will meet her. I will not spend the next four years living like this. Now, either you give me some freedom to do my schoolwork, to make friends . . . to breathe, or . . ."

"Or what? Everything you do is my business, Rami. Everything! Be careful. You have a family back in Syria and some very lovely sisters."

"Are you threatening to harm my family?"

Attempting to calm the escalation, the imam asked Rami and Omar to step out of the office for a few moments.

* * *

Alone with Abdallah, the imam said, "We must not unsettle Rami. Al-Shahid has big plans for the boy. Slowly, we will indoctrinate Rami and prepare him. Patience, Abdallah. Rami is not like Omar. Rami is strong-willed. He won't respond to threats the way you would like. Abdallah, you must not interfere with their time at school . . . neither of the boys. Yousef has made this clear."

Summoning the two students back into the office, Abdallah pulled his chair close to them. "The imam is a wise man. Listen to him. Omar, do what it takes to help Rami get a driver's license. Provide him with use of the car when he needs it. You both can work out the details of sharing the car."

Making it known that he was pleased to have any differences settled, the imam counseled, "As Muslims, we must stand together. Disturbances among ourselves are frowned upon. I hope this will not happen again." He rose, extended his hand, and led Rami and Omar to the door. "I expect to see you Friday for prayers. Salaam."

* * *

On the ride back to the apartment, alienation overtook Rami. Alone in a strange country, he yearned for his family. By some twist of fate, a Jew had captured his heart. The apartment he lived in was bugged and the phone was tapped, if what Omar said were true. He hated Abdallah. He could not trust the imam. His relationship with his best friend was quickly deteriorating. "Omar, did you tell them about Rayna's call this morning?"

"No, I did not. But I am concerned for your safety."

"Do not be. Al-Shahid needs us more than we need them."

"If you want your driver's license, you will need to get a permit so you can practice. There is also a booklet you must study. I will help you. When do you want to start?"

"Tomorrow."

* * *

Hurrying out of Spanish class, Rami shielded his eyes from the bright sun and scanned the grounds, hoping to spot Rayna. As he slowly turned, she came into full view. Striking in her purple jeans and hot-pink stretch tee, her long dark hair was pulled back with a large pink barrette. She slipped on a pair of sunglasses and walked toward him. Rami's heart stilled.

"You need some shades," she smiled.

"Shades . . . window shades?"

"No," she laughed, "shades as in sunglasses."

"Oh . . . sunglasses are called shades in America?"

"Sometimes."

"Do you mind if I walk with you?"

"I don't mind."

"You mentioned that you are taking advanced Spanish conversation. You must speak the language well."

"Fluently. I'm carrying a full load this semester, so taking Spanish makes my life a little easier. My major is journalism."

"I am fluent in Arabic, French, and English. Spanish is very new to me. But I am told I must learn the language for my future."

"Why do you need to know so many languages? Will you be an interpreter?"

"Something like that. Would you be willing to help me with Spanish?"

"Sure."

"How was your weekend home? Did you have a good Rosh Hashanah?" Rami had practiced the correct pronunciation to impress her.

"It was okay. How was your weekend?"

"Also, okay." Rami wanted to tell Rayna how much he longed to see her again, how each minute that passed had seemed like an eternity. He wanted to know about her ride home with Jonathan. He wanted to trust her with the burden he was carrying. But he spoke none of this.

Entering the philosophy lecture hall, they found two seats together. Professor Nolan was already on the platform pacing back and forth, stroking his beardless chin and pushing back his black spectacles as they slipped down his nose. Students rushed to take their seats. Nolan started his lecture. Rayna leaned over to Rami and whispered, "He's a nerd."

"In Syria, we would never make fun of a teacher."

* * *

"Today, I want to talk about abortion. Why would a woman choose abortion? Perhaps the mother's life could be at serious risk. Her physical or mental health might be jeopardized. The pregnancy could be the result of incest or rape. Maybe the woman is unmarried and cannot care for a child. Maybe the child would be born deformed. What if the baby were to be a financial burden? Or interfere in some way with the happiness of the woman? Or with her career? Or her family? Or maybe, she just doesn't want a child now, or ever."

Nolan signaled his assistant to turn off the lights and start the projector. "Conception takes place when a male sperm combines with a female ovum resulting in a single cell that embodies the full genetic code donated by both parents. Twenty-three pairs of chromosomes."

With his red laser pointer, the professor expounded on his discourse. "During the first eight weeks, this cell is known as an embryo. After the first eight weeks, it is known as a fetus. The fetus undergoes a continual process of change and development during its life span. Movement of the fetus is felt somewhere around the sixteenth week. By the twenty-fourth week, the fetus reaches viability, the point at which it is capable of surviving outside the womb."

Professor Nolan had the students spellbound. "So . . . at what point of fetal development, if any, and for what reason, if any, is abortion ethically acceptable? Or is it never acceptable? Does a fetus have the right to life? Does a woman have the right to control what is done to her own body? Whose rights take precedence, the mother or the fetus?"

Rami leaned over to Rayna and whispered, "He is not a nerd. He has given us a lot to think about."

Still pacing back and forth, Nolan pressed on, "We have a precedent case known as *Roe versus Wade*. A young single woman challenged a Texas law on the constitutionality of a criminal abortion law. The case went before the Supreme Court under Justice Harry Blackmun. In concurrence with six of the other justices, it was determined that a woman has the right to terminate her own pregnancy during the first trimester. After that, the state has the legitimate right to protect both the mother and the potential life inside her."

Rayna raised her hand. Nolan signaled for her to speak. "What about birth control? A lot of unwanted pregnancies could be curtailed if . . ."

"Good question. But who is going to be there to guarantee that a woman, or a man, will always use birth control? And isn't abortion a form of birth control?" After several more minutes of class interaction, Nolan stopped the exchange. "I would like you to break up into groups of six and discuss this issue. Pull your chairs to form circles. Each group is to choose a leader. Keep to the topic. You have forty minutes. Don't box yourselves into the Supreme Court ruling. Expand your horizons. You can go as conservative or as liberal as you see fit. Take notes and be prepared for a lively discussion during our next class."

* * *

Rami was looking forward to a challenging debate until Jonathan approached and pulled up a chair beside Rayna.

"Hi, Jonathan. This is Rami. I told you about him, remember?"

"Yes."

Rami nodded politely, wishing for Jonathan to disappear. Three more students joined them. After all introductions were made, Rayna was chosen to be leader. An energetic dialogue began. Rami sat silently, stewing in a jealous rage. At the end of class, Jonathan placed his hand on Rayna's shoulder, "I'll come by and get you at six."

"Great. Thanks. See you later."

That exchange drove Rami into deeper resentment.

Without another word, Rayna straightened her chair, picked up her things, and darted out the door. Grabbing his books, Rami ran after her. "Wait! What is your hurry?"

"I'm trying to ditch you," she yelled.

"Ditch me? What does that mean? Ditch?"

"*Ditch*. Like get far away from you," she hollered.

"But we have an assignment to finish . . . remember?" Rami picked up his pace until he reached Rayna's side. She stopped. Their eyes locked. Gently, Rami took her arm.

"Let go of me!" she demanded, pulling away.

He stood back and studied her.

"You are very moody! What's wrong with you? On the way to class, you were so pleasant. Then, in the group, you didn't open your mouth, didn't contribute one word to the discussion. You sat and sulked. I don't think I like you." Rayna reached into her book bag, pulled out the notes from the other day, and shoved them at Rami. "Here. I don't want to work with you. I can handle the bacteria assignment on my own." She took off.

Rami found her irresistibly sensual. An insatiable craving for Rayna devoured him and he ran after her. When she picked up speed, he called out, "Rayna, please. Let me apologize. Let me explain. I am really sorry."

Coming to a standstill, Rayna turned and faced him. Impatience flickered in her huge hazel eyes. "I'm listening. You have five minutes and this better be good."

"Can we find a quiet place to talk?"

"No!"

"Please, Rayna . . ."

"Five minutes. You have five minutes and your time is ticking away."

In a panic and without a convincing alibi, Rami impulsively blurted, "I am in love with you. I knew it the instant I saw you in line registering for classes. I cannot take you from my head . . . from my body. The harder I try, the more intensely you hold on. I went crazy knowing you and Jonathan traveled together to New York for your Jewish holiday. Then, when I saw him join our group and sit down next to you . . . I was jealous. Rayna, I am so sorry. I do not know what else to say." Embarrassed and feeling exposed, Rami prayed she would not poke fun at him and turn away.

Unexpectedly, she touched his hand. "Thank you for being honest. I would not have confessed so courageously. And don't be jealous of Jonathan. There's no romance between us, at least not one I'm aware of."

"I want to have your heart."

"You already do." For a moment, there was only silence as their eyes held. "I'm hungry. I'll race you to the Student Union."

* * *

Eating salads and veggie melts, both tried to focus on the assignment, engaging in a long exchange over the oil-devouring bacteria. Rayna took notes and Rami agreed to type the report.

"I have a three o'clock class," she said as the time grew closer.

"When can I see you again?"

"Thursday in philosophy."

"You are seeing Jonathan tonight?"

"Rami, you're a Muslim, yes?"

He nodded, "A Shi'ite Muslim."

"A terrorist? A militant?" she teased.

"No," he grinned. "I am neither. I hope you do not think all Muslims are that way."

"I don't." She paused, trying to figure out how best to explain so Rami could understand. "I come from a very religious family. I eat salad and veggie sandwiches for lunch because I keep kosher. It's part of my being Jewish. I don't eat pork or shellfish or meat from any animal unless it has been slaughtered in a certain ritualistic way. We must take care that the animal is healthy and feels no pain when it is killed. The jugular is severed, spilling the blood, and the animal dies instantly. Only then is the meat certified kosher for us to eat."

"I also come from a religious family. Islamic law is similar, but we do not call it kosher. We call it halal. We, also, are not allowed pork, and the only meat we can eat follows the same ritual slaughter you just described." Rami was finding it difficult to comprehend why Muslims had such a profound hatred for Jews. He recalled his layover at Heathrow Airport, when another Muslim traveling alone befriended him. In the course of their conversation, the stranger told Rami that if he could not find halal food in the United States, then he should look for kosher food. At the time, Rami did not understand the meaning. "What does your telling me about kosher food have to do with your seeing Jonathan at six o'clock tonight?"

"On campus, there's a Jewish Student Center, a Hillel. Jonathan lives in the same dorm as I do and we eat our kosher meals at Hillel. Jonathan and I, and some other Jewish students in the dorm, we walk over together for dinner. I only just met Jonathan a couple of weeks ago and discovered that he lives near me in Brooklyn. He's been kind enough to offer me rides home. That's all."

"Can I see you over the weekend? A movie? Dinner somewhere?"

"I'd like to say yes, but I'm going home for Yom Kippur. It's our holiest day of the year. From sunset to sunset, we fast, we pray, and we make peace with God and with our fellow man. It is our day of repentance. On Rosh Hashanah, the fate of each man for the coming year is written. And on Yom Kippur, it is sealed. I'm leaving this Friday afternoon and won't be back until Tuesday morning, but I'll see you in class on Thursday and we can have lunch afterward."

"I would like that." What Rami did not like was Rayna traveling alone with Jonathan. "What about the following weekend? Are you going home again?"

"No . . . yes . . . I mean *yes*, we can go out then."

Leaving the Student Union, Rami carried Rayna's books and walked her to class. "One of our holy times is Laylat al-Baraa, Night of Repentance. Forgiveness is granted to those who repent. Allah sets the course for each of us for the coming year. Something like Yom Kippur."

"I'd like to learn more about Islam."

"I will teach you. And Judaism . . . will you teach me?"

"We have a deal," she smiled. They approached the journalism building. Rayna took her books from Rami. "Thank you. See you on Thursday." She started for the entranceway.

"Wait!"

Rayna turned back.

"I need your trust. I have no one else in America. When you return, I will explain everything. For now, please accept what I ask. Do not call me. I think my apartment and phone are bugged. It is something I have to deal with. I need a cell phone. Will you help me get one?"

Rayna started to ask a question, then stopped. "When I get back next week, we'll make time. We can take the metro and go shopping."

Rami took her hand and clasped it firmly in his. He felt her pulse quicken and her hand tremble. Looking into her remarkable face, he lifted her hand to his lips and kissed her palm.

"I really have to go, Rami." She eased her hand from his grip and hurried into the building.

* * *

In the classroom, Rayna plopped down in a vacant seat. Her pulse beat rapidly and she felt her head spinning. An unexplainable force was thrusting her toward him. *My destiny is bolted shut*, she was convinced. *There is no way to get free of him.* Rayna prayed to God to give her the strength to fight this predetermined path befalling her.

* * *

For the next two days, she struggled in vain to keep Rami out of her thoughts. On Thursday, she tried to avoid him and left early from Spanish class, but Rami caught up with her. In philosophy, Rami surprised her by apologizing to the group for his behavior, which made him more endearing.

* * *

After class, Rami and Rayna got their usual from the coffee bar and sat out in the grass with their lunch. "Do you wear mascara?" she chuckled.

"*Mas-ca-ra?*" he sounded out the word. "What is that?" When Rayna amused him with a detailed description of the cosmetic, he asked, "Do you really see mascara on my lashes?"

"Yes," she giggled. "I see mascara."

"No. No mascara."

"No one could possibly have such long, curly black lashes without mascara," she teased.

"It is my natural beauty," he bantered, bringing a burst of laughter from both of them. "Now, let me look at your lashes." He moved his face close to hers. "Mmm-hmm."

"What? What do you see?"

He took her hands. "I see the two most captivating eyes on this planet . . . and mascara is on your lashes." He wanted to kiss her. "One day, I will marry you."

"No!" she shouted, then lowered her voice. "Muslims and Jews don't . . ."

"Do not what, Rayna?"

"Just do not. That's all. I can't . . . my family."

"I am sorry there is no peace between Muslims and Jews. Can we just not get caught up in all that ugliness?" This time, when Rami leaned in to kiss her, she did not resist. The delicate smell of her warm breath sent a current of energy through his body. Rami wanted more. "Have you ever been intimate with someone?" he asked clumsily.

"You mean sex . . . with a man?" she blushed.

"Yes," he bumbled over the word.

"Of course not. My parents would kill me. Not until I'm married."

"Good," he smiled.

"Have you?"

"No, I never have. Until now, there was no one I wished to be . . . you know . . ."

* * *

Over the next several weeks, the bond between them deepened. Every night before sleeping, Rami called Rayna on his new cell phone. Extra cautious, he spoke in whispers.

Rayna tutored Rami in Spanish. He helped Rayna with her algebra. She learned about al-Shahid. He discovered Hillel and the Jewish sabbath. With an outpouring of tolerance and acceptance, they explored each other's faiths. On weekends, they took the metro into Washington. The Woodley Park Zoo became a favorite place for them to marvel at the animals. When Rami got his license, he and Rayna often drove to Brookside Gardens, a treasured place where they strolled hand-in-hand, shared long, soul-searching talks, and trusted one another with their deepest thoughts, feelings, and fears. Never at a loss for words, they learned from one another, growing both in wisdom and in spirit.

* * *

Rami and Omar had no choice but to continue their mandatory, weekly indoctrination meetings with Abdallah and the imam. However, Rami's inner strength persevered and he would not allow his mind to be manipulated by abhorrent ideas. In contrast, Omar was fearful and obedient. Mistrust and alienation cast a dark shadow on their friendship.

* * *

By December, students were busy preparing for final exams and term papers, and making plans for the month-long winter break. Rami and Omar would be returning together to Syria. Rayna was going home to Brooklyn.

SEVEN

A warrior never betrays weakness in the face of adversity.—A Samurai saying

Ten days before Rami's departure to Syria, Abdallah had left for a meeting at al-Shahid headquarters in Lebanon's agriculture heartland, the Bekaa Valley. The ringleaders in al-Shahid had joined forces with two other militant organizations and had begun to infiltrate a region in South America known as the Triple Frontier, a place notorious for its lawlessness and for being a haven for terrorists and drug lords.

* * *

On a blustery December morning, Rayna tossed her jacket and tote on top of the pile of books and clothes in the back seat of the car. Easing herself into the front passenger side, she glanced at Jonathan and sighed, "Whew! I thought we'd never make it."

Jonathan smiled, started the engine, turned on the heater, and steered the white Legacy off campus. From a distance, Rami watched them drive away.

Slipping off her shoes, Rayna drew up her feet and crossed them over one another into the lotus position that so often brought her comfort. She chatted about taking extra classes in order to graduate early and about going on to Columbia University's School of Journalism for advanced degrees. Jonathan expressed hopes of getting accepted into Columbia also, but in the College of Physicians and Surgeons. His family expected him to go into practice with his father, a renowned surgeon. "Jonathan, that's wonderful. You'll make a terrific doctor." Rayna gave him an encouraging squeeze on the shoulder. Expecting the conversation to continue in a light vein, she was taken aback by Jonathan's question.

"What's going on between you and Rami?"

"What do you mean?"

"Come on, Rayna, we're not stupid. We all see it."

"Who is *we*?"

"Me, the rabbi, our whole group of friends . . ."

"Is it that obvious?" Rayna was feeling alarmed.

"Yes, it's that obvious." With his eyes on the road, Jonathan proceeded to give Rayna stern warnings about the inherent hatred that Muslims have for Jews. "Did you ever read the Quran? Its violent passages read more like a war manual than a religious text. It depicts Jews as being sub-human . . . monkeys . . . pigs. From the little I know, Muhammad had a vision. He went to the Jews of Medina wanting them to accept him as one of their prophets. When the Jews refused, Muhammad turned on them. His fury shows up all through the Quran. Jews are slime and Muslims must rid the earth of us all."

"Oh really? Didn't something like that happen when Jews refused to accept Jesus? Christians tried to annihilate us, and almost succeeded. Let's not forget the Crusades, the

Inquisition, the Holocaust, and every atrocity in between. Yet, amazingly, today, there are Jews and Christians who befriend one another, conduct business together, and even intermarry. Tell me Jonathan, how do you explain that?"

"Have you slept with him?"

"What! That's none of your business."

"Wrong. Your involvement with that Muslim will devastate your family. Especially your parents. Or don't you care about anyone but yourself?"

"Rami is a good person. He doesn't hate Jews. Not every Muslim hates . . ."

"So . . . have you slept with him?"

"No, I have *not* slept with him." She pulled out a CD of Elton John and shoved it into the player in the dashboard.

Brusquely, Jonathan ejected it. "Rayna, be careful. You may want to believe that Rami is a good person, but he's still a Muslim. In the real world, Jews and Muslims don't mix and I don't want to see you get hurt." Purposefully, Jonathan put on his flashers and eased the car onto the shoulder, bringing it safely to a stop. He unbuckled his seat belt, leaned over, and forced an impetuous kiss on Rayna's lips. Startled, she pushed him off.

* * *

Settling into their seats for the flight back to Syria, the conversation between Rami and Omar was strained and surrounded by long periods of silence. "Four months ago, I was excited for you to arrive. Now, we are like strangers." Omar waited for a response. Rami withdrew more into himself. An hour into the flight, Omar tried again in a voice barely above a whisper. "Abdallah knows of your friendship with Rayna."

"So?"

"I assured him that Rayna is of Syrian blood."

"Oh? And what else have you assured Abdallah of?"

"Rami, they know you have a cell phone. Be careful."

Omar knows more about me than I care for him to know.
Rami was grateful that Rayna had put the cell phone in her
name and that she had insisted on keeping it while he was
in Syria. Hoping to block out Omar, he closed his eyes. His
thoughts drifted to Rayna, and a heaviness overshadowed his
spirit. Watching her drive off with Jonathan had refueled his
jealousy. He ached to be with her. With every part of his being,
Rami craved Rayna.

* * *

Inside Damascus International Airport, Ibrahim waited
for Rami and Omar to arrive. He spotted them approaching
and rushed toward them, first embracing his son, then Omar.
With luggage in hand, the three started out to the car. The
cold misty air and dark clouds hanging overhead fanned
Rami's melancholy. Ibrahim drove the old Mercedes north on
Highway 5 toward Aleppo. Two hours later, he stopped the
car near Omar's modest dwelling. From inside the courtyard,
Omar's mother rushed out. She had prepared a big lunch and
invited them all inside. Graciously, Rami refused. He wanted
to get home to see his own mother.

* * *

Salha stood outside in the cold, crying with joy at the sight
of her son. "This is my happiest day . . . to have you home.
We missed you. Your sisters are anxious to return from school
and welcome you. They have been counting the days."

Inside the meager home, Salha served lunch—rice with onions and lentils, and a yogurt sauce with cucumbers and mint. Rami and his parents talked non-stop, catching up on the past four months. Afterward, Salha cleaned the dishes, then apologized for having to leave. "Abu and Zakieh are helping out at the souq so we could spend some time with you. Your eby and I must go and relieve them. But we will not be home late. We will close the stand early. When your sisters come from school, they will prepare a special meal to celebrate your return. But now, my son, you must rest after such a long trip." Lovingly, Salha looked at Rami.

"Tomorrow night, we have a special treat. A party at the Grand House restaurant," Ibrahim announced.

His parents left, and Rami found solace in the quiet of the afternoon. Tired from the long voyage, he unpacked and then lay down on the cot that used to be his bed. He tried to sleep, but his mind was active with thoughts of Rayna.

* * *

Inside the large heated tent at the Grand House, Rami was surrounded by family and friends, and his favorite Syrian foods. He carried fond memories of the many gatherings at this restaurant. Steady dialogue, hearty laughter, and a barrage of questions about the United States saturated the table. Rami's spirits soon lifted. Ibrahim and Salha announced Ayisha's upcoming marriage and introduced her future husband. Like most Syrian unions, the match had been arranged with the blessings of both sets of parents. The nuptials were to take place before the month of Ramadan.

She is so young. Just fifteen. Rami found it hard to fathom his sister being intimate with a man at her delicate age, especially a man eleven years her senior. Speculating on how Ayisha could possibly know about love, Rami's mind wandered back to Rayna. He reflected on one of their long walks at Brookside Gardens, recalling their pledge of love. They had agreed that sex would be a cherished destination to come only within their marriage.

* * *

On Friday, Salha stayed home to work on Ayisha's wedding preparations. Rami and his father attended the mosque for noon prayers, then went to the souq. While waiting on a customer, Rami caught sight of a man in military garb lingering nearby. Instantly, he recognized the long jagged scar etched into the officer's left cheek. *If I did not know better, I would thank him*, Rami mused. *If it were not for him sending me to the University of Maryland, I might never have known Rayna.*

Rami nodded, acknowledging the man. Yousef gestured to him. Rami finished with the shopper and approached Yousef, who told him to prepare for a four-day conference in the Bekaa Valley. "On Monday morning at nine, a car will meet you and Omar on the south side of the Citadel. Be there. And Rami, just so you know, Abdallah and the imam take their orders from me. So do you and Omar." Yousef turned and left.

* * *

In a drizzling rain, with the Citadel's tower and moat directly behind, Rami and Omar waited in silence. Rami pulled up his hood to stave off the dampness. He glanced over at Omar, remembering when, as young boys, the two had played at this fortress. A black limousine pulled up. The driver rolled down the window and motioned to them. Rami rushed ahead and took the front passenger seat. Omar was left to sit in the back.

The vehicle weaved in and out between the contrasting old narrow streets and new wide roads. An hour into the trip, they passed through the city of Hims. From there, the driver followed signs to al Biqa, curving around the statuesque Anti-Lebanon Mountains that form the boundary between Syria and Lebanon. Looking up at the snow-capped peaks, Rami recalled them well. With a softened heart, he turned around, "Omar, remember when we used to ski here?"

Omar smiled, "Yes, I remember. In these mountains, we thought we could conquer the world." Pointing to the red tile-roofed houses clinging precariously to the mountainside, the two reminisced about their fantasies of some day living in one of those dwellings.

Skirting around the Litani River, the chauffeur veered off toward the Lebanese town of Zahle, famous for its good restaurants and wonderful shopping. After passing through Zahle, the automobile snaked in and out of several back streets until reaching a long, winding dirt road. At the end of the path, they reached a heavily fortified complex. Men with assault rifles signaled for the car to stop. "Salaam," said one of the officers, ducking his head into the open window. He scrutinized Rami, then Omar. He ordered the two to step out. Guards frisked them. Satisfied about finding nothing, the officer waved them back into the automobile.

* * *

Inside a two-story edifice constructed from Jerusalem stone, Rami and Omar were led into a large meeting room filled with men seated around a long cedar conference table.

"*Fahdal*," Abdallah welcomed them, pointing to two empty seats.

Yousef's dominant figure stood at the front for all to see. "Anyone opposing Allah's will shall be dealt with accordingly. That includes both infidels as well as disloyal Muslims." An authoritarian figure in his military uniform, Yousef spoke in Arabic, emphasizing the dominant themes of spreading Islam throughout the world, infiltrating Western culture to stop its filthy cancer, and purging the earth of Israel and the Jews. "This is our jihad dictated by Allah. Every Muslim must attack these issues through whatever means necessary."

Rami felt sick to his stomach and feared he would vomit. Staring down at the wood parquet floor, he struggled to balance himself.

* * *

During the ensuing days, Yousef informed the group of their assignments in the Triple Frontier, where counterfeiting, bribery, murder, illegal immigration, and trading arms for drugs were the norm. He laid out the logic of suicide terrorism, highlighting the best places to target. "Public transportation. Airplanes. Buses. Trains. Also office buildings, shopping areas, schools, restaurants, and places of worship. Strikes are to be carried out anywhere substantial numbers of people gather and move freely. Breaking down the social structure of a society is the ultimate bomb. It is uncomplicated, inexpensive, and guarantees media coverage. It works. Little by little, we shall change the face of the world. Muslims are a patient people, not like impetuous Westerners." Yousef paused, keeping his listeners waiting. Satisfied with how his lecture was progressing, he continued. "Let's not forget the water supplies, food supplies, and nuclear facilities. These strikes are part of our final plan. Like a Spanish bullfight, taunting and weakening the bull before the final slaughter . . . nothing shall interfere with Muhammad's teachings and Allah's will."

Scrolling down a large map hanging on the wall, Yousef highlighted the territory where Argentina, Brazil, and Paraguay meet. "Fifty thousand Muslims inhabit this region known as the Triple Frontier, and our numbers are growing. We conduct business in Cuidad del Este in eastern Paraguay. Some of our people live in Foz do Iguaçu on the Brazilian side. Some live in Puerto Iguazú on the Argentine side. Linking these three cities is the Paraná River, which is harrowing to cross." Stopping, Yousef calculated his next move. "From here, we can easily launch terrorist activities on the Americas, negotiate lucrative drug deals with Colombians, and raise money for our cause. The authorities can easily be bribed to look the other way and provide us with protection." Yousef approached Rami. Addressing him personally, he stressed the importance for Rami to master the Spanish language. "You will do whatever you must to make this happen. Eventually, your position with al-Shahid will surface in the Triple Frontier." When Yousef instructed Rami to take another class with Professor Nolan and to befriend the teacher, Rami was aghast.

* * *

"Tell me, Rami, you're smart. Why do you think we need Doctor Nolan?"

All at once, Rami understood. Blood drained from his head and his face lost its color. The room began to spin. *Get hold of yourself. Do not let Yousef see weakness.* "I do not know. You tell me."

Yousef's face stiffened and his voice turned sharp. "Do not challenge me, Rami. Those who do meet unfortunate outcomes. Now, tell the group what you know."

Rami looked defiantly into Yousef's eyes. He searched the faces of the others in the room. Next to him, his gaze fell upon Omar. Omar looked away. Standing alone with all eyes on him, Rami felt like a meal for a group of vultures about to swoop down on him. Several times, he cleared his throat. He gulped once, then again more strongly, before proceeding. Providing an account of Professor Nolan's very first lecture on the oil-eating bacteria, Rami was careful about not revealing Rayna's name.

"Tell us about the assignment Nolan gave you."

Guarding Rayna's role, Rami responded, "I had to analyze the positive and negative ramifications of the bacteria. My report is on the computer if you want a copy."

"Yes. By all means. Be sure I receive it."

Instantly, Rami regretted making the offer.

"Now, I will tell you all about the infamous Doctor Nolan," Yousef gloated confidently. "Doctor Quintin Nolan was a chemist long before he became a philosopher. After working twenty-one years for Bryson Research, he was forced to resign. Top management in the multi-billion-dollar corporation did not approve the funds he needed to pursue research on bacteria that would very quickly and effortlessly eradicate oil spills. Western conglomerates that have been making millions on oil cleanups lobbied heavily for Bryson not to take this direction. Bowing to pressure and American government enticements that would sway more business in its direction, Bryson backed off and forced Nolan out. To keep Nolan from talking, they offered him a substantial severance package with strict conditions. Nolan used those funds to secretly pursue his obsession. However, six years ago, the good doctor ran low on funds and had to stop the project. For a while, it looked like he would give up entirely. He pursued a doctorate in philosophy and secured a teaching position at the University of Maryland." Yousef paused when someone handed him a glass of water. "Now, for whatever reason, Nolan is searching for backers. He wants to raise cash and complete the project. We're going to provide him with what he needs to succeed. And we must reach him before anyone else does." Maintaining his focus on Rami, Yousef went on, "Nolan is fifty-two and divorced. The breakup of his marriage hit him hard. He has one daughter, Anna, who attends Princeton University in New Jersey. The two are very close."

It unsettled Rami to know just how much Yousef could find out about a person. The thought of his own life being so exposed unnerved him. He worried about Rayna. *How much does Yousef know about her? Does he know she is Jewish?* Rami vowed to always protect her from harm.

"This is your first assignment, Rami. If you do nothing else, delivering the bacteria into our hands will be your major contribution to the spread of Islam. We will provide you with money and with whatever else you need. In your next life, Allah will reward you greatly."

Rami did not want to live for the next life. He wanted to live for this life, the life he knew. He mumbled, "Why do you hide behind Allah to brainwash others into doing your bidding?"

"Speak up. If you have something to say, let us all hear it."

Rayna's voice pierced Rami's consciousness: *Do not let your strength and courage be wasted. Find what you need and use it.* Courageously, Rami stood up and looked Yousef straight in the eyes. With the sagacity of a great warrior, Rami boldly asserted, "I am not flattered by your motive for selecting me to do this job. However, I will deliver the bacteria into your hands. In six months . . . in six years . . . however long it takes. You said Muslims are patient people. I assume that includes you. So do not pressure me, Yousef. It will be done. In return, I want something back. I want my privacy and my freedom. I do not like being spied upon. If there are monitoring devices in the apartment that I do not know about, remove them. I will do it myself if I have to. And I want my own car." Rami slumped into his seat. Wisdom told him he had said enough.

In the end, Yousef conceded to all of Rami's demands. For the time being, he needed the young man, and Rami knew it.

* * *

Returning home, Rami found his family squeezed around the kitchen table eating supper. Excitedly, they were discussing Ayisha's upcoming marriage and the approaching month of Ramadan. Salha stopped when she noted the anguish in Rami's eyes and the slouching of his shoulders. "Come. Sit down and eat, Rami."

"I am not hungry. Go on without me."

Salha gestured to her husband. "Talk with your son. Something is wrong."

* * *

Seated on the worn, mustard-colored couch in the dimly-lit parlor, Rami disclosed everything to his father. He spoke of al-Shahid and Yousef, of school, the apartment, Abdallah, the imam, Omar, and Rayna. For a long while, Ibrahim did not respond. When he did, Rami felt his father's words sear like a branding iron imprinting a permanent scar into his brain.

"The Jew is a bad omen," Ibrahim warned. "She is a fungus that is defiling you. She is the devil in disguise, discreetly luring you into her web. You must keep away from her. Do not ever go near her again . . . ever." He preached about how Allah was testing Rami, and beseeched his son to adhere to the teachings of the Quran and to fervently practice more discipline. "Allah has chosen your path. Your life is now with al-Shahid. In the name of Islam, you must do whatever must be done."

Rami could hardly believe his father's words. Trying to reason with Ibrahim was useless. His mind was already set. Before their dialogue ended, Rami extracted a promise from his father to utter not one word of their conversation to anyone. To himself, Rami vowed never again to discuss anything with his father.

* * *

The following Friday, Rami joined the men who were gathering at the mosque for pre-ceremonial prayers prior to Ayisha's marriage. Over that weekend, he tried hard to be joyous. His sisters painted themselves with henna—their palms, their feet, their hair. Relatives threw parties. The *kitab* was signed. Ayisha looked beautiful, but far too young to be a bride, Rami thought. After the rituals, Ayisha changed into a gown for the big feast. The celebration lasted late into the night. When the newlyweds departed, guests threw handfuls of rice and candy-coated almonds at them.

The long weekend of revelry failed to lift Rami's depression. He yearned for Rayna. Family and friends who had always been a close and dear part of his life now seemed unfamiliar. Rami no longer knew them and wondered how many were cemented in the same intolerant, hateful mindset as his father.

EIGHT

A season is set for everything, a time for every experience under heaven. ––Ecclesiastes 3:1

During the last weeks before Christmas, Rayna helped Abe in one of his lighting supply stores. From the time she had turned seven, working with her father during the busy Christmas season had always been a high point and a fun time for her. Abe taught Rayna well and she proved to be a quick learner.

* * *

Sarah had grown fond of Jonathan and was grateful to him for bringing Rayna home on his frequent visits back from school. She cultivated a friendship with Jonathan's mother and liked the social prominence it offered her. Jonathan's father was a well-known and respected surgeon with big-name patients from all over the world.

Until now, Sarah had been adamant about associating only with Sephardic Jews. She was steadfast about her five children marrying within the Syrian Jewish community. Yet, for such a notable and wealthy family as Jonathan's, she would accept an Ashkenazie Jew into the family, and she encouraged a relationship between her daughter and Jonathan.

* * *

On New Year's Day, the two families left the hustle and bustle of New York for a week's vacation at a kosher resort in Curaçao. Rayna and Jonathan went swimming, banana boating, snorkeling, and jet skiing in the calm waters of the Caribbean. Evening entertainment and good food enhanced the blissfulness of the warm climate and the relaxing and friendly atmosphere. Sarah watched with delight as her daughter and Jonathan took pleasure in being together. She secretly hoped for a full-fledged romance to blossom.

* * *

Returning from their vacation, the Mishans were greeted with bitterly cold weather and freshly fallen snow as they emerged from Kennedy Airport. On the drive home, they made a stop at the post office to pick up the mail being held for them. Entering the house, Rayna dropped her luggage on the floor and excitedly attacked the mound of envelopes until she found, buried at the bottom, the letter from *InterContinental Weekly*. Snatching it, she dashed upstairs to her room. A loud shriek followed. The family bolted up the steps, not knowing what caused Rayna's sudden outburst.

"I got it! I got the job!" She was euphoric. After competing with more than five hundred other journalism students across the country, Rayna had captured the coveted summer internship with the most widely circulated weekly magazine in the world. Working during the upcoming summer at the

World Trade Center Towers in New York City would earn her six college credits and a chance to get one of her pieces published. "They want me to come in and sign some papers and discuss the scope of my internship." Rayna could hardly wait to tell Rami. He had helped her with the application and with writing the three short stories required for submittal.

* * *

That night, lying in bed with a myriad of thoughts vying for her attention, Rami's energy persisted in dominating her senses. Rayna yearned to be with him, while at the same time praying not to love him so. *Jonathan is right*, she tried convincing herself. *Mixing a Jew with a Muslim is like mixing water with oil; they are compelled to separate.* Yet Rayna could not separate herself from Rami. In just a few days, she would ride back to school with Jonathan. In just a few days, she would begin her second semester. In just a few days, she would see Rami.

* * *

Rami and Omar began the last leg of their journey, boarding a London flight back to Washington. The jet taxied out to the runway and was soon airborne. Omar dozed. Rami tilted his seat back and closed his eyes, but he could not sleep. Greatly anguished over events of the past few weeks, Rami was experiencing the hollow sensation of living on borrowed time.

The special connection he had always shared with his father was gone. Never again could he trust Omar, his once closest friend. Al-Shahid had him locked into an unsettling situation. Yousef now ruled his life. And a Jew had captured his heart.

* * *

On a bright Sunday morning in early January 1997, Jonathan arrived to pick up Rayna for the trip back to Maryland. Sarah insisted he come into the house for some breakfast. Jonathan wanted to get on the road. Sarah's persistence won out.

Half an hour later, Abe marched out to the driveway with his youngest son, Eli. Each man carried an armload of Rayna's belongings. With the two back car doors open, they calculated how best to cram the stuff in the back seat.

"Sorry the trunk is so full," Jonathan apologized.

Eli handed Rayna's hair dryer to Jonathan and chuckled, "Don't drive away without this. It's my sister's lethal weapon. If her hair doesn't look good, she becomes deadly."

Smiling and shaking her head, Rayna approached the car, "Are you making fun of me?"

"Never in a million years would I dare to make fun of you," Eli teased.

Jonathan opened the car door and gallantly gestured, "Enter, beautiful lady." He then slipped into the driver's seat and started the engine.

Sarah bounded out of the house dragging a big red cooler filled with Syrian food. "Wait! You can't leave without this!"

"Mom! Rayna purposely forgot the cooler. Leave her alone. There's no room left in the car." Eli attempted to reason with his mother. Abe, Rayna, and Jonathan joined the protest.

Ignoring them all, Sarah swung open the back door, "I'll find room. You men just don't know how to pack."

In disbelief, Jonathan watched as Sarah began pulling out Rayna's things, piling some into Abe's arms, more into

Eli's, and the rest into Jonathan's. She slid the chest onto the back seat, retrieved Rayna's stuff, and stacked everything on top. "Can you see out the rear window?"

"No, Sarah, but what difference does that make?" Jonathan made it known that he was not thrilled about having anything Arabic in such close proximity.

"It'll be worth it. You'll both thank me. Syrian food is the best." Closing the rear door, Sarah moved to the open window where Rayna was sitting and reminded her daughter to give a safe call home when she arrived.

* * *

Relieved to be on the road and out of her mother's clutches, Rayna turned around and readjusted things so Jonathan could have a clearer view out the rear window. "I apologize for my mother's behavior. Is this better now?"

"Yes." Jonathan rolled his eyes and shook his head.

"She has been known to make us all crazy. My mom and I have our clashes, but she means well." Rayna slipped off her shoes, settled into her lotus position, and turned up the heater.

Crossing the Verrazano Bridge, she watched as Jonathan carefully concentrated on the many vehicles darting in and out of lanes. *He is handsome.* Jonathan's curly blonde hair framed his suntanned face. His deep blue eyes danced. His smile was relaxed and warm. His straight nose gave him a near-perfect profile. Being together in Curaçao had been fun. Their match could not have been more idyllic if it were not for the fact that someone else was tugging at Rayna's heart.

NINE

They constitute a universe of their own in which dreamers go beyond their dreams, beyond their desires, swept away by their quest for imagination and salvation and an infinite craving for innocence and wonder.—Elie Wiesel

There was one last thing to unload from the car. "You go on in. I'll park and bring up the cooler . . . with the Syrian food," Jonathan made a distasteful face.

"Thanks, Jonathan, but you've done enough already. Really, I'll get it . . ."

"I don't mind. I'll be right up . . . just don't ask me to eat that stuff."

* * *

Out of breath, he lugged the cooler up to Rayna's room and dropped it on the floor. "Shit! This thing is heavy."

"Sorry, I would have done it."

"It's okay. It's done." Easing the door shut with his foot and turning the lock, Jonathan cast his eyes upon Rayna.

His breathing was slow and deep. Fire blazed in his eyes. Swiftly, he moved toward her, circling his arms around her waist, inflicting a long, coercive kiss on her lips. She fought to release herself from his grip. He tightened his hold. "Don't fight me, damn it. You owe me!" In the heat of raging hormones, Jonathan pushed Rayna onto the bed, pinning her down. "Start acting your age, for Christ sake. You're not a little girl anymore. Grow up."

Straining to get free, she cried, "Jonathan, please don't do this. You're hurting me." The more Rayna resisted, the greater was Jonathan's resolve. His boiling lust scared her. She did not want him. Jonathan's kisses drooling over Rayna's face repulsed her. Feeling his hand wrestling down to unzip her jeans, she screamed. The zipper caught in her skin, tearing it below her navel. "Ouch!" Blood trickled from the open wound. "I'm begging you, Jonathan. Don't . . . please don't." She felt herself sinking. Her breathing was uneven and she gasped for air. Rayna was not physically strong enough to fight off Jonathan's determined, brute force.

"You like it from Rami, don't you? Tell me, is a circumcised Muslim better than a circumcised Jew? Here's your chance to find out." Panting heavily, Jonathan suffocated her with beastly passion.

"Don't do this to me," Rayna sobbed. "I never had sex with Rami . . . or anyone. Don't take away my virginity," she wailed hysterically. "No Jonathan . . . no. Please. No . . . don't."

Very slowly, Jonathan raised himself up. "I was sure . . . I thought . . . I'm sorry. I didn't know." Without another word, he turned and walked out, pulling the door shut behind him.

The next few hours were a blur. Over and over, Rayna scrubbed herself in the shower, trying to wash away the shame of Jonathan. She cried. She unpacked. She wanted Rami.

* * *

The phone rang. "Yes, Mom . . ."

"I've been waiting for you to call."

"I'm sorry. I forgot." Rayna looked at the clock, then out the window. It was already dark. The streetlamps reflected on the falling snow.

"You forgot? You should have called hours ago."

"I apologize. Mom, I have a really bad headache. I need to lie down."

"Did you eat?"

"Mom, I'll call you tomorrow . . ."

"Where's the food I sent?"

"In the refrig."

"Is Jonathan there?"

"No, Mom, Jonathan's not here."

"Where is he?"

"I have no idea where he is."

"It's snowing here. Is it snowing there?"

"Yes, it's snowing."

"I hope you're not planning to go out tonight."

"No, Mom, I'm not planning to go out tonight. Bye, Mom." Rayna lowered the receiver into the cradle. A knock at the door startled her. Thinking it was Jonathan, she did not respond. Another knock. Then another.

"Rayna. From the street I saw your light on. I cannot imagine you are out in this weather."

The voice. The accent. It could only be Rami. Her knees weakened and her lips went dry. Trembling, she opened the door. For several seconds, the two of them did not move. They stared without speaking.

Rami took Rayna's hand and put her palm to his cheek. His face warmed to a tender smile. "I missed you so much. Please, may I come in?"

This was the first time Rami had been inside her room, the first time they had been completely alone. Rayna locked the door. Instinctively, she knew he would not harm her. Rami placed a gentle kiss on her mouth. She clung to him, then shivered from his cold, wet jacket. "Your jacket. Here, let me help you off with it. I'll hang it on the door hook to dry."

"It is a blizzard out there. The weather report predicts more than three feet of snow before it is over." He slipped off his wet boots.

"How did you get here?"

"I walked. The roads are really bad. The news on the radio says not to go out unless you have all-wheel drive, and even then, only if it is an emergency."

"Four miles, Rami. You walked four miles in this weather?"

"To see you, I would walk a thousand miles in this weather."

"You're not going back tonight. I won't let you."

Rami did not need persuading.

"Your clothes. They're drenched." She went to the closet and took out her oversized purple terry robe. Handing it to Rami, she awkwardly pointed to the tiny private bathroom where he could change. "This is all I have to fit you. You can't stay in wet clothes. You'll catch pneumonia."

Minutes later, he appeared in Rayna's garment. Laughing, he said, "I feel ridiculous, but it smells so good." He held the right sleeve to his nose and took a deep whiff. "Mmmm. It is filled with your scent."

Rami's presence was soothing and Rayna felt safe with him. Shutting her eyes, she silently thanked God that Jonathan did not penetrate her. *In time, Rami will be the one I give myself to.* Taking his wet clothes, she spread them out to dry. "When did you return from Syria?"

"Yesterday. And you . . . from Brooklyn?"

"This afternoon . . . around one o'clock." Rayna's stomach growled. "Ooops!" She giggled nervously. "I'm hungry. I haven't eaten since early this morning."

"I have not eaten since last night."

"Ramadan?"

Rami nodded. "Yes. I will go out and try to find us something . . ."

"No, you won't. You're not going anywhere." Kneeling down, Rayna took out the food from the little refrigerator. "I have *kibbeh, lahamageen, mihshee, baba ghanouj, spanekh, tabouleh*, Syrian bread, and chicken salad. My mother insisted on sending all this Syrian food back with me in a big cooler." While fussing with the food, Rayna babbled uneasily. "Do you know that my mother has her hooks into Jonathan? She insists he will make a perfect husband for me. Syrian Jew or not, he has her full approval. Jonathan is her wish for . . ." Rayna faltered.

"And you? What is your wish?"

"Jonathan is definitely not my wish. I . . ." The incident from earlier in the day vividly rebounded. Turning to hide her emotions, Rayna warmed the food in the microwave.

* * *

Slowly scanning the small dormitory room, Rami liked
that it was clean and tidy. In the far left corner sat a mini-
refrigerator. On the shelf above it was a small microwave. A
computer, a printer, a small stereo, and books occupied the
space on her desk. A compact device containing a television,
radio, alarm clock, telephone, and answering machine sat
atop a four-foot high multi-shelved black PVC unit. Neatly-
folded towels, sheets, and clothes filled the shelves beneath.
Colorful travel posters decorated the walls. A purple and
pink valance framed the window. A matching comforter lay
across her bed. There was a black leather recliner and one
wooden desk chair. Plush purple and pink towels hung in the
bathroom. "I like your room."

"I'm glad you like it. Now, I have a surprise for you."
Looking directly into his eyes, she recited, "Ramadan is the
ninth month on the Islamic calendar and the fourth Pillar of
Islam. Muslims fast from sunrise to sunset during the whole
month. It is a time for inner reflection and devotion to God."

Rami had taught Rayna about the Islamic holy month
of Ramadan and delighted in her eagerness to learn. "I am
impressed that you remember." For the first time in weeks,
he was feeling joy. As Rayna laid out the food on two paper
plates, Rami gently massaged the back of her neck, sensing
her pleasure at his touch. When she pivoted to face him, he
lowered his mouth to meet hers and, for a moment, the world
withdrew from around them. "It hurts to be away from you."
Rami brushed the hair back from her face.

She blushed, then eased herself from him. "Let's eat
before the food gets cold." Rayna laid one plate on the desk

with a small bottle of grape juice. She picked up the other plate and took it to the recliner.

Studying Rayna's face as she ate, an insatiable desire for her consumed him. Still, Rami would only give his love if she wanted him. After the meal, he helped her clean up, tossing the paper goods and plastic utensils into the trash. Rayna dimmed the lamp, creating a warm glow in the room. Gracefully, she moved back to the recliner. "Come," she gestured, making a place for him to squeeze in next to her.

Rami reached into the pocket of his wet jacket hanging on the door hook. He removed a small package, then edged into the space she had made for him. Rayna handed Rami the cell phone she had kept for him while he was away. "This afternoon, I needed so much to call you, but I knew it wasn't safe to do so. I needed you to come." She lowered her eyes, unable to go on.

"Something is wrong. Tell me what it is."

She shook her head and forced a weak smile. "I'm just glad you're here." Quickly, she changed the subject and showed Rami the cell phone her parents had given her for Hanukkah. "Now we can talk whenever we want, anywhere we are."

He jested, "Two phones will surely put us on some new ground." Taking her hand, he kissed each finger. "Can I tell you about Hanukkah?"

Squeezing his hand, she encouraged him on.

"On Hanukkah, Jews light candles for eight nights to celebrate a miracle. About two thousand years ago, the army of the Syrian King Antiochus desecrated the Temple with idols. The Maccabees fought the Syrians and reclaimed the Temple for the Jews and for Allah . . ."

"For God. *Hashem*."

"Yes, for Hashem. The oil left in the Temple was only enough to light a flame for one day, yet the flame in the Temple burned for eight days. This was the miracle."

"I'm impressed at how well I taught you," she smiled. "I like that we learn from each other."

He kissed her forehead, then each eye, then her nose, then her lips. "I have something for you. I found it in an old shop in Halab." Rami held out the little package. "It reminded me of you. I had to buy it."

Rayna removed the wrapping. Slowly, she examined the little music box of delicate purple and pink glass inlay "Oh, Rami, it's so beautiful."

"Wind it up."

She turned the knob and lifted the lid. Rayna's face lit up, "It's the Arabic wheat song." Bubbling with pleasure, she sang to the music. "Ya rra bee barrek ee barrek weezeedawn, ya rra bee barrek ah ah, ya rra bee barrek ah ah, ya rra bee barrek . . ."

Rami joined in, "Lalala lalalala, lalala lalalala, lalalalaaaaaa . . ." They were laughing and singing and full of joy. "How do you know this song? It is so ancient."

"It's one of my favorites. My *jidaw* taught it to me. When I was a little girl, whenever I was sad, my grandfather sang this song and insisted I sing with him. We would clap our hands and dance and then I would be happy."

"I am glad my gift brings you good memories." Rami curled his fingers into Rayna's. "Tell me about your month."

"You first. I want to hear about your month in Syria."

"No, no, you first, then me. My month in Syria is a very long story."

So Rayna began. She spoke about the final weeks in December working with her brother Eli at their father's Manhattan store during the busy Christmas shopping season. When she told Rami of the summer internship at *InterContinental Weekly*, he squeezed her hand, genuinely excited for her. "I knew you would get it."

"Thank you for your encouragement and support."

"Some day you will be a famous journalist and win all kinds of awards, and I will be by your side."

"Yes," she whispered, "you will be by my side."

"Now, tell me how you got this beautiful suntan."

She tried making light of the vacation in Curaçao, but still it disturbed Rami to know that Jonathan had spent a fun week with her. He said nothing. Then, at once, Rami watched Rayna's expression precipitously change. He felt her body shudder. Sitting so close in the dimly lit room, he observed Rayna's lower lip quiver and her eyes well. "Something is wrong. Tell me what it is. Why did you need me to come this afternoon?"

Rayna's breathing went ragged. A series of quick intakes followed. Her voice broke and she began to cry. Rami brushed the droplets from her cheeks and comforted her, patiently waiting to hear her story.

Gradually, she revealed all that had happened earlier in the day. "I was so scared. I thought for sure Jonathan would not stop. He had me pinned down and I couldn't budge from under him. His physical strength . . . he is much stronger than me. I couldn't defend myself," she cried.

Cradling Rayna snugly, he gently rocked her in his arms until he felt her body soften. *The bastard*, Rami flared in silence. *With my own hands, I will murder that filthy slime.* An uneasy feeling tugged at him and he wrestled to crystallize a memory that flirted with his consciousness. This was not the first time he had failed her, but he knew not when. *If only I had come by earlier.* "From now on, when you go home to Brooklyn, I will be the one to take you. When you go to Hillel for dinner, I will meet you and walk you back to the dorm. I am going to protect you always. And, one day, Jonathan shall pay for what he did. He will not come near you again."

Having Rami there, Rayna felt safe, and she told him so. "Tell me about your month in Syria."

Into the wee hours, Rami spoke of his family, Ayisha's marriage, Abdallah, Yousef, and his diminishing friendship with Omar. He described the three days in the Bekaa Valley, educated Rayna on the Triple Frontier, and confirmed the existence of Doctor Nolan's project on the oil-guzzling bacteria. After relating the tale of his father's contempt for her and for all Jews, he cleaved to the security of her nearness. "I feel like I am trapped on the edge of something I cannot escape from. You are all I have in this entire world. There is no one I can trust but you."

Running her index finger along Rami's troubled face, Rayna traced his majestic features until, exhausted, they both fell asleep.

* * *

The howling of the wind wakened Rayna. Rami felt her stir and held on more strongly. She glanced at the clock. It was after four in the morning. "We can't shut out problems. We must live the life we are born to know." She took Rami's hand. "Come. The sun will soon rise. We need to sleep." Rayna rose from the recliner and went to the window. "It's getting worse out there." In the dimness, he came to her side. The streetlamps illuminated the winter scene. Big white snowflakes fell softly. Tree branches hung heavily. Fierce winds created high drifts. Rayna closed the slats in the blind. Rami's hands braced both sides of her face and they kissed. Awkwardly, she eased herself from him and went into the bathroom. Twisting up her hair, she fastened it with a clip. Rami stood in the doorway. His eyes could not leave her. Rayna washed her face and brushed her teeth. She handed Rami a clean towel. Then, holding up a new toothbrush, she smiled, "I got this from my dentist. I almost didn't pack it."

Stepping back into the room, Rayna hesitantly removed her clothes. She released the clip from her hair, and reached onto the shelf for a nightgown. Rami came to her side and steadied her hand. *Her body is just as beautiful, just as sensuous as her face.* Needs, emotions, new sensations tumbled together. Then his eyes fell to the gash below her navel. "Did Jonathan do this to you?"

"Yes."

"As long as I am alive, he will never again touch you." Rami knelt down and caressed her wound, then lifted Rayna to the bed. "This past month, you were with me every minute. No matter where I was, no matter what I was doing, you occupied my heart and my thoughts." His warm breath brushed against her lips.

Rayna's small hands moved inside the purple robe, helping Rami slip it off. On her narrow bed, under the down comforter, they lay naked. Rami began to laugh.

"Whaaat?"

"I must love you very much, but . . ."

"But . . . what?"

"Do you know that no Muslim man would be caught sleeping in a purple and pink bed?" Their laughter filled the room. The wind howled, rattling the window panes. Rami stretched his body over hers. "Rayna Mishan, will you marry me?"

"When?"

"Right now."

"Right now?"

"Yes, right now. Remember in the fall when we were walking at Brookside Gardens? We made a pledge that this would be a special time, saved for our wedding night."

"I remember."

"I want to honor my pledge to you. We only need Allah to bless our union." Passion surged through their warm bodies and they hungered for each other.

"In the presence of Allah, will you marry me, Rayna Mishan?"

"In the presence of Allah, I will marry you, Rami Mahmoud. In the presence of Hashem, will you marry me, Rami Mahmoud?"

"In the presence of Hashem, I will marry you, Rayna Mishan."

Together, they recalled God's blessing to Abraham that his seed would be as numerous as the stars. "One day we will have lots of children . . ."

"Yes. One day," she smiled.

"Above all others, I will cherish only you. I will protect you and love you all the days of my life and forever after."

"With my love, I give you my trust and my commitment. Trust, so you will never doubt my love. Commitment, so you will always know that I belong to you alone. Until my death and forever after."

"May Allah of our Prophet Muhammad bless our union. May the God of Abraham, Isaac, and Jacob . . . and Ishmael . . . bless our union."

"Amen." A powerful energy flowed, their bodies locked, and Rayna gave herself to him.

"Uhhhhh," her body tensed and she cried out in pain. Leaning into Rami's shoulder, she masked her sounds.

The rapture of breaking Rayna's virginity sent a surge of virility into Rami's being. He was determined to be the only man in her life. Feeling Rayna's spasms, he instinctively slowed the pace of his thrust as she clutched to him. Rami had not wanted to hurt her. Gently, their bodies swayed rhythmically. He moaned. Culmination gushed in a stream of sublime pleasure, uniting their fate and elevating their souls to a higher world. Intertwined in a lover's knot, they fell into a deep and blissful sleep, unaware that their destinies had already been drawn.

TEN

Nothing in this world comes easy. Nothing comes without a price. Each hurdle is a journey with bruises and scars. Every pleasure is accompanied with a sense of pain.—Lao-tzu

The phone rang, awakening the lovers from a peaceful slumber. Reaching for the cordless, Rami handed it to Rayna. "Hello."

"Hi. Did I wake you?"

She leaned her head and angled the phone, enabling Rami to hear. "Yes, as a matter of fact, you did wake me. Goodbye, Jonathan."

"Wait! Don't hang up! I want to come over and apologize . . . make things right."

"I bet you'd like to come over, you despicable piece of scum. Stay away from me!"

"Rayna, I'm sorry. I don't know what got into me . . ."

"Stay away from me!"

"I'm on my way up. It'll take me two minutes to climb the steps."

Rami took the phone. "You heard the lady. Stay away from Rayna. If she wanted you, you would have had her yesterday when you tried to rape her."

"I don't know what you're talking about, you fuckin' Arab."

"Jonathan, we have a witness. Rayna is prepared to report the incident and bring charges. That should look good on your record when you apply for medical school. Think of the publicity. Son of famous surgeon . . ." Rami winked at Rayna.

"You goddamn Muslim . . ."

"I suggest you stay away from Rayna, or I will make your life a living hell."

"Are you threatening me?"

"No, Jonathan, I am forewarning you. Do not under-estimate what a *goddamn Muslim* is capable of doing. Keep away from Rayna." Tracing the line to the wall, Rami disconnected the phone. "I hope he will not be stupid enough to bother you again." Rami brought Rayna back into his arms.

"It would devastate Jonathan if his parents found out. Once he told me that he doesn't want to be a doctor, but would not dare disappoint his parents."

"Good. Let us tuck that information away. We may need it someday." Rami ran his hands along the curves of Rayna's body, then gently rolled her over and massaged her back.

* * *

By late Tuesday morning, the sun's rays broke through the clouds, the snow stopped falling, and the blustery winds lost their momentum. After two crippling days, the

Washington area began digging out from under a white blanket. Around campus, snowplows were in full motion. Student life rekindled and the march to classes was on.

Rayna tilted the slats in the blind. Beams of light brightened the room. *The past two days have been so wonderful. Never could I have imagined it to be this way.* Easily, she and Rami had shifted into a reassuring level of comfort with each other—never closing the bathroom door, never bashful about their bodies, and never hesitant to speak their minds. The two were now solidly secure with each other. Rayna crawled back in bed.

"I hope you will agree to a decision I just thought of," Rami smiled. "From now on, the only time I will spend in my apartment is to do laundry. Yours and mine. There is a washer and dryer in the kitchen. I do not want you going alone to wash your clothes. I will do all of it. Every week." Grinning, he joked about how he would explain this to Omar.

"And just where do you plan to sleep every night?"

"On this small purple and pink bed right next to you." His eyes lingered on her face.

"It's going to be very uncomfortable." She rolled on top of him, smothering his neck with kisses.

Rami laughed, "You are tickling me."

* * *

While showering and dressing, they discussed Nolan and the bacteria, agreeing together to take another of the professor's classes. Rayna persuaded Rami to enlist Nolan in defining firm working parameters with Yousef. "An exclusive, only with you," Rayna coached. "If Abdallah or anyone else interferes, Nolan is to be clear that the deal is off and he'll find other sponsors."

"That should make Yousef go crazy."

Their dialogue drifted to Nolan's abortion lecture and to their own new level of intimacy. Rayna verbalized her concerns about the past two days of lovemaking. "Today, I'll go to the Health Center and see a doctor about getting birth control pills, and hope I'm not pregnant." Professor Nolan's lecture on abortion had prevailed.

Rami pressed for a legal marriage, saying he did not want anything or anyone to come between them. Responding to his wishes, Rayna spoke of her friend Marisa, a back-to-school mom pursuing journalism. "I met her last semester in one of my classes. We studied for exams together and I've been to her house several times for shabbat dinners. She has a great husband and three sweet children. I'll talk with her. I think she'll help us." Rayna opened a snack-size box of Cheerios and dribbled a small container of soy milk over it. "I'm grateful my mother thought of more than just Syrian food when she packed the cooler." She poured orange juice into a plastic cup and swallowed a multi-vitamin. "Sorry to be eating in front of you during Ramadan, but I'm hungry."

"Please. Do not starve yourself on my behalf."

"Don't worry, I won't," she grinned. "Would you like to come to Hillel and have dinner with me tonight? Break your day of fasting with a bunch of Jews."

"If it will not cause a problem, I would like that very much."

* * *

Rami donned his navy down jacket and helped Rayna on with her purple wool coat. They pulled up their boots and slipped into their gloves. Rayna wrapped a pink angora scarf around her neck and slipped the extra room key into Rami's pocket. "We can finally get out of here."

"Get out of here?" Rami was bewildered. "What do you mean? These past two days have been paradise. The best two days of my entire life. You are magnificent and I would much prefer to stay right here with you forever."

Adoringly, she pecked his lips. "Tonight you can have more."

"I do not know if I can last until tonight."

"You'll last until tonight because you have no choice," she teased. "Let's meet back here at five and we'll walk over to Hillel together."

* * *

Outside, the fresh cold air and bright sunshine brought a rush of new energy. Rami ran ahead, picked up a handful of snow, molded it, and tossed it at Rayna.

"Now you're asking for it." She swooped up some of the white powder, shaped it, and threw a snowball back at him. It hit his shoulder and broke apart. She burst out laughing. Invigorated, they indulged in a playful snowball fight until Rayna's pink scarf came loose and she tripped over it.

"Had enough?" Catching her before she hit the ground, Rami picked up the scarf and gently wrapped it around Rayna's head. He took hold of her gloved hand and they walked to the Health Center.

* * *

On February ninth, Rami celebrated the holy day of Eid al Fitr, the end of Ramadan that concluded the month of fasting. On Valentine's Day, Rami innocently showed up with a big love-card and a gray knitted scarf that a student in one of his classes had given to him.

"Rami Mahmoud, you give that right back to her!"

"But that would be rude."

"How would you like it if I accepted a gift and love card from a guy in one of my classes?"

Immediately, he understood the ramifications. "Uh-oh, I gave her the wrong message, yes?"

"Yes . . . unless you want her for your girlfriend."

"Never! I want only you. I will give it back."

"Just know that I'll kill you if I catch you with somebody else."

His hands encircled her waist and he kissed her. "Good. I am glad you are jealous," he teased affectionately, conscious of his own possessive feelings for her.

* * *

On Tuesday, the fourth of March, Rayna confided to Marisa that she and Rami wanted to secretly marry. Marisa choked on her sandwich. "How could you? He's a Muslim. What you want to do is sheer lunacy. Think, Rayna. Think with your head, not with your hormones."

"But we love each other . . ."

"At eighteen, you love each other? Have you been sleeping with him?"

Lowering her eyes, Rayna looked away.

"You don't need to respond. I already know the answer."

Rayna's face turned red.

"Is Rami your first?"

"Yes. And he will be my only . . ."

"He's taking advantage of you, Rayna. He's a Muslim. Don't confuse sex with love. Think of what you're doing. Do you have any idea how Muslim men treat their wives? Most are physically and emotionally abusive. Women are beneath them. And you'll have it even worse because you're Jewish. Marriage between a Jew and a Muslim? No, Rayna, don't be foolish. Open your eyes and look. You come from an orthodox family. Think of the consequences. What you want to do is so wrong."

"I'm sorry to have bothered you." Rayna rose to leave.

"Sit down, Rayna. You asked for my help and that's what you'll get."

Visibly reluctant, Rayna eased back into the chair.

"Do you know that Muslims believe we Jews kill non-Jewish children and use their blood to make our Passover matzoh? Do you know that Muslims believe we Jews, even though we are in such a small minority, are positioned to take over the world? They want to rid the planet of us before we succeed in accomplishing world dominance."

"That's ridiculous."

"Have you read one page, one word of the Quran?"

Rayna shrugged her shoulders.

"The book is full of ugly stuff. It gives Muslims the right to murder infidels, non-believers like us." Marisa took her forefinger and ran it horizontally across her throat. "It's their jihad. And what's more, their population is exploding. They plan to take over the world with Islam."

"Marisa, how can you make such blanket statements and narrowly judge a group of people? You're telling me that over one billion Muslims in this world are evil. You're telling me that there is not a good one in the bunch."

"Rayna, you're in denial. Like the story of *The Emperor's New Clothes*, you don't want to see the truth. You see only what you choose. What will your family say when they find out?"

"I don't plan to tell them."

"That won't last long. I guarantee they'll find out. This kind of secret does not stay hidden. What if you have children? What if . . . there are so many 'what ifs.' You're Jewish, Rayna. It's bad enough when a Jew marries a Christian . . . but a Muslim? Rayna, don't do it. Turn and walk away before. . ."

"So you won't help me?"

"Not with this. I'm sorry, Rayna. I can't."

"Marisa, your narrow way of thinking and your pre-judgments don't make for good journalism. Maybe you better consider changing your major."

"Rayna, I'm offering you some guidance . . . some words of wisdom from a friend who is several years older than you. Please listen to me."

"If you met Rami, you would know that he is a good human being. He is gentle and kind with a great capacity to love. He's also very smart. Never would he hurt me. I'm sure of it. We'll find another way. Thank you, Marisa." Rayna stood and gathered her books. "I can't help who I fall in love with. All I know is that I love Rami and he loves me." She walked eight steps, stopped, turned back, and sat down again. "I want to tell you about one of my cousins. She had met someone, an orthodox Syrian Jew just like herself. They were deeply in love and planned to marry. One month before the wedding, he told her he had genital herpes. He had told no one else.

He caught it from a girl he dated in college and regretted the whole affair. Sometimes he's okay and sometimes he has flare-ups. With no one to turn to, my cousin confided in me because we had been close growing up. I was seventeen at the time, she was nineteen. Initially, my advice to her was the same as your advice is to me—turn and walk away."

Pausing, Rayna considered Marisa's demeanor, then continued. "My cousin asked, 'If he were crippled and doomed to a wheelchair, would you tell me to turn and walk away because my life would be miserable with him?' I thought for a moment and then advised her to listen to her heart. They married, are ecstatically happy, adore one another, and their first child is due this summer. Because of their love, they found a way. Not all people who have herpes are sexually promiscuous. Not all Muslims are bad people."

Again, Rayna stood to leave.

"Wait!"

"Marisa, this is difficult enough on me, and on Rami, too. But something is drawing us together. Call it *basheert*. Fate. God's intervention. I don't know."

"Can I meet him?"

"Why? You've already made up your mind."

"Let's start over, Rayna. I'm inviting you and Rami for shabbat dinner on Friday night. Allow me to come to a decision with an open mind."

Rayna hugged her friend. "Thank you."

* * *

Reaching into her tote, Rayna withdrew the ringing cell phone and put it to her ear. "Where are you?"

"The meeting with Abdallah lasted much longer than I expected. I am on campus and walking over now. I should be there in ten minutes. Did you have lunch with Marisa today?"

"Yes. I'll tell you about it later. Rami, I'm going to start back. I've got a paper due tomorrow and I have to finish it tonight. I'll meet you on the same path we always take."

"Rayna, no. Wait until I get there. I do not want you walking alone in the dark."

"I'll be okay, really. You worry too much. I'll see you in a little bit. I love you." Rayna ended the call and dropped the cell phone into her tote. She was at Hillel. Most students had finished eating and were gone. Rayna did not want to wait any longer.

* * *

Jonathan had been hanging around eyeing her. Rayna sensed it. Subtly, she looked at him, trying to gauge the situation. Thinking he would not bother her, she buttoned up her coat, collected her things, and left.

Following her, Jonathan called out, "Rayna."

She walked faster. Jonathan increased his pace, again calling to her. She ignored him. He caught up and grabbed Rayna's arm. She jerked away. Again, Jonathan grabbed hold of her arm, determined not to let go.

"Ouch! You're hurting me!"

"What's the matter? Has your Muslim protector deserted you?" Jonathan's fingers dug into Rayna's elbow.

"Ouch!" she screeched again, trying to free herself from his strong hold. "Let go of me!"

Hearing Rayna's outcry, Rami rushed toward her sounds. From behind, he grabbed Jonathan's left arm and twisted it behind his back. Startled, Jonathan dropped his grip on Rayna and spun around. He lunged at Rami, but Rami was quicker. Drawing up his knee, Rami rammed it into Jonathan's groin, leaving him doubled over in pain and spewing out a mouthful of profanities.

"Next time, I will not be so gentle. Stay away from Rayna. This is your final warning."

* * *

After having just come from a harrowing meeting with Abdallah, Rami's tolerance was on a short leash. Taking Rayna by the hand, he led her across campus and back to the dorm. "I asked you to wait. In all these weeks, have I ever been late for you? Patience! Do you know the meaning of the word? Is it too much to ask of you?" For the first time, Rami was angry with Rayna.

"I should have waited."

"Why are you unable to see that I am concerned for your safety? I could not help being late. Sometimes it will happen. The meeting with Abdallah was beyond my control. I was not late on purpose. Next time I ask something of you, do not disregard me."

"I'm sorry."

"What if I had not arrived when I did? Do not do this to me again."

"I won't."

"I care too much about you. I wish you could see that."

ELEVEN

May the fires of your love keep you happy and warm. May the strength of your love keep you safe from all harm. May the light of your love guide your pathways together. May the joy of your love keep you happy forever.—Indian marriage blessing

From the onset, there was mutual trust and respect between Rami and Nolan. Both were of the same mindset—the bacteria were never to fall into Yousef's hands. However, Nolan needed Yousef's financial backing to continue the project, and Rami needed Yousef to continue perceiving him as the indispensable link to Nolan. So the professor and the student made a pact to extend the duration of their undertaking for as long as they could get away with it.

* * *

On March 7, after Friday noon prayers, Abdallah summoned Rami into the imam's office. "But I have classes this afternoon and need a ride back with Omar," Rami grumbled.

"This won't take long. Omar can wait. Now, sit." It was no secret that Abdallah and Rami did not like each other. Early on, Abdallah pushed to get rid of Rami. It was Yousef who had decided that Rami was to stay. "Yousef is upset. And when Yousef is upset, then I'm upset. We don't like your rebellious nature. Now, I want to know who instructed you to form an exclusive relationship with the professor, or did you come to that arrangement on your own? Nolan won't even take our calls . . . you will pay heavily for this. I'll make sure of it."

"An agreement was made last December in the Bekaa Valley. Remember? You give me my freedom and my own car. I give to Yousef the perfected bacteria from Doctor Nolan. I am living up to my end of the deal. Are you?"

"No, you are not! We never agreed for you to be the only contact with Doctor Nolan."

"I cannot help what the professor chooses to do. Do you want me to deliver the final product or not?" Rami was keenly aware of Yousef's consuming desperation for the bacteria.

"Yousef wants you in the Triple Frontier. We've arranged for a brief trip."

"How long is a brief trip? I have classes."

"Well, maybe we can end your schooling here and make your brief trip a permanent one."

Anxiety pulsated through Rami's veins. The last thing in the world he wanted was to be separated from Rayna, so he lied. "Abdallah, there is something I failed to mention. Something you and Yousef should know. Yesterday, Nolan received a tempting offer from other backers. If you or Yousef object to Nolan's parameters, then al-Shahid is history. Another sponsor is waiting to usurp you."

"Yousef doesn't like those kinds of messages. Here, you be the messenger." Abdallah lifted the phone and dialed Yousef. After a brief exchange, he passed the handset to Rami. "Why don't you tell Yousef what you just told me?"

In Arabic, Yousef exploded at Rami, ordering him to the Triple Frontier.

"I have classes . . ."

"And a very beautiful girlfriend, I hear."

A chill shot up Rami's spine. "How much longer do you intend to keep me under surveillance? I thought we had an agreement. The perfected bacteria in exchange for . . ."

"No, Rami. You will not make demands on me or the organization. Your position is to do what you're told."

Rami had to do something fast. His brain jumped into full gear, assessing the situation and betting on a new strategy. "You want me in the Triple Frontier? Okay, Yousef, I will not argue with you. Book me on the next flight. And while you are at it, I suggest you find a replacement for me before Nolan supplants al-Shahid with the new backers waiting at his doorstep."

A long silence infused the phone lines. "I don't believe you, Rami."

"Refresh my memory, Yousef. How many men have you already put on this assignment, including Abdallah? At least five that I know of. All have failed, if my facts are correct. Right now, I am your only hope. Nolan *will* work with me. But this is your call." Rami waited.

"Who are the other backers?"

"Oh, no. I am not so stupid to lay all my cards out for you to see. You only have to know that you asked me to do a job and I am doing it. When I make an agreement, I keep it. The choice is, either you trust me or you do not." Rami reveled in how well he had taken the lead, not aware of the false sense of security ensnaring him.

Yousef's vile rage, cursing Rami in the most profane of Arabic damnations, caught Rami completely off guard. Rami's blood curdled. He said nothing. The sounds of Yousef's heavy breathing were interrupted only by periods of ghostly silence.

"You've backed me into a corner, Rami. Know that I have a long memory."

With an evil smile distorting his face, Abdallah took the phone from Rami, conversed with Yousef, then looked back up at Rami. "Yousef wants you to stay and work with Nolan. You will provide him with weekly progress reports."

A temporary reprieve. Rami pushed his luck. "The spying must stop."

Abdallah nodded.

"A car was promised. I do not want to keep sharing Omar's car. When do I get my own?"

"Yousef said you will have a car next week." He scribbled something on a piece of paper and handed it to Rami. "The number for Yousef's direct line. You're to call him weekly with updates on Nolan's progress. And, Rami . . ."

"Yes, Abdallah . . ."

"Don't think this is over. Your trip to South America has only been postponed until summer. It is *not* canceled."

* * *

Later that day, Rami sat in the dorm room and waited. The time was five o'clock. Rayna was late. The key turned in the door.

"Sorry. I was at the library and lost track of time." Rayna bent and kissed Rami. He did not respond. She kissed him again. Nothing. "What's wrong?" she asked, hurrying to freshen up and change clothes.

"*Patiently.* I have been waiting for you, *patiently*," he said, reminding Rayna of her impatience a few nights earlier when he had asked her to wait for him at Hillel.

"Your point is well taken. I said I was sorry. Now, can we please drop it?"

"How much longer will you be?"

"Ten minutes. I'll be quick."

"We still have to stop and pick up challah and dessert . . . and fight rush-hour traffic. You did say Marisa was expecting us at six?" Rami looked at his watch.

"Yes." Observing Rami, Rayna saw that he seemed troubled. She kicked herself for snapping. "Do you not want to go?"

"Did I say that?"

"No."

"Then why would you assume . . ."

She put her arms out, "I need a hug."

"Me, too."

* * *

Rami slowed the car to a crawl in the bumper-to-bumper traffic. Rayna reached over and touched his hand. "You had a hard day, didn't you?"

"Yes."

"Tell me what happened."

As Rami related all that had transpired at the mosque that afternoon, Rayna lovingly kneaded the back of his head and neck. "I marvel at your diplomatic skills. You should be working for the United Nations. I bet you could solve the Israeli-Palestinian conflict."

"Really?"

"Mmmm." She leaned over and stroked him between the legs.

"You better watch out or I will have to pull over and we will be late for dinner."

"In that case, I should stop."

"Did I say you should stop?" He pulled her close. "I adore you."

She kissed his cheek. "Rami . . ."

"What?"

"Rami . . ."

"What, *rrawhee?*" He hit the brake as a minivan cut in front of him.

"Don't you find it strange that Yousef has never come here to Washington . . . to the United States? If he is so bothered about your having this exclusive relationship with Professor Nolan, and if he wants his own personal connection with the man, wouldn't you think Yousef would come here himself? Something is not right. Yousef caved into you much too easily."

"Tell me what is going on in that gorgeous head of yours."

"Well, maybe Yousef can't come to America. Maybe he would be arrested. Maybe he's a wanted man . . . by the FBI or the CIA. Do you know his last name?"

"No."

"Find out. When I start my internship at *InterContinental Weekly* this summer, I'll do some investigating."

* * *

"Come on in," Marisa greeted the couple.

"Sorry we're late. The traffic . . ."

"No, no. Your timing is perfect. We haven't lit the candles yet."

Three-year-old Miriam jumped into Rayna's arms. Jason appeared in the entranceway and kissed Rayna on the cheek, "The children have missed you."

Rayna beamed, "Everyone, this is Rami."

"Is he your boyfriend?" inquired six-year-old Joseph.

"Yes, Rami is my boyfriend," she smiled with amusement. Then pointing to the family of five, Rayna introduced Rami to each one.

"I got an air-hockey table for my birthday. You wanna see it?" Eight-year-old David had taken Rami's hand and was eagerly coaxing him downstairs to the finished basement.

"I would very much like to see your new hockey table." Rami followed David down the steps.

"I wanna play, too." Joseph made his wants known as he trailed behind.

"I can see the boys have hooked Rami into playing," Jason laughed.

"Thanks for the challahs and dessert," Marisa called out as she put the two whole loaves on a large silver platter and covered them with a decorative Israeli weave.

Jason filled a small silver goblet to the brim with Manishewitz blackberry wine and called down to the boys. "Okay guys, it's time to come up. Everyone wash hands."

* * *

They all gathered in the dining room. Two silver candle-sticks stood regally on the long buffet. A quiet reverence descended over the room. Marisa loosely draped a white-lace scarf over her head. She lit the candles, encircled the flames three times with her hands, and in Hebrew chanted the prayer welcoming in the light of the sabbath.

Rayna whispered in Rami's ear, "Ashkenazie women circle the candles three times, not Sephardic women."

Soon, everyone took their seats around the elegantly set table. Little Miriam insisted on sitting next to Rayna. In Hebrew, Jason recited the blessing over the wine, drank from the chalice, then passed it around for all to sip. Rayna looked at Rami, knowing that Islam forbade the imbibing of wine or any alcoholic beverage. When Marisa handed the half-empty goblet to Rami, Rayna tactfully took the cup from him. She touched her lips to the rim, then passed it to the children.

Jason held up the challah platter and delivered the Hebrew prayer thanking God for the bread they were about to eat. The children's eyes were intent on their father as he broke off a piece for himself, then pulled out chunks of the soft fresh dough and passed around portions for everyone at the table. Rami watched with delight as the children devoured their pieces of challah, then enthusiastically attacked the balance of the loaf, ripping out the insides.

Rayna helped Marisa bring in the meal. There was chicken soup with matzo-balls, salad, roasted chicken, potato kugel, and carrot tzimmes. Noisy chatter from the children saturated the room. "Me first," Joseph demanded as his big eyes zeroed in on Rayna slicing the lemon meringue pie.

"No, Joseph. You know better. What have you learned about patience?" Marisa reprimanded.

"Patience is not so easy," Rayna said to Joseph while serving him a piece of pie. "Even I sometimes have a hard time being patient." She glanced at Rami and winked.

With each spoonful, the children smacked their lips with pleasure, then asked for seconds. "Your dessert made a big hit. Thank you," said Jason.

"Thank you for inviting us," Rami reciprocated. "You have a wonderful family."

Miriam climbed onto Rayna's lap, fingering her diamond pendant. "Mommy, I want Rayna to give me my bath."

When Marisa nodded her approval, Rayna hugged the little girl, "I'll race you upstairs." Giggling, the two made a wild dash for the steps.

"Come on guys, shower time," Marisa signaled to Joseph and David, who clearly preferred to go back downstairs with Rami and play table hockey.

* * *

In the kitchen, Rami and Jason were left to clean up. "Marisa says the two of you want to marry. Other than Rayna's beauty, why would a Muslim marry a Jew? Are you aware of all the difficulties this will cause her . . . or don't you care? Marriage to a Muslim is not in Rayna's interest, and it's unfair of you to toy with her life. You will only hurt her. For Rayna's sake, I'm asking you not to do this."

Not expecting this invasion, Rami was disturbed at Jason's assessment and decided to leave as soon as Rayna came down the steps. His day had been difficult enough with Yousef and Abdallah. He did not need more turmoil. "Why is it that people must be categorized? Good, bad. Black, white. Jew, Muslim, Christian . . . or whatever else. History is rampant with religious wars, hatred, intolerance. From childhood, we are taught. Our innocent beginnings are contaminated. How sad for all of us that we live in such a divided world. I only know that I love Rayna. We accept each other for who we are. She has taught me a lot about Judaism and I have taught her a lot about Islam. Our religions are not so far apart."

"Intellectually, you make a lot of sense, Rami. But reality is what you must live with. I'm thirty-eight years old. You're only eighteen. You and Rayna are too young to take this kind of drastic step. Twenty years from now, when you're my age, you both will regret this, if you survive that long. There are consequences to everything. Why don't you just date while you're in college and enjoy your few years together? Then you can easily go your separate ways and no one gets hurt."

"Do you love your wife?"

"Yes, of course I do."

"Did you marry her because she is Jewish or because you love her?"

"I married her because I love her."

"If she were not Jewish, would you still have married her?"

Jason did not answer.

Rayna descended the steps, informing Jason that his children were waiting to be tucked in. Jason smiled, "I'll be fifteen minutes. They'll get extra-long storytime tomorrow night. Marisa should be down in a minute and we'll have tea and talk more." Jason climbed the steps.

* * *

Rami placed his hands on Rayna's shoulders and looked directly into her face. "Coming here was a big mistake. I want to leave now."

"What just happened between you and Jason?"

"He opposes our marriage." Tugging at Rayna's arm, he edged her toward the door and reached for their jackets.

Marisa descended the steps. "You're not leaving?"

Visibly upset, Rami turned the doorknob. "It appears that you and your husband have your minds made up. A Jew and a Muslim do not belong together. Thank you for your hospitality. I enjoyed meeting the children."

"You're wrong. We're going to help you. Come into the living room and sit down. Please."

Rami lingered. *Maybe Marisa and Jason have had a change of mind.*

Suddenly, Rayna seemed eager to leave. "It's getting late, Marisa. Rami and I are both tired. We've had a long day." She gave her friend a hug. "Thank you for inviting us. The evening was delightful. I'll call you soon."

Rami was baffled by Rayna's anxiousness to leave just when a ray of hope might be on the horizon.

Jason came down the steps. "I'm getting too old for this," he grinned. "The three of them keep us hopping . . . you're not going, are you?"

"Jason, thank you, but we really have to get back."

"No, Rayna. We want you and Rami to stay. Marisa will make tea."

* * *

In the living room, sitting on a navy-blue, brushed-suede loveseat, Rami and Rayna shifted restlessly. On a matching sofa, Jason sat opposite them. Marisa carried in a tray with a pot of tea and four mugs. She set it down on the large oval coffee table and took a place by her husband.

"Do you fully understand the consequences of what you are about to do?" Jason asked. "A *fatwa* could condemn both of you. Islamic legal opinions issued by fundamentalist clerics are not to be taken lightly. Rayna could be killed for marrying a Muslim. She could be accused of seduction, of defilement. Look what happened to Salman Rushdie just for writing *The Satanic Verses*. For years, he had to go into hiding to safeguard his life. And his problems are not over yet."

Rami glared at his host, knowing there was truth in Jason's pronouncements. "Not all Muslims are bad and not all Jews are good."

Marisa moved closer to her husband. "We care about Rayna and what this will do to her." She looked at Jason, who nodded. "When do you want to marry?"

Rami found Marisa's question unsettling. "Do not dangle a carrot in front of us and then hit us with a stick." He stood to leave.

"Jason and I are asking you a question. Isn't love the reason you came here?"

Rami sat down, drawing Rayna closer.

"You'll need to go to the courthouse and apply for a marriage license. Go to the one in downtown Rockville. You can use our address. In about a week, you'll have the license and . . ."

Rami could not believe what he was hearing. A chance to be forever with Rayna. "Go on. And what, Marisa?"

"We would like for you to have a meaningful ceremony to hold in your memories. Will you allow us to make the arrangements?"

"I don't know how Muslims marry," Jason jumped in, "but there's a reform temple here in Rockville with a very open-minded rabbi. As long as one of the partners is Jewish, he will marry you. Can we speak with him?"

Rami was not sure why a door was opening. "Is there something I missed? Just a while ago, you were telling me to walk out of Rayna's life."

"At times, Marisa and I tend to be judgmental, but we're working on it. Thank you for shining a light into my tunnel vision. You know, Rami, earlier you asked me a question. I want to give you an answer. If Marisa were not Jewish, I still would have married her, because I love her." He smiled, "Now, when do you want to marry?"

"This month. Tomorrow. Next week. Two weeks. But sometime this month." Rami was elated. He squeezed Rayna's hand. It went limp. *Something is not right. Rayna is too quiet.*

* * *

Inside the dorm room, Rayna silently got ready for bed. She slipped under the blanket. Rami undressed and inched in next to her. Rayna shifted, turning away from him. Rami massaged her back. "What is it, rrawhee? You did not say one word in the car. If I did something wrong, I apologize." No response. "Rayna, please talk to me. Rayna . . ."

"Getting married is so . . . so final. I'm petrified. Jason is right. What if those Muslim fundamentalists disapprove and take out a fatwa against me? Against us? We won't be safe anywhere. What if you get tired of me and want someone else? Muslims are allowed four wives. What if I get sick . . . very sick? Who will take care of me? What if Yousef sends you to South America permanently and I'm left here by myself? I'll be damaged goods. I'll be ruined. All alone and ruined. My whole family will have disowned me. I won't have anyone. No one. I will be ostracized from my community, from everyone I know, from all that I know. No one will want me. I'll have no one. My life will be over. No, I can't marry you. I can't marry a Muslim. You can't marry a Jew. Do you understand?"

Desperation met Rami head on. The essence of his life was at stake. Without Rayna, his heart would surely stop beating. "Do you have any idea how much I love you?" Gently, Rami nudged her to look at him. "I love you too much to ever hurt you. I love you too much to ever want anyone else but you." He stroked back her hair with his fingers. "Before I ever knew you, I knew I loved you. From the first instant I saw you, I was sure I wanted to marry you. *Four wives*? What would I ever do with four wives?"

A tiny smile crossed Rayna's lips.

"And South America? I do not want to live in South America. I do not want to return to Syria. I want to stay here and make my life with you, to have children and grow old with you."

"We're so young."

"I am not too young to know that the thought of you with another man . . . it would be less painful if you plunged a knife through my heart." Rami felt her body soften. From Rayna's cheeks, he kissed her salty tears. "Who knows where this journey will lead. A Muslim and a Jew. I cannot promise it will be easy. But it will be our journey, and it will be blessed with our love." Rami closed his palm around Rayna's fingers. "I give you my heart. I give you my soul. Take them. Without you, they are of no use to me."

Rayna strayed from Rami's gaze, then looked back up into his eyes.

"It is in your hands now. The decision is yours to make." Rami drew in his breath, afraid to close his eyes, afraid that if he did, Rayna would be gone when he opened them. Invoking Allah, he prayed for Rayna's love not to be taken from him. He begged for this night together not to be their last.

* * *

Rayna shut her eyes and kept them that way until the first rays of morning light flickered through the blinds. Lifting her huge hazel eyes to him, she wiped a tear from his cheek. "Living without you would hurt so bad, more pain than I could endure. We'll take this journey together, wherever it leads us. Just never let go of my hand. Swear to me in front of your Allah. You'll never let go of my hand."

"On my life, I swear this to you." He took her hand and held it.

* * *

In a simple ceremony on Sunday, March 30, 1997, Rami and Rayna were married by Rabbi Damian Heschel at Temple Beth HaTorah in Rockville, Maryland.

> *In sickness and in health. In poverty and in wealth.*
> *In sadness and in joy.*
> *I entrust to you my heart, for the rhythm of its beat*
> *will forever nourish our love.*
> *I commit to you my soul, for it is the other half*
> *of yours.*

TWELVE

You must do the thing you think you cannot do.
—Eleanor Roosevelt

One season passed into another, and spring brought the smell of blooming honeysuckle and flowering dogwoods. On a weekend in mid-April, Rami and Rayna celebrated their marriage by being tourists in Washington. They delighted in the cherry blossoms at the Tidal Basin, marveled at the panda bears in the National Zoo, and climbed the steps to reach the massive figure of America's sixteenth president. They munched down pizza for lunch, poked fun at the art in the Hirshhorn Museum, rode the elevator up the Washington Monument to view the city from its highest point, dined on a maza platter of Syrian appetizers at Lebanese Taverna, and treated themselves to a night in a luxurious room at the upscale Hay-Adams Hotel.

* * *

In late April, Rayna found the eight days of Passover closely approaching. She felt pressed to spend the holiday with her family in the Catskill Mountains, an experience she was dreading for several reasons, one of which was Sarah's bombardment of daily phone calls, insisting that she get a ride home with Jonathan.

* * *

"Well, here goes," Rayna sighed as Rami pulled into the Mishans' driveway. The couple removed their wedding rings and placed them inside the zippered pouch of Rayna's tote. "The first gauntlet of married life awaits us." She put her hands together as if in prayer.

"You are not alone. We will do this together." He gave her a quick smooch, then grabbed her belongings and carried them up the eight stone steps to the front porch. "Wow!" Rami was overwhelmed by the lavish, modern exterior.

Rayna rang the bell and punched in some numbers on the keypad to the left of the door. As she depressed the latch, Rosa, the live-in housekeeper, appeared in the doorway. "*Hola, Rosa.*" Rayna hugged the maid and introduced Rami.

Inside the house, Rami was taken aback by the big two-story foyer with marble flooring, intricately finished walls, and elaborate crystal chandelier. The wide-arched portal led to a stepped-down family room with an impressive hand-painted tray ceiling. Royal blue tie-back drapes decorated the multi-faceted leaded-glass windows. A plush Oriental rug accented the exquisite parquet floors.

Rami gawked and tugged at Rayna's sweater, "You never told me your family was wealthy." He remembered Rayna mentioning her father's lighting supply business, but Rami never comprehended the extent of her family's fortune. "Why did you not tell me?"

"If I had told you, would it have made a difference? To me, it wasn't important."

"*Not important*? I thought we tell each other everything."

"Rami, you're right. We have no secrets. I should've told you about my family's affluence. And when my parents find out about my marriage to a Muslim, I will never see another penny from them. That's what I have given up for you. Now you know why I didn't tell you."

Rami was stunned, not at the wealth but at learning what Rayna had abandoned for him.

"Rosa," Rayna called out, "*dónde están mis padres?*" In Spanish, Rosa said that Abe and Sarah were due home momentarily and that she had to go finish cooking dinner. "Rosa is the reason I'm fluent in Spanish. She came to this country from Chile and has been living with us for over twenty years, from before my birth. She still speaks very little English. Come on, Rami, help me up with my bags."

Up the steps, Rami followed her. Rayna swung open the door to her room. Rami put the bags down. "Whoa! So this is the famous purple and pink bedroom."

"Like it?"

"I love it because it is so . . . so you." He shut the door, drew her close, and instinctively kissed her lips. "I do not know how I will survive the week without you."

Hearing the sound of the garage door opening, Rayna yanked Rami by the hand. "Hurry, my parents are home. They can't find you up here." Running down the steps, they made it to the landing just before Abe and Sarah entered the house.

* * *

"We appreciate your bringing our daughter home," Abe said.

Sarah gave Rami a disapproving once-over. "I don't understand why Rayna had to inconvenience you when she could easily have gotten a ride home with Jonathan."

Rami held his tongue.

"Mom, I invited Rami to stay for dinner."

Sarah started to object but Abe quickly outweighed her. "Yes, of course. Rami, where are you from?"

"Syria."

"Then you're Syrian?"

"Yes."

Sarah glanced harshly at her daughter before going into the kitchen to check on Rosa. The phone rang. Abe picked it up.

"Come on, Rami, I'll give you a tour of the house."

Rami's eyes widened with awe as Rayna guided him through the rooms. Every piece of furniture dripped with lavish stateliness. The walls and ceilings were decorated in a myriad of colors, finishes, and murals. Each lighting fixture was a finely detailed work of art. The window treatments had been scrupulously coordinated with the decor. Everywhere Rami walked, he stepped on marble, ceramic tile, wood inlay, and rich carpets. Every bedroom had its own luxuriously appointed private bath. The house was immaculate, not a thing out of place. Rami now understood where Rayna got her meticulous discipline.

As he was led from room to room, it gnawed at Rami that he had not envisioned this opulence. Rayna was always dressed well, but her clothes did not appear to be indulgent. Her jewelry had consisted of a delicate gold bracelet watch and a diamond pendant that rested just below the hollow of her neck—and now the gold band on her finger.

* * *

Eli exuberantly flung his arms around his sister. "Come here. You've never been away for such a long stretch of time. I've missed you."

Rami cringed at the male affection shown to his wife.

"Rami, this is my brother Elijah, known to us all as Eli. Eli, this is my friend Rami. He gave me a ride home." The two men exchanged a courteous greeting.

Sarah called everyone to the table. Rami studied the kitchen. It was bigger than any he had ever seen. There were two ovens and so many cabinets and drawers. He remembered, in detail, how Rayna had described the kosher laws of Judaism that require meat and dairy to be separate. In his mind, he drew images of the innards of the kitchen. *Two sets of pots, two sets of dishes, and two sets of flatware—all for everyday use. Fancier dishes for the sabbath and holidays. And even more of everything for the week of Passover, just in case any of the family were at home.*

* * *

Over dinner, the conversation began quite innocently. Rayna talked about school. Eli also spoke of school. He was working on a master's degree in business at New York University. Sarah updated Rayna on the latest news of her three oldest brothers and their wives and children. "You're going to be an aunt again. Daniel's wife is expecting."

"Number six, if I'm counting correctly," Rayna jested.

"Yes, number six. Gita says she is closing up shop after

this. Says she's contributed enough to the family tree," Eli laughed.

Abe informed Rayna that her grandfather was not well, news that unsettled Rayna. "Will Jidaw be with us in the Catskills?"

"Unfortunately, no," Sarah answered. "Your grandfather's kidneys are failing."

Tears mounted in Rayna's eyes and she promised herself to spend more time with him this summer. "Tomorrow, I'll visit with him before we leave."

"He's not at home. He's in Deal spending Passover at your Auntie Livia's," Abe said.

Just as Rami was getting comfortable listening to the family exchange, Sarah started in, "So, Rami, tell us where you're from in Syria? Your accent is very strong."

"Halab. Aleppo."

"Really! All four of our grandparents were from Halab." Eli was excited to make the connection and prodded Rami into telling them about the city.

"Then you're Muslim?" Sarah was not going to let up.

"Yes, a Shi'ite Muslim."

"I have been told that Syrians hate Jews and would like to see Israel wiped off the map."

"To be honest, many Syrians do believe that way. It is what we are taught, from early on." A deafening silence shrouded the table.

Eli broke the awkwardness of Rami's response. "Mom, why can't you accept that Rami was nice enough to give Rayna a ride home? Just say 'thank you' and let it go."

"Rayna, you said on the phone that you would explain why this . . . this . . . ."

"Muslim." Rami smiled, helping Sarah find the right word.

"Yes, Muslim. Why has *he* brought you home instead of Jonathan?"

Rayna stammered, trying to say something. No words came out. Under the table, Rami took her hand and held it. Their eyes made contact. Rayna nodded.

"There is good reason why your daughter came home with me instead of Jonathan."

"Rami, you don't owe us an explanation."

"Eli, butt out! Now, Rayna, I want an answer."

"Jonathan tried to rape Rayna, and almost succeeded." Rami's words brought gasps from around the table.

"That's a lie! Jonathan would never do something like that. I know him. I know his parents. And the only thing I know about you is *you're a Muslim.* I don't need to know any more. Rami, it's time for you to leave. And you are to stay away from our daughter." Sarah pushed her chair back, but she did not rise. Rayna's next words kept her in her seat.

"Rami is not lying, Mom. Last January, after Jonathan and I returned to school, Jonathan carried the cooler up to my room. Remember the cooler filled with your Syrian food?"

With a nod, Sarah glared at Rayna.

"Well, Jonathan put down the chest, kicked the door shut, and locked it. Before I could react, he forced me onto the bed and . . . and . . . pinned me down."

"Rami, is holding my daughter's hand under the table a habit of yours?" Abe asked.

In reaction to her father's confrontation, Rayna tried pulling her hand from Rami's grip, but he held on.

Sarah disregarded Abe's probe. "Rayna, I don't believe you. I think you're exaggerating what really happened. Jonathan is a fine young man from a well-respected and prominent family. He's going to be a surgeon like his father. You are to find a way to work this out with Jonathan. It wouldn't kill you to please your family."

"This is exactly why we didn't want you to leave home," Abe scowled. "We were afraid of something like this. School is over! You can't return to Maryland. Until you get married, you'll live at home. Aaron Yedid is crazy for you. He's been waiting a long time. His family is a pillar in the community, and very wealthy. We'll make a match and you'll be married before the summer is over. We've tried it your way and it didn't work. Now it will be our way." Abe turned and gave his wife a stern look, "You've been infatuated with Jonathan and his family from the beginning. It is to stop right now. My daughter will marry a Syrian, not a J-Dubb."

Rami concealed a smirk. *Your daughter married a Syrian.*

"Get your hands off my daughter!" Abe screamed.

Rayna twitched, yanking her hand from Rami.

"I didn't agree on Aaron Yedid," Sarah defied her husband.

"Well I did! Ezra Yedid and I have already agreed on the match for our children, so . . ."

"Without consulting me! How dare you! I'm the one who carried your precious daughter for nine months and labored to deliver her. I will not have Rayna's chances with Jonathan messed up."

"Wait a minute! This is insane. Mom, you're asking my sister to embrace her attacker. What's wrong with you? And Dad . . . you've agreed to marry off Rayna without giving her any say in who she will spend the rest of her life with. My vote is for Rami. He's the one who has been watching out for Rayna . . ."

"I'll just bet he has, Eli!" Abe pushed away the plate of food in front of him. "No more University of Maryland. I forbid it!"

"I have your hand," Rami whispered. "Do not pull away this time."

"Rami, you better leave now. I'll see you to the door." Sarah rose.

Rami remained firmly in his seat. "Let me remind you, Mister and Missis Mishan, that it was a Jew, not a Muslim, who almost raped your daughter."

Eli sought to diffuse the uproar, "*Stop this*! Jonathan tried to rape my sister. Rami was good enough to bring her home. Instead of thanking him, you throw him out. Something is very wrong with this picture."

Rayna thanked her brother, then made a plea on behalf of her husband, explaining that this was Rami's first trip to New York and it would be cruel to force him out to face a long ride back at night on unfamiliar roads. "If he got into an accident, it would be on your heads." She turned to Rami. "I'm inviting you to stay the night. It's the least we can do."

"You can have one of the guest rooms," Eli volunteered, following Rayna's lead. "Our three older brothers are married, so their rooms are available. And the bathrooms are stocked."

"Thank you. One day I hope to repay you with the same kindness," Rami said graciously.

Abe grumbled, "This is not over yet."

Sarah seethed. "Did I ever tell you about the daughter who dug a grave for herself? She made it so deep, she wasn't able to climb out."

* * *

Ascending the steps, Eli led Rami to his brother Micah's old room. Rayna unwillingly went to her own room and began packing for a week in the Catskills. Purposely, she left the door open. There was a knock. She looked up. Rami smiled. He sat down in the rocker and watched Rayna neatly pack her pink suitcase.

"I'm sorry you had to witness my dysfunctional family."

"Rayna, rrawhee, do not be sorry. In some ways, your family is not much different than mine." Rami knew well about Syrian culture. Daughters were sheltered and kept at home until they married, hopefully long before the age of twenty. Parents played a major role in the choice of a prospective mate. Rami reflected on his trip back to Halab in December when his sister, at age fifteen, was consigned to an arranged marriage. Keeping his voice low, Rami encouraged his wife not to go to the Catskills with her family. "You will be miserable there and you will be too far away for me to hold your hand. Tomorrow, I am taking you back to Maryland. Your life is with me now. You can have your Passover seders at Hillel. Gather your things for school. In the morning, we leave."

Eli knocked on the open door. "Mind if I join you?"

Rayna smiled. "Sure. Come talk with us."

Plopping himself down on the carpet, Eli did not mince his words. "It's obvious the two of you are more than friends. Be careful, Rayna. The consequences can be horrendous for you." His eyes shifted to Rami. "My sister and I have always been close. I care about her a lot and she depends on me to protect her. I don't want to see Rayna suffer because of a wrong choice . . . and she will suffer greatly if she's involved with you. Don't do this to her." Eli pulled himself up from the floor. "It's late and time for us all to turn in. Rami, you look like you're about my size. Come on into my room and I'll give you a change of clothes."

* * *

It was long after midnight before Rami was sure everyone was asleep. The doors to both Sarah and Abe's bedroom and to Eli's room were shut. Rami detected quiet and darkness behind them. Silently, he treaded down the hall. He turned the doorknob, grateful to find it unlocked. Securing the door behind him, Rami slipped into Rayna's bed. Lying beside her, they cuddled, whispering like two children with a deep secret, concocting a scheme to maneuver their morning departure together. In the wee hours, after feeling their young hearts beat as one, Rayna fell into a sound sleep. Gently, Rami released himself from her grip and tiptoed back to the guestroom.

* * *

Awakened by the sound of the clock radio, Rayna dallied in bed, listening to John Denver sing "Annie's Song." She shuddered to think of the inevitable confrontation with her parents. Drawing in a deep breath and ejecting a long exhale, she rose, showered, dressed, then softly knocked on Rami's door. "Ready?"

"I am ready. My hand is in yours. Although you may not always feel it, know it is there." They descended the steps with Rayna's luggage.

From the kitchen, Sarah called out, "Rayna, is Rami leaving?"

Setting the overpacked suitcase by the front door, the couple approached the kitchen. Rami thanked his Jewish in-laws for their hospitality.

"I'm not going to the Catskills . . ."

"What! Sit down, Rayna. Your dad and I have something to say . . ."

"I have classes all week and I don't want to miss them. Hillel has kosher-for-Passover food. I'll take all of my meals there and have both seders there. Going to the Catskills will be miserable for me, especially without Jidaw."

"You heard your mother. Sit down! You're spending Passover with us in the Catskills." He looked at Rami. "Thank you for bringing Rayna home. I'll show you to the door . . . and keep away from my daughter. Muslims and Jews don't . . ."

"I always hated the Catskills. The entire holiday revolves around food and obeying rules . . ."

"Yes! Life is full of rules." Abe's anger escalated.

Rayna turned to leave.

"If you walk out the door with . . . that . . . that . . ."

"Say it, Mom. With that Muslim."

"Rayna, if you walk out with him . . . the Muslim . . . then don't come back. You're on your own. We will no longer be responsible for you."

"I don't need your money, Mom. I don't want your money." Rayna's knees were shaking, but when Rami took hold of her hand, a boldness mushroomed. "I can finish school without your money. I'm leaving with Rami. Goodbye."

"No! Wait! Let's talk."

"No, Dad. I'm tired of talking. I don't want to marry Aaron Yedid or Jonathan Klezman or anyone you or Mom decide for me. I'll choose my own husband. Rami, let's go."

As the couple headed to the front door, Abe made a frantic dash after them. "Rami, come have coffee. Do you know that Rayna doesn't drink coffee?"

"Yes, I know."

"Rami, let's go."

"So what do you want me to do?" Abe questioned.

"Nothing, Dad. I want you to do nothing. We're leaving. I'm eighteen. You can't stop me."

"So go," Sarah sarcastically encouraged. "Good riddance. We're not begging you to stay."

"Sarah, will you please shut up!"

"No, Abe. Don't you tell me to shut up."

"Rami, I need to get out of here . . ."

* * *

Yawning and rubbing his eyes from just waking up, Eli descended the steps. "What's all the commotion? What's going on?"

"Your sister refuses to go to the Catskills with us. She's going back to school with her . . . her Muslim friend."

"She's a big girl, Dad . . ."

"Enough, Eli," Sarah admonished before turning her wrath on Rayna. "We've given you everything. *Everything*! What have we denied you?"

"You've denied me love, Mom. Love is important to me. I'd much rather have your love than . . ."

"You ungrateful brat!"

Sarah's words stung. Rayna swallowed back tears. Rami grabbed Rayna's hand and started for the door.

Abe yelled, "Get your hands off my daughter!"

Ignoring the man, Rami picked up the luggage and, holding onto Rayna, made a quick exit.

Barefoot and wearing only jeans, Eli ran after the couple, calling out to Rayna. She stopped and turned. Eli hugged her. "Rayna, this is not a good situation. You're walking directly into a land mine that will explode and kill you."

"Thank you for the warning, Eli." She opened the car door and slipped into the front passenger seat.

Eli kneeled down to face Rayna. Rayna looked up toward Rami. Rami walked away, giving them space. Eli handed Rayna a folded check. "Dad said to put this into your account at school."

Rayna looked at it. *Twenty-five thousand dollars.* She ripped it in half and gave it back to Eli. "I'll be fine." She forced a smile. "I have my trust fund."

For all of his five children, Abe had set up irrevocable lifetime trusts. Each child, upon turning eighteen, began receiving, in monthly payments, one hundred thousand dollars per year.

"Does Rami know about the trust fund?"

"No, he doesn't. But I plan to tell him on the ride back."

"Are you sleeping with him?"

Rayna glanced away.

"Look at me, Rayna." With his finger, he lifted her chin. "You are, aren't you? Rami has found a gold mine . . ."

"No, you're wrong. Rami knew nothing about our family's fortune until he came here yesterday and saw the house. I've told him nothing."

"Just how deep have you and Rami gone?"

Rayna stared silently at her brother, but did not respond.

"Answer me, Rayna. How deep?"

"Deep."

"Is it too late for me to stop you?"

"Yes."

Rami shut the trunk, slipped behind the wheel, and started the engine. Eli walked around to the driver's side, "Rami, I beg you to release this hold you have on my sister."

"I cannot. She owns my soul."

THIRTEEN

Concern for man himself and his fate must always form the chief interest of all technological endeavors.—Albert Einstein

In mid-May, Doctor Quintin Nolan spent the weekend at Princeton University visiting with his only child. Anna was the light of his life and, until he met Rami, the only person he trusted. It had been several years since Nolan's wife left him for another man. While he was falling apart over the divorce, it was Anna who sided with her father, providing him the impetus to move on with his life.

As the two hugged goodbye in front of the University Bookstore, Anna took her father's hand and placed a diamond ring in his palm. "I have held this for a long time now. When Mom wanted to hock it, I threw a fit and took it from her." She closed Nolan's fingers over the gem and smoothed his brow. "I know this represents a lot of sadness, but perhaps there are some happier memories also."

Nolan struggled to mask the pain and shook his head, indicating that he did not want it. He tried to give it back.

"No, Dad, it's time you worked through Mom's betrayal. This ring will help. Do with it what you wish. Keep it. Flush it down the toilet. Hock it, if you like. I don't care. I just don't want her to have it. And I want you to find peace."

Nolan did not believe that he would ever come to terms with the devastation of his ex-wife's rejection. Repeatedly, he asked himself how he could have been so stupid not to see what was happening right in front of his eyes. With a troubled expression, he put the stone in the left pocket of his trousers and kissed his daughter one more time before driving back to Maryland.

* * *

Nolan lived in a middle-class neighborhood in Silver Spring. He had reconstructed his two-car garage so that it was no longer a place to park, but rather a place for him to work. After eliminating the two front automatic doors, he had bricked in the room. At the rear entrance, he installed a two-inch thick solid oak door with a tamper-proof lock. Heating, air conditioning, and electric wiring were built in. Lighting and a security system were set in place. A floor-to-ceiling wall split the large room in half, making one side the laboratory and the other side Nolan's office. Bertha, his part-time secretary, kept him organized.

The morning after Nolan had returned from visiting Anna, he sat in his laboratory gazing into the powerful microscope. The bacteria inside the glass cube were shriveled and clustered together. To Nolan, it appeared as if the organisms were retreating, almost fleeing from a life-threatening force. Never had he seen the microbes in such a state. He was at a loss as to what could have caused the change. He knew that if the bacteria were to break loose, untold destruction would follow. To avoid such a catastrophe, Nolan kept close scrutiny over whom he allowed in the lab. For the past several months, only Bertha and Rami were permitted entry, and only when he was present. Nolan, alone, had the key.

Redirecting his eyes, Nolan slowly studied the room. Nothing had changed. Nothing new added. Nothing deleted. Everything seemed to be as he had left it on Friday morning before leaving to visit Anna. *Something has changed. But what?* The professor picked up the phone.

* * *

In her dorm room, Rayna was at the computer typing a term paper for her social-psych class. Rami sat in the recliner intently studying for a Spanish exam. His cell phone rang. He ignored it. By the third ring, Rayna looked up and shook her head.

"What? Let it ring. This subjunctive tense is very confusing and I need your help."

She lifted the phone off the desk and handed it to her husband.

He hoped it was not Yousef. "Hello."

"Rami, something's wrong with the bacteria. They're dying. How soon can you come?"

"What is happening, Nolan?"

"Rami, I need you. Hurry, please . . . how soon?"

"Nolan . . ."

Listening to the conversation, Rayna asked, "Rami, what is it?"

Rami put his hand over the mouthpiece. "Nolan says something strange is happening with the bacteria. He needs me there now."

Rayna nodded, indicating that Rami should go to Nolan.

"Nolan, I'm leaving now. Give me half an hour." He hung up the phone.

"I keep telling you there's a reason you were chosen for this mission." Adoringly, she kissed him. "I'm wild about you."

Rami flooded her with affection. "There is only one interruption I would like to have right now, and it is *not* Nolan."

"You're a sex maniac. Do you know what that is?"

"Yes," he grinned. "It means I am crazy in love and cannot tear myself away from you."

"That's a pretty good definition. Now, go see what's happening at the lab. I'll be here when you get back . . . and so will your schoolwork."

"After finals, I have a surprise. You and I are going far away for a whole week."

"Really?"

"Really. It is our . . . what do you call it?" Twice, he snapped his fingers trying to summon the word. "Moon . . . something . . . moon . . . moonhaven. That is it! A surprise moonhaven."

"A what?"

"Moonhaven," he repeated. "You know . . ."

"Oh, a honeymoon. We're going on a honeymoon!" Enthusiastically, she jumped into his arms and wrapped her legs around his waist. "Where?"

"If I told you, it would not be a surprise."

"I love you."

Rami started for the bed, "Forget about Nolan . . ."

"Uh-uh. Later." She wriggled out of his arms. "Go see Nolan."

"Must I?"

"Yes. And when you come back, I want to hear all about our honeymoon."

* * *

Inside the lab, Rami peered into the microscope. "This is really strange." He scanned the room. "Nolan, are you thinking what I am thinking?"

Nolan raised his brow. Rami began removing things from the room, item by item. Nolan monitored the bacteria. The microbes were on the verge of extinction. "My project, all my work down the drain." Nolan was in a panic.

Rami looked intently at Nolan, "Your clothing."

"My clothing? That's ridiculous. I wear the same kind of clothes all the time. This has never happened before."

"Your pockets? Do you have anything different in your pockets?"

"No, I don't." Nervously, he took out his wallet and key chain. To prove his point, he pulled his pockets inside out. As he did, the diamond ring rolled across the floor. "Ohhh . . . I forgot about that. But it shouldn't affect the bacteria."

"Are you sure?" Rami bent over and snatched up the jewel. While holding it in his hand, he peered into the microscope. The bacteria seemed lifeless. "Quick, take this ring out of here."

Nolan had forgotten about the ring and began to explain, but Rami cut him short and pointed to the door. Nolan returned without the ring. Through the lens, Rami witnessed a slow rejuvenation of the bacteria. "That is it! I think we have our answer. But let us be certain. Bring the ring back, just not too close." Again, the bacteria began to shrivel. "Hurry, Nolan, get it out. We have solved the problem."

A relieved smiled tugged at the professor's lips. "Me, with two doctorate degrees and I couldn't figure out a simple thing like this."

Rami beamed. "You are welcome. I am glad to be of help."

"Thank you, Rami. You do have a brilliant mind."

"I know," he acknowledged with a broad grin. "Now give me a quick refresher course on the bacteria and then tell me about the properties in a diamond."

Nolan presented Rami with a brief review on decoding the DNA of geo-bacterium for oil-spill remediation, then deliberated on how the genome of this tiny microbe, once perfected, could safely and quickly perform even in the most difficult of oil cleanups. "The bacteria, while capable of eradicating an oil spill, right now, in its present state, will also destroy everything around—marine life, plant life, human life, animal life, and who knows what else. Rami, you already know this stuff. I don't need to go into more detail."

"Nolan, I am trying to find a link. Let us see if the diamond might hold some answers?"

"Okay, Rami. You want to know about . . ."

"The diamond."

Nolan proceeded to list the characteristics of the gem-stone. "Diamond is the hardest natural material and also the least compressible. It is an exceptional thermal conductor, has an extremely low thermal expansion, and is chemically inert with respect to most acids and alkalis. Diamonds are one of only a few materials with a negative work function."

"Negative work function? What does that mean?"

"A work function is an electron affinity. One consequence of a negative electron affinity is that diamonds repel water, but readily accept hydrocarbons such as wax or grease."

"Uh-huh." Rami diligently took notes, then paused to contemplate how to fit the pieces of the puzzle together. Just when he was sure the diamond might provide the link, his thoughts abruptly challenged that theory and his expression reflected another mind search.

"What is it now, Rami?"

"The metal?"

"What metal?"

"There is another component to this ring. What is the metal that the diamond is set in? Is it gold, silver? What?"

"It's platinum."

Intentionally, Rami smiled.

"Okay, now you want a lesson on platinum?"

"Yes. I do."

"I think you're not going to let sleeping dogs lie, are you?"

"What does that mean?"

Nolan was amused at Rami's question. "It's just an expression, one of the nuances of American English. It means not disturbing what you are not sure of."

"Oh, I must remember that," Rami laughed.

"I'm not going to get into a lengthy discourse on platinum because we'll be here until midnight. For now, it will suffice to cover it very briefly." The professor explained the atomic number, weight, standard state, and color. He spoke about platinum's coefficient of expansion being almost equal to that of soda-lime-silica glass and its usefulness in making sealed electrodes in glass systems. "The metal doesn't oxidize in air."

Fascinated, Rami was writing as fast as Nolan was speaking. Phonetically, he spelled out many of the technical terms and struggled to understand it all.

"In its finely divided state, platinum is an excellent catalyst . . . such as a catalyst for cracking oil. That's why it's used as a catalyst in fuel cells as well as in anti-pollution devices, and catalytic converters for cars." Nolan looked at his watch. "We've been at this for almost four hours and I'm beat. More another time."

Rami did not want to stop. He had more questions. "Where is this metal found?"

"In Colombia, Ontario, the Ural Mountains, the United States."

When Rami started to ask another question, Nolan stopped him. "That's all I have left in my head to give you today. We can pursue this later. Take some of my books to read."

"Thank you. Now . . ."

"Rami, I know what you want. I'll work on the diamond's components first, then the platinum's. My research will be extensive. I will leave no stone unturned. No pun intended," he chuckled. "This work may take months, but more like years, if I can stretch it out."

"Good," Rami smiled. "We must extend this for as long as possible. Our lives depend on it. We will continue to meet once a week, more often when needed. And each week, a full report, directly to me. No one else."

"Of course, Rami. No one else."

"And your loyalty. To me and no one else."

"You already have that."

Pleased with the solid relationship forged with Nolan, and with securing the professor's commitment to extend the life of the project for as long as possible, Rami reflected on how he looked forward to presenting Yousef with the weekly reports, loading them with technical terms that Yousef did not understand. But Rami knew that the leverage he now enjoyed, and the generous monthly stipends from Yousef, were to be short lived.

FOURTEEN

In each journey of your life you must be where you are. You may only be passing through on your way to somewhere more important. Nevertheless, there is purpose in where you are right now.—The Rebbe Menachem Mendel Schneerson

"The Triple Frontier! You want to take me to the Triple Frontier for our honeymoon? You must be out of your mind!"

Rami could not understand why Rayna was reacting so vehemently. At the library, he had mulled through books about the place and had spoken to two different travel agents to learn more. Rami wanted to show Rayna the most spectacular waterfalls in the world and the greatest hydroelectric dam on earth. He wanted her to experience a place she had never been, a place where Yousef intended him to be. *I want Rayna to know everything about me. Why does she not see this?* "Okay, if the Triple Frontier is not the place you want to go, then tell me what your idea of a moonhaven is."

"Honeymoon! The word is *honey-moon*! There's no such word as moonhaven. Get it straight!"

"Then where . . ."

"The beach . . ."

"The beach? You can always go to the beach. You were at the beach for a whole week during winter break. Remember . . . with Jonathan in Curaçao?" Rami's stabbing words added fuel to the fire.

"That's a low thing to say to me."

"Well, I think what you said to me was also low. I went to great efforts to plan a very special trip for us, something you would always remember . . ."

"Oh, you bet I would always remember. How could you even think of taking me to such a lawless place?"

"Maybe you should have married Jonathan. He would have taken you on a Jewish honeymoon to the beach and . . . and may . . ." Impulsively, Rami stopped. He did not like where their harsh words were leading.

"Don't you ever bring Jonathan into our disagreements. *Ever!* This is between you and me. No one else."

Rami regretted their bickering. "I apologize. I was wrong to say what I did. Please, I do not want to argue like this." He wrapped his arms around Rayna. "I love you more than my life. You are my life. I would not ever knowingly put you in danger. In your heart, you must know that." He kissed her mouth.

"Then why did you choose such a place for our honeymoon?"

"We will be staying on the Brazil side . . ."

"I don't care which side it's on. Argentina. Paraguay. Brazil. It's all the Triple Frontier to me."

Rami pulled out captioned pictures from his bookbag. "Look." He attempted to show her the beauty of the region.

Rayna ignored the prints. "What else? What is the real reason?"

"I want you to know everything about me. Everywhere I am . . ."

"What about our safety? My safety?"

"No harm will come to you. You will be with me every minute. I promise. The place attracts over a million tourists each year, maybe more. Do you think so many people would visit if it were unsafe?"

"What if we bump into Yousef or . . ."

"We will not be anywhere near Yousef. He will never know that you and I made this trip."

"Something tells me we shouldn't . . ."

"Have I steered you wrong, yet?"

"Don't even ask me that question."

Rami did not want to linger on the subject. He knew she was right. "If you really do not want to go, it is okay." Still, he hoped she would reconsider. "You choose a place for our *moonhaven*," he smiled. "I trust your judgment."

"Honeymoon," she rectified with an easy grin.

"Yes, honeymoon."

* * *

After completing final exams and securing visas for their trip to South America, Rami helped Rayna move out of the dorm. Packing the car with her belongings, they were going to Brooklyn. Thanks to Eli, Rayna was on her way home and Rami was joining her as a guest in the Mishan house. Eli had championed his sister's cause, just as he had done so many times before. Grudgingly, Abe and Sarah caved in, just as they had done so many times before. The family dynamics continued as usual.

* * *

"We'll have dinner around eight when your father gets home," Sarah said to Rayna.

Rami promised himself to be on his best behavior and appreciated Rayna's family tolerating him, a Muslim, as a guest in their home. He would not take advantage of their hospitality and reminded himself of his own father's fanatic intolerance. He understood Abe and Sarah's strong expectations for all of their children to marry Jews, preferably religious Syrian Jews. Rami felt a tinge of remorse about the devastating blow his marriage to Rayna would cause them once they found out. "Sarah, you and Abe are more than kind to welcome me into your home. From my heart, I thank you."

"Welcome isn't the right word, Rami. It's more like coercion. You can thank Eli, not me."

I owe Eli a lot for this, he noted.

* * *

"Aha, you're all out here in the sunroom." Eli pecked his mother's cheek, put his arms out for a hug from his sister, gave Rami a high-five, and plopped himself down on the large curved sectional. "I just finished my last exam and I'm zonked." Eli had received his undergraduate degree from New York University and had one more year left for his MBA at the same school. Between studies, he worked for his father, who was growing more and more dependent on Eli.

Rosa, the housekeeper, brought in a tray of cinnamon iced tea and Syrian pastries. The conversation politely centered on school, family, and the upcoming summer. Fidgeting from lack of physical activity, Eli rose from the leather furniture. Subtly, he coaxed Rami. "I really need to unwind. Traffic was nerve shattering coming home from the city."

"Uh-oh. Until my brother finds himself a serious girlfriend, there's only one way for him to unwind," Rayna laughed.

"Rami, how would you like to shoot some baskets?" Eli wheedled.

"Shoot baskets?"

"Basketball," Rayna laughed. "Eli wants you to play basketball with him at the gym."

"Ahhh, yes, basketball." Looking to Rayna, Rami shrugged his shoulders.

"I guarantee you have never played basketball until you have experienced the game with Eli. Go enjoy yourself."

"Give me ten minutes to get out of these clothes." Eli gestured to Rami, "Come on up. I've got plenty for you to change into."

* * *

"Mom, we'll be back by seven-thirty. That'll give us half an hour to shower before dinner."

Observing her husband and her brother leaving in their shorts and tank tops, Rayna noted their similarities. *Slender, strong physiques. Closely matched height and weight. Olive skin. Soft, curly dark hair. Large brown eyes.* She smiled to herself. In very different ways, she loved them both.

Growing up, the bond between Rayna and Eli was unmistakable. Of all her brothers, Eli was the one who always sheltered her. She hated deceiving him now, hated not telling him the truth about her marriage. *Soon, when I come back from the Triple Frontier, I will tell Eli everything.* "Mom, can I help you with dinner?"

"No, thanks. Everything is prepared and Rosa is here to help." On the sofa, Sarah moved closer to her daughter. "Your absence was noticed over Passover."

"Has Dad calmed down?"

"Well, you know how your dad gets when it comes to you. Why don't you go up to your room, unpack and get settled while there's some quiet time in the house."

"Mom . . . Mom . . ." Rayna hesitated. "Mom . . . some of my girlfriends from school are going to the beach this week to relax after finals and term papers. They invited me to join them and I'd like to go, especially since I'll be working in the city all summer." *A lie.*

"Rayna, is that necessary? Why must you go away to a beach when we live at the shore all summer? We have a magnificent house in Deal and the whole Syrian community will be there and . . . no, you can't go. I don't know these friends you're talking about. No!"

"But, Mom, I have an internship at *InterContinental Weekly* working five days a week all summer long. These are really close friends from school and . . ."

"You already said that. Are they Jewish?"

"Of course they're Jewish. I know them from Hillel. Please, Mom. Just for one week, before I start work." *A bigger lie.*

"What beach?"

Ummm . . . Charleston." *Another lie.*

"What Charleston?"

"Charleston, South Carolina."

"South Carolina? Rayna, do you know how far that is? How do you intend to get there?"

"Rami will drive me back to school. From there, I'll ride down to Charleston with my girlfriends. We're renting a condo for the week. We'll be together the whole time." *More lies.*

"Rami is driving you back to school?" Sarah's tone turned harsh. "Just how much of a friendship is this with you and Rami? I'm not stupid, Rayna."

"Mom, we're just friends. That's all. Honest. He's a really nice guy. Why do all of my friends have to be females and Jewish?"

"Because it doesn't look good the other way, that's why. Think of our reputation in the community. Think of your own reputation as an unmarried female. Your friendship with that Muslim will end. Tomorrow, he leaves. And you're not returning to Maryland. I suggest if you want to continue with school, you better find one here in New York. You'll live at home. No more away. And, no, you're not going to Charleston, South Carolina, and Rami is not driving you back to school."

"But, Mom, I plan to leave tomorrow and . . ."

"Tomorrow? The only one leaving tomorrow is Rami."

"Mom, *please.* I've already told them I would go. They're counting on me as the fourth."

"I want to know why you suddenly have become so dependent on Rami to drive you around? For God's sake, Rayna, he may be Syrian, but he is a Muslim. You're not going to muddy our reputation. I will not have people gossiping behind our backs. Never should we have allowed Eli to talk us into this."

Not wanting to lie further, Rayna went upstairs to pack for her honeymoon.

* * *

Over dinner that evening, Eli expressed delight in learning from Rami that Rayna had made so many good friends at school. "I think it's a great idea for Rayna and her girlfriends to have a week together in Charleston before starting her internship."

"Who are these friends? We don't know them. I know nothing about where she'll be staying, who she'll be staying with. No! That's my final answer. Eli, what is it with you and your sister? Why are you always doing her bidding, always defending her?" Abe turned back to his daughter. He was not yet finished. "Rayna, you're not going to Charleston, South Carolina. If you want the beach, come to Deal. Your friends are welcome to stay at our house. We'll supply food, beds, and a beautiful beach. End of dialogue."

"But, Dad, that's so unfair . . ."

"Go spend the week with your grandfather and do something constructive. He's not well and has been asking for you."

Rayna's eyes glossed over. She loved her grandfather. "I'll go tomorrow and see him. Is he still at Auntie Livia's in Deal?"

"Yes, he is." Sarah's tone bristled with irritation.

* * *

Amid much household uproar, Rami and Rayna left early in the morning and made the hour drive to upscale Deal, New Jersey. Stopping the car in front of the extravagant house of Rayna's aunt Livia, Rami waited. Rayna walked up the front steps and rang the bell. The live-in maid came to the door, "Nobody home, Missees. Only grandfather."

"You can go, Rami. My grandfather's here," she called out and waved goodbye. They had agreed that Rami would return by three o'clock, which would give them enough time to drive to Kennedy Airport and make their evening flight to Brazil.

"See you at three." He threw her a kiss and drove off. Rayna had given him suggestions on how to pass the time.

* * *

Isaac was a wise old man. He had a full head of white hair and a devilish grin that sometimes got him into amusing trouble. Rayna and her grandfather sat out on the screened-in porch, sang Syrian songs, and played backgammon. She told him about her year at school and her internship at *InterContinental Weekly*. He cried over the loss of his wife, still not able to accept her death. "It's been three years. I miss your grandmother more than ever. She was my life. I loved her so much. One day you will understand."

Rayna reflected on Rami, who often expressed those same words of love. "I do understand. More than you know." Their interaction switched to one of lively discussion. She knew how much her grandfather always enjoyed debating the Bible. Isaac justified God's flood and defended Noah for building the ark. Rayna argued for the people and questioned God's actions to destroy what He had created. The maid served lunch. Rayna helped Isaac eat when his hands became too unsteady. They played more backgammon. The doorbell rang. It was three o'clock. "Jidaw, I have to go. My ride is here." She gave her grandfather a strong hug and kissed his cheek. "I love you with all my heart. See you next week."

* * *

Inside JFK International Airport, just before boarding, Rayna swallowed a Dramamine to avoid motion sickness and warned Rami that she would sleep most of the trip. The pair plunked down into their seats, ready for the all-night flight.

* * *

Hours later, early the following morning, they landed at Guarulhos International Airport in São Paulo. From there, Rami and Rayna boarded a domestic flight into Foz do Iguaçu. Two hours later, the small Rio Sul aircraft began its descent, flying directly over the mammoth Itaipu Dam. Leaning across Rayna to view the spectacular structure, Rami gently coaxed her from sleep. "Look. Look." Rami pointed from the window. "It is the dam."

Bleary-eyed, she peered down. From the air, the sight of the massive structure straddling the Paraná River was overwhelming.

FIFTEEN

Neither is it allowable to the sun that it should overtake the moon, nor can the night outstrip the day; and all float on in a sphere.—Surah 36:40

The old colonial style pink-stucco resort, nestled inside the subtropical forest, shimmered against the contrasting backdrop of the glowing afternoon sun. "Ahhh! It looks pink. It looks violet. It looks . . . beautiful. It's elegant."

Rami sighed with relief. *Good, so far.* Emerging from the taxi, he valiantly took Rayna's hand, helping her out. "Shhhh. Listen." The tranquil sound of running water welcomed them.

"It's the waterfalls." Rayna squeezed Rami's hand.

Lifting his brow, Rami smiled, paid the driver, rolled their one large piece of luggage through the entranceway, and checked into the Tropical das Cataratas. The spacious lobby glistened with splashes of pastel colors that highlighted the surrounding dark woods. The guest rooms were spread out over a number of wings and Rami and Rayna were happy for the exercise, taking the long walk through the corridors in search of their accommodations.

"There it is!" Rayna pointed, waiting for Rami to open the door. "Ohhhh! Wow!" The deluxe room with hardwood floors, dark wood furniture, accents of vibrant colors, and modern bath with granite countertops met with Rayna's approval.

Contrary to the gloom Rayna had initially expressed about the trip, this early enthusiasm was more than Rami could have hoped for. Raising his eyes toward the heavens, he silently thanked Allah.

They unpacked, made love, and fell into a sound sleep. It was nighttime when they woke. Their stomachs growled. Rami called the hotel's concierge. "If you would like to eat out on the terrace, we can seat you in forty-five minutes," said the man at the other end of the line.

* * *

After showering and dressing, they dined leisurely on Brazilian cuisine. The food was not what they were used to. Keeping to their religious dietary laws took some thought. They settled on a meatless Brazil nut soup, a meatless black bean stew with rice, kale fried in olive oil and garlic, and a green salad. For dessert, they ordered one flan and shared it. Rami had coffee. Rayna drank tea.

Afterward, they strolled the grounds. "Look," Rayna pointed upward. The moon and stars in all their splendor lit up the night sky. Rami took Rayna's hand. In the vastness, they tried to grasp the enormity of space. "It's magnificent. I have never experienced the sky quite like this." In awe, they breathed in the universe, not wanting their euphoria to end.

A strong breeze soon whipped up, and Rayna felt chilled. They returned to the hotel and browsed in the gift shop.

Rayna set her eyes upon a Brazilian carnival doll. Rami observed her admiring it and bought it for her.

* * *

Having breakfast out on the terrace the next morning, the couple were calmed by the sounds and views of the waterfalls, and the serene isolation from the outside world. "Look, Rami. Look at the bright colors and the large bill. It's a toucan. Have you ever seen one before?"

Rami smiled. "Never."

* * *

Leaving the resort, the couple caught the bus crossing the Tancredo Neves Bridge connecting Foz do Iguaçu in Brazil with Puerto Iguazú in Argentina. They showed their visas, checked through border patrol, and began the trek into the jungle of Argentina's Iguazú Falls National Park.

Hand-in-hand, Rami and Rayna walked down the path to where the Iguazú and Paraná rivers converge. Captivated by the two waterways plunging off the plateau, separating the Triple Frontier boundaries of Argentina, Brazil, and Paraguay, the couple stood mesmerized by the breathtaking display. To them, it seemed like an ocean pouring into an abyss.

Along the rim of a two-mile-long crescent-shaped cliff, disconnected cascades plummeted three hundred feet straight down into the gorge below while others sent up clouds of mist and spray, creating a dazzling spectacle of rainbows. Never had Rami and Rayna known such beauty. Everywhere they turned, they were stimulated by the surroundings. "Rami, I'm sorry for giving you such a hard time about coming here. You were right. I'll never forget this place."

Rami was happy to see Rayna in such good spirits. He thought of how he had almost canceled the trip when she had so fiercely protested. Now he was glad they had come.

* * *

The next morning, they went for a swim, indulged in a buffet breakfast on the terrace, and returned to the room to gratify their hunger for one another. Afterward, they showered and dressed, then set out to view the five-mile-long Itaipu Dam that harnessed the waters of the westward flowing Paraná River. The colossal concrete structure soared high into the air. Rayna wrapped her arms around Rami's neck, "This is humongous! Thank you for bringing me here."

"Allahu akbar," Rami murmured under his breath.

* * *

Late Monday morning, they set out for Parque das Aves, the bird sanctuary. Rayna got carried away when they came upon two giant otters. "Just look at them, Rami. Look at them playing. In my next life, I want to come back as an otter. They eat, sleep, play, and make love."

* * *

On Tuesday, they hurried through breakfast and rushed out to make it on time for the Macuco Safari tour. They rode in an open wagon towed behind a jeep, hiked the trail to Macuco Falls, and traveled in a motorboat to the base of the falls. They were not prepared to get so wet.

* * *

The honeymooners saved their last day to venture into the most notorious region of the Triple Frontier, the place where Rami would return to meet Yousef. Not far from their hotel, on Rua Almirante Barroso, they caught the bus marked *Ciudad del Este*. They were warned to prepare for long delays crossing the Paraná River via the Puente de la Amistad.

From a distance, Rami and Rayna caught sight of the decaying iron overpass and the miles-long backup of cars crawling at a snail's pace. Before reaching the infamous city, they jumped off the bus and walked the rest of the way, realizing they could get across much faster on foot. They zigzagged through the congestion of hundreds of people traipsing across the bridge, pushing carts filled with black market merchandise or carrying large bags of contraband. Rami and Rayna followed the narrow walkway that ran along the outer edge until they arrived on the other side. The sharp contrast from where they had come unsettled them. Here, in Ciudad del Este, they found dirty streets, blatant crime, drug trafficking, and illicit merchandising—all exposed like bright red flags. Anything in this infernal tax-free pit could be had by haggling. One could buy sex, murder, drugs, weapons, passports, visas, and bogus American dollars.

Tourists from Porto Alegre stopped to talk with Rami and Rayna. They spoke of the billions of dollars in drug money that moved through the city each year. A strangulating knot formed deep inside Rami's stomach.

A man in a drug-induced stupor stumbled out of a decrepit doorway, shouting incoherently. A bedraggled prostitute came out after him, demanding her money. The panderer pushed her to the ground and stomped on her. Seedy-looking people gathered around, cheering him on. Three teenage boys sat on a corner sniffing cocaine. A young woman stuffed a handful of jewelry into her bag and walked off. She was shot in the face by the vendor.

Frightened for Rayna and conscious of the sleaze and lasciviousness spewing forth from the streets, Rami firmly grasped her hand, "We are getting out of here right now." Before she could react, he pulled her down the street and onto one of the white buses marked *Línea Urbana Internacional* that would carry them back into Brazil.

* * *

Totally unnerved by the experience, Rami and Rayna were relieved to be safely back in the center of Foz do Iguaçu. Tired and hungry, they wandered into a coffee shop. While sipping on maté, Rami apologized. Rayna intertwined her fingers into his. "I'm afraid for you. I don't want you coming back here this summer. Promise me you won't."

"I am the one who is afraid for you. Today, I put you in danger. How could I have been so stupid?" Rami withdrew into quiet contemplation.

Rayna reached under the table and softly squeezed his knee. "A kiss for your thoughts."

"Al-Shahid has made major inroads here, trading arms for drugs and carrying out hundreds of executions each year. Also, many suicide bombers are trained in this place. I am only just beginning to understand it all. Rayna, I want no part of this, but I do not know how to free myself from Yousef's clutches without putting us both in danger."

Disturbed, they left the coffee shop and returned to their room to pack.

* * *

All week, Rami and Rayna carefully monitored their food, eating no meat, since they had found none to be kosher or halal. On this last evening of their honeymoon, they discovered a Syrian restaurant in the center of Foz do Iguaçu. Seated at a small round table, they discovered at the top of the menu printed in Arabic: *All our food conforms to the most stringent rules of halal.*

The couple shared a large maza platter filled with an array of their favorite appetizers. Casually, they ate every morsel until they were stuffed. "I do not know where I can put another bite, but shall we split a dessert?"

"Rami, I think I gained five pounds tonight. Tomorrow is diet time." She looked down and loosened the tie in the waist of her slacks.

"Uh-oh," Rami teased, letting out a notch in his belt. Thinking this hilarious, they both burst forth in laughter.

"Mmmm. Yes, dessert. But only if you promise to love me when my tummy is no longer flat."

"Hmmm. I have been keeping a secret from you. It is your tummy that I love most. If that changes, well . . . I cannot be responsible for my feelings." Their playfulness had lightened the heaviness of their encounter earlier in the day.

Sharing a custard-rice pudding, they took pleasure in feeding each other from one another's spoons. Rami sipped Turkish coffee from a demi-tasse cup, and Rayna drank cinnamon-spiced tea from a clear, narrow glass. The week appeared to be ending on a good note when, in an instant and without warning, everything changed. All color drained from Rami's face. Partially digested food trickled up his esophagus and he choked.

"What's wrong, Rami? Something just happened. What is it? Are you okay? Are you in pain? What is it Rami?" With a look of fear, she rose from the chair.

"Rayna, sit down. Do not say one word. *Not one word.* Let me handle this."

"Whaaat?" she lowered herself back into the seat.

He muffled his voice. "Yousef, Abdallah, and Omar just walked in. They are coming toward us." With his heart racing, Rami grappled to find a way to cope with the advancing threat. *I must protect Rayna. I must not leave her vulnerable to these predators.*

"Well, well, well," sneered Yousef. "What brings you to this part of the world? We did not expect you until July."

At first Rami said nothing. He observed Abdallah's obvious contempt and Omar's weak smile. "Hello, Omar. It has been a while. How are you?"

Omar responded clumsily, "Fine, Rami, and y . . ."

"Mind if we join you?" Yousef intruded, signaling for Abdallah to pull up three chairs.

"We were just leaving."

"No, Rami. You're not going anywhere." Scrutinizing Rayna, Yousef's lips curled sardonically. "Tell me, Rami, what brings you here with this stunning lady?"

Rami attempted to leave, but Abdallah moved to block the couple. "So Rami, I didn't catch the reason for your visit. Business or pleasure?" Yousef baited.

"Pleasure."

"Oh. Using my money to vacation? How nice of you."

"Yousef, I have been doing everything you ask of me . . ."

"And I have been generous with you." Yousef spoke to Rami, but his covetous eyes were all over Rayna.

Tension mounted and Rami's awareness sharpened. "Yousef, the professor and I have reached a critical point. It seems we shall soon have a breakthrough. I will provide you with an update on Monday."

"Good. You do that. Now introduce me to your friend."

Rami kept still. Rayna slowly put down the glass of tea she was holding. Yousef snatched her wrist and held it firmly. "Is this your wife or someone else's wife?"

Rami's discomposure magnified. *Yousef has spotted the gold band on Rayna's finger.*

Yousef maintained his firm grip on Rayna, addressing her personally. "All that I have heard of your beauty does not do you justice. Yet, if you are an American, your loveliness is wasted."

"Rayna is Syrian," Omar blurted.

"Ahhhh, Syrian," Yousef toyed in Arabic. "*R-a-y-n-a*," he deliberately articulated her name, sounding out each letter. "Where are you from in Syria?"

"Halab," she answered.

Thank you, Allah. Rami was grateful she responded with Halab and not Aleppo.

"Are you Muslim?"

Again, Omar protected her. "Yes, she is."

Yousef's nostrils flared with lust. "If I were you, Rami, I would have my wife cover herself like a proper Muslim woman, so as not to tempt men such as I." Still fixated on Rayna, Yousef continued, "I see you know her also, Omar. Tell me, are you as familiar with Rayna as Rami is?"

Impulsively, Rami shoved the table against Yousef. "I have no idea how strongly you want the bacteria in your possession, but it must not be much of a priority since you persist in provoking me. Now, get your sleazy hands off my wife!" He thrust Yousef's hands off of Rayna and pulled her up. "As I said, we were just leaving before you so rudely interrupted." Rami grasped Rayna by her waist, discreetly gave a nod of gratitude to Omar, threw some money at the waiter, and led Rayna to the door.

"I'll go after him, boss," Abdallah lunged forward with a depraved twist extending across his face. "Let me at him!"

"No, Abdallah. Let him go. You know I have other plans for Rami. I need him to negotiate that arms-for-drugs deal with Carlos el Negro. After that, he's all yours. Be patient until July when Rami returns. And Abdallah, find a replacement to work with Nolan, someone who will not fail us this time."

* * *

That night, as Rayna slept, Rami lay awake wishing he had never brought her to this place, wishing he had hearkened to her initial protests about the trip. Visions of Yousef's wanton eyes casing Rayna sent him into silent madness. *I must shelter Rayna from him. If I could kill the beast, I would.* Bringing Rayna into the contours of his body, he thought it impossible to love her more. "Rayna, rrawhee," he whispered, "I never meant to pull you into this mess. As long as I am alive, you will be safe. I swear this to you."

* * *

Rayna opened her sleepy eyes and turned to him. She felt his hands against her skin. *From the beginning, Rami has shared all of his life with me. No other man would trust me so completely or cherish me so intensely.* No longer could Rayna exist without Rami's love. Nothing in the world would ever change that.

SIXTEEN

What good to us is a long life if it is difficult and barren of joys, and if it is so full of misery that we can only welcome death as a deliverer?—Sigmund Freud

On Monday morning, the second of June, the R-train from Brooklyn pulled into the station under the World Trade Center. Rayna fought her way through the crowd, emerging onto the platform. Following the masses up the escalator to ground level, she stepped out onto the grand concourse that connected the north and south towers and housed the largest shopping mall in Lower Manhattan. More than seventy-five stores and restaurants beckoned to Rayna. She looked at her watch. There was little time. She continued to the main corridor of the south building and made her way to the express elevators. With people pushing rudely, she found herself crammed into the next available lift. Its last stop was the upper sky lobby on the seventy-third floor. Scurrying to keep up with the group, she followed them to a second set of elevators. Squeezing into one, she rode it to the ninety-first floor. Finding her way to *InterContinental Weekly*, Rayna proceeded through a set of glass doors.

* * *

She approached the receptionist, and introduced herself.

"Mr. Newborn will be with you shortly. Can I get you some coffee?"

"No. Thank you." Rayna took a seat and waited. On the brass-and-chrome coffee table lay the latest copy of *InterContinental Weekly*. She picked it up. "Turkey Adamantly Denies Armenian Genocide." The headline caught her eye. She thumbed through the pages and found the article.

"Good morning. You must be Rayna. I'm Simon Newborn." He extended his hand. Her fingers buckled under his strong handshake. The magazine fell from her lap. He bent and picked it up. "For you to keep," he smiled. She scrambled to rise. "Come on in my office," he gestured.

Rayna followed the tall, burly man into a handsomely appointed suite. She waited for him to settle into his black leather executive chair before sitting down opposite him. As he reviewed her file, she scanned the room. A floor-to-ceiling bookcase stretched across the wall behind his desk. A round conference table with six chairs occupied space by the span of windows. A large caricature hung on the left wall; it depicted Simon surrounded by various plaques, each with a different inscription: *President, Publisher, Chairman, CEO.* Simon was portrayed in a dilemma as to which title to choose. The illusion of God's voice beaming down, commanding him to take all, illustrated Simon's powerful and influential position.

The phone rang. "Yes." Simon put his hand over the mouthpiece. "I'll be just a moment. It's my wife."

Rayna walked over to the windows. *He does have beautiful views.* It was thrilling to look out onto New York Harbor and see the Statue of Liberty, Ellis Island, and the Verrazano Bridge. *Rami would love it up here. I can't wait to bring him into the city and show him the sights.* She missed Rami, yet believed in the importance of sacrificing for the future. It was at her insistence that he was at the University of Maryland taking summer classes so he could graduate early with her. Rayna intended to live at her parents' house in Brooklyn during the summer months and commute into Manhattan for her internship. The weekends would be theirs—rotating between Washington and New York.

"Isn't the view spectacular? You're lucky to have caught it on such a clear day." Simon's booming voice projected like that of an actor on a Broadway stage.

"Oh, yes," she acknowledged, jarred by the interference with her thoughts.

"We have a lot of ground to cover and not a whole lot of time." Glancing at the clock on the wall, he said, "I've got a plane to catch. We're opening a new office in Istanbul."

"Turkey?" She quickly recalled the front cover headline: "Turkey Adamantly Denies Armenian Genocide."

"That's the country." Leaning back in his chair, Simon's commanding figure was intimidating. Rayna maintained her composure. A half hour passed. Their talk was going well. Again, Simon looked at the clock. "Rayna, I carefully hand-pick my staff members. Our people are the best in the business. Some were once interns like you. *InterContinental Weekly* is the most widely circulated magazine in the world. Every issue is translated into thirteen languages. We are constantly growing and fortunate to have advertisers clamoring for space."

"Advertisers keep you in business . . ."

"You're darn right! They pay our bills. But we don't compromise for them. Our reporting is factual and ethical. I demand it. Now, your first six weeks on the job will be to study media law. That's all you'll do. Everything is set up. We don't like lawsuits. Whatever we print must be accurate and verifiable. It's our policy."

"Can I write something for the magazine after . . ."

"Kamil and I chose you from among the hundreds of candidates because your writing samples were crisp and clear and your topics well researched and relevant."

"Did you say Kamil? Kamil Adjmi?" The name sparked Rayna's intellect. She and Eli had often watched his interviews on television and avidly read his weekly column.

"Kamil will be delighted that you know of him, especially since he'll be your mentor this summer." Simon stood. "We're pleased to have you on board. Call me Simon, everyone else does. Now let me show you to your office and introduce you to Kamil before I get going."

* * *

Rayna's office was narrow. It had no windows. The white walls were bare. A television monitor, a VCR, and a printer filled the space on a metal table. A computer and telephone sat on the desk. Opening the drawers of the two file cabinets, Simon showed Rayna the many disks and videos. He pointed to books and magazines cramming the shelves of a tall bookcase. "I urge you to make use of every available resource. You have six weeks . . . and a lot of learning to do if you want to write for *InterContinental Weekly*."

* * *

Kamil Adjmi was a respected and world-renowned journalist. He was of medium height and weight. His black hair was cropped and his hazel eyes sparkled when he smiled. Kamil coached Rayna on operating the equipment and walked her through the material at hand. "We can take lunch together and talk more. Come by my office at twelve-thirty."

* * *

Just before noon, as Rayna was deep into a tutorial, her cell phone rang. "Hi, Mom."

"Rayna, I'm at the hospital with your grandfather. New York Presbyterian. How soon can you get here? I'd like to go back to Deal and was hoping you could help out . . . spend the evening with him . . . someone from the family should . . ."

"I get off at five. I'll take a cab and come straight from work. What's the room number?" Rayna jotted down the information. "Tell Jidaw I love him and I'll be there soon. Mom, is he going to be alright?"

"No, he isn't. My father's dying. His kidneys . . . it's just a matter of time. The family . . . me and my sisters and brothers . . . we were hoping you would spend the evenings with him . . . a few hours after work every night. Maybe the weekend, also. We'll take turns coming into the city from Deal to spend the days with him."

"Of course I'll be there for Jidaw. See you later. Bye."

* * *

At twelve-thirty, Rayna appeared at Kamil's door. She knocked, then peeked in. "Ready?"

Making their way down the elevators, Kamil led Rayna through the lunchtime congestion to Gemelli's Italian Restaurant. They looked over the menu and ordered. While waiting for the food to arrive, Rayna pulled out a list of questions. Kamil laughed. "All these questions and it's only your first day. Simon didn't warn me about you."

Regarding him intently, she said, "I never miss reading your columns. And my brother Eli and I have watched so many of your interviews. It's an honor to work with you."

"Ah! So you know of me?"

"Yes, I do. People say that you have a gift for shedding light on the darkness that wishes to remain hidden. How do you choose what to write about? Aren't you concerned for your safety when you expose so much of the world's injustices?" Energetically, Rayna rattled off one question after another before coming to a halt. "You're grinning at me."

"I am." Kamil was amused at her inquisitiveness and taken with her unique beauty. "I could stay a while longer this evening and respond to all of your questions."

"Thank you, Kamil, I would really like that, but I can't tonight. My jidaw is in the hospital and I must go see him after work."

"I understand . . . uhhh . . . did you say your jidaw?"

"Yes, I'm sorry. My grand . . ."

"I know. Your grandfather. I hope he will soon get well. Have you always referred to your grandfather as your jidaw?"

"Yes. Always."

"And your grandmother?"

"*Sitaw*. But she died three years ago."

"I'm sorry. Tell me, where are your grandparents from?"

"Syria. From Halab . . . Aleppo."

Kamil was delighted to make the connection. "I, too, am from Syria. From Hamah. But now I'm American."

"Are you Sunni or Shi'ite?"

"Sunni."

"I'm Jewish."

"I won't hold it against you. Simon is also Jewish."

"Hamah . . . didn't a massacre occur there?"

Instinctively, Kamil tensed.

"Will you tell me about it?"

"Another time. Right now we both have work to do."

* * *

Later, back in his office, Kamil was tapping at his keyboard when he caught sight of Rayna in his peripheral vision. She stood by his desk. Stopping, he looked up at her and spoke softly. "Rayna, what now? I have a column to write and a deadline to meet."

"Please, Kamil." She mumbled nervously and sat down. "I need a favor. There's a terrorist from Syria . . ."

"Speak up, Rayna. I can't understand you."

"There's a terrorist . . . a militant . . . from Syria," she stated more boldly. "His first name is Yousef. I don't know his last name. He's high up the ladder in al-Shahid."

"How do you know of this man?" Kamil gave her his full attention.

Rayna fidgeted. "I need Yousef's last name and a profile on him. Please, can you help me?" She held her breath.

He looked at her intently and asked again, "How do you know of this man?"

"I've met him."

"*You met him?*" Kamil did not suspect such an answer. "Are you going to tell me?"

"Please. Can you help me?" Rayna waited as Kamil clicked away at the computer.

"Is this the man?" He handed her a profile and picture of Yousef Mugniyeh. "Is this the Yousef you met?" Kamil studied her face.

Rayna examined the picture. She remembered him vividly, right down to the long jagged scar etched into his left cheek. "Yes."

"You owe me something in return. I want to know what you know. Tell me about him. Where did you meet Yousef Mugniyeh?"

"I can't . . ."

"You can't or you won't? What's holding you back, Rayna?"

"Please . . . I can't."

Until that moment, Kamil said nothing of the gold band Rayna wore. "Are you married?"

She clutched at the profile, using it to obscure the ring on her left hand. "Is it customary to ask personal questions of your interns?"

"No, it isn't, Rayna. But it is also not customary for an intern to ask for a profile of a prominent Muslim terrorist that she has met. You, a Jew . . ."

"Yes."

"Yes, what?"

"Yes, I'm married."

"Is your husband mixed up with Yousef?" Rayna did not answer. Instead, she stood to leave. Kamil jumped up and blocked the door. "Is he?"

"No," she lied.

There's a connection between Yousef Mugniyeh and her husband. For years, Kamil had been chasing slippery clues. Now he would pursue Rayna until he got answers.

"Your husband? Jew or Muslim?"

Silence.

"Jew or Muslim?"

"Muslim."

"Sunni or Shi'ite?"

Again, she kept silent.

"Sunni or Shi'ite?"

"Shi'ite."

"Lunch tomorrow. Be at my door at twelve-thirty."

* * *

On the phone, Rayna told Rami about Kamil and the profile on Yousef Mugniyeh. "Yousef is on the government's ten-most-wanted list of terrorists. He can't enter the United States. There's a ten-million-dollar bounty on his head. We'll talk more when you come." She then told Rami about her grandfather. "After work, I'll take a cab and go see him. I'll call you later. I miss you. Bye."

"I am starving for you. I do not think I can last until Friday."

* * *

In a private room in the geriatric wing of New York Presbyterian, Rayna's eighty-four-year-old grandfather lay dying. Sarah had been waiting for her daughter to arrive. She stiffened when Rayna approached to hug her. "I must get back to Deal, and I don't look forward to the rush-hour traffic. Your grandfather is sleeping, so let him rest." Sarah walked out to the elevator and pressed the button. Rayna followed behind.

"Mom . . ."

The elevator door opened and Sarah stepped in. "Eli will come by around nine to pick you up. You and your brother can grab a bite to eat on your way home." The elevator door closed.

* * *

Alone now in the room with her jidaw, Rayna felt the strong connection flow between them. *He has aged so much since my sitaw died.* Rayna was fully aware of the intense love her grandparents had for each other. She witnessed Isaac's suffering after he lost his wife. "Jidaw, I love you so very much," she whispered to herself. Of Isaac's thirty-three grandchildren, Rayna had always been his favorite. The two used to spend hours debating portions of the Tanakh. They played backgammon, sang Syrian songs, and took long walks together. Whenever there had been flareups with her mother, and Eli was not around to provide a cushion, Rayna would run down the street to her grandparents. Always, Isaac was there with open arms.

Approaching his bed, she thought he was sleeping. Tubes carrying medicines and nourishment into Isaac's body delayed the inevitable. She leaned over and kissed his cheek. Affectionately, she took his hand. It was mottled with brown age-spots, and it was cold. "Jidaw, it's me, Rayna. I'm here." She felt him squeeze her hand. "I love you, Jidaw."

"Rayna, come close." He opened his eyes. His voice was weak.

"I'm right here," she moved her face nearer to him.

"You're so much like your sitaw. You have her beauty and

her determination. Do you know how much I still love her? She was my life. I'm starving to death without her."

Rayna remembered how, earlier that day, Rami used that word starving to describe how much he was missing her. The death of Rayna's grandmother three years earlier had devastated Isaac. Rayna still remembered his inconsolable grief. Until Rayna went away to school, she had spent long hours comforting him, crying with him, loving him.

"God will soon grant me my wish to join your grandmother. I miss her so much. Promise me, Rayna, not to cry when I'm gone. Be happy for me. I will finally be at peace."

Rayna stroked Isaac's head and kissed his brow.

"I want you to do something for me," his voice was barely audible.

She strained to hear him. "Anything . . ."

"The safe in my house. Do you remember the combination?"

"Yes."

"There's a large pink envelope. I made sure it was pink so you would know it." Isaac's breathing grew heavier. "I don't have much time, so you must bring it to me tomorrow."

"On the way home tonight, Eli and I will stop by your house and get it."

"Rayna . . ."

"Shhh. You need to rest."

"Let me say this one thing, then I'll rest." He held onto her hand. "I pray that you find a man who will love you as intensely as I have loved your grandmother. I so much want that for you." Isaac closed his eyes and slept.

Please, God, let him live long enough to meet Rami on Friday evening.

SEVENTEEN

Job was right. Life is warfare. But for the true survivor, the worst that can happen is merely another obstacle that must be hurdled.—Baltasar Gracian

For the second day in a row, Rayna and Kamil were having lunch at Gemelli's. From his shirt pocket, Kamil took out a small map of Syria, unfolded it, and smoothed out the creases. "Here is Hamah," he pointed. "It sits between Aleppo and Damascus. Sunnis make up seventy-five percent of the Syrian population. In Hamah, my people lived peacefully with their Christian neighbors. President Hafez al-Assad and his family rule. They are Alawaites and comprise about twelve percent of the Syrian population."

"Who are the Alawaites? Are they Sunnis? Shi'ites? What?"

"They're Shi'ites, but not quite. They deviate from pre-scribed Shi'ite practices and are more lax about Quranic interpretation. Some Muslims regard them as unbelievers . . . heretics."

"Really? Muslims consider other Muslims to be unbelievers?"

"Oh, yes."

"Tell me about the Shi'ites." Rayna thought about Rami.

"Shi'ites are in the minority. Five or six percent of the Syrian population." Kamil did not elaborate. Instead, he continued the tale of the Hamah massacre. "Most entitlements, better housing, good jobs, the right to own businesses, and government and military positions have consistently gone to the Alawaites, ever since al-Assad came into power in 1970. Sunnis have been treated like second-class citizens, even though we are in the majority."

"The Shi'ites . . ."

"The Shi'ites, to use an American phrase, are very low on the totem pole. Hasn't your Shi'ite husband told you?" A hint of sarcasm embodied his question.

"Yes. Yes, he has." Goosebumps erupted on her arms and neck. "Please go on."

"Is he involved with al-Shahid? Is your Shi'ite husband part of Yousef's gang of terror? Yesterday you said no, but I think differently."

With her hands unsteady, Rayna looked down. "Rami would never hurt anyone. He's a good human being." She lifted her head, "The answer to your question is *no*."

"Oh. He has a name. Rami. Rami the Shi'ite who knows Yousef the Syrian terrorist. Do I have that correct?"

Cautiously, she nodded.

"You, a Jew, tell me that your Muslim husband is not involved with Yousef Mugniyeh or al-Shahid. Yet, you ask for a profile on Yousef and tell me you have met him. Something is missing from this picture."

A wave of nausea swept over Rayna. "I don't feel very well. I need to leave."

"No. Stay. I want to tell you about Hamah."

Uneasy about divulging more information, Rayna guardedly stared at Kamil. "I'll stay."

"The Sunnis in Hamah staged a well-organized, peaceful protest against the government. Equality for the majority, my people had demanded." Kamil paused, anticipating another question. When it did not come, he resumed. "On February second, 1982, President Assad sent in the Elite Defense Brigade to quash the demonstrators. Tanks rumbled in, accompanied by fighter planes flying low overhead. Shells were fired from every direction. Citizens, young and old, had nowhere to hide. People . . . children lay dying in the streets. Soldiers carried out executions in cold blood. My father's head was blown off in front of me."

"Oh, God!"

"The brutality lasted four weeks. By the time it was over, my city was devastated, flattened by bulldozers, and drowned in bloodshed. The stench of decomposed corpses permeated the air. Mosques, markets, schools, and homes were in ruins. Witnesses have said that as many as fifty thousand people were killed and an equal number were wounded."

"I'm so sorry, Kamil." For a long moment, their eyes held. Rayna could almost feel his agony. "Where is the rest of your family now?"

"They're gone. Dead."

"You're the only survivor?"

He nodded. "I lost my parents, four sisters, and three brothers. My youngest brother was just three years old at the time. Frightened and crying, he had clung to me for protection. I held onto him as tightly as I could, gripping him against me, trying to shelter him from the carnage. Then, in an instant, he was yanked from me. It all happened so fast. His tiny hands reached out to me, but I couldn't grasp them. I never again saw my little brother."

"How old were you when this happened?"

"Sixteen. Yousef Mugniyeh murdered my father. Yousef Mugniyeh tore my brother from my arms. I'll never forget that man's face."

Rayna wanted to touch his hand but restrained herself from doing so. "Then what? How did you survive?"

"For weeks, I was crazed. I searched everywhere for my brother. Everyone loved him. He was adorable. A happy child, and extremely bright for a three-year-old. He was attached to me. I remember one morning when I was leaving for school . . . he grabbed hold of my leg with his little hands and body. He wouldn't let go." Tears welled. Kamil swallowed hard to keep them from flowing. "I looked all over for my family. I prayed to find even one of them alive. In time, I fled to Tarsus, a city in southern Turkey. I have an uncle there, my mother's brother. I found shelter with him and his family. After that, I went to the university. Then I got a job writing for an English newspaper. Simon found me, offered me a position with the magazine, and here I am."

"My God, Kamil, how did you endure it all? In the Bible, there is a story about a man named Job. He loses his children, his home, everything. Then, because of his faith, God restores Job's life and . . ."

"Rayna," Kamil briskly interrupted, "nothing can ever replace the family I lost. I live with it every day of my life. Why was I the one to survive? That question will forever haunt me. Only death will bring me peace. I loved my family. I still do. We were very close. So don't preach to me about Job, and God, and faith until you have walked in my shoes."

"I'm sorry . . . I'm sorry about your family." Rayna noted the gold band on Kamil's finger. "Are you married?"

"Yes, to an American. My wife is a teacher. In November, we'll have our first child."

"Before my internship ends this summer, you will know about Yousef."

* * *

After work, Rayna emerged from the south entrance of the World Trade Center. She stood on Liberty Street in the middle of rush-hour traffic and hailed a cab. "New York Presbyterian Hospital," she instructed the driver.

* * *

Entering her grandfather's private room, Rayna approached him quietly. Isaac's eyes were shut and she thought he was asleep.

"Rayna, is that you? Come closer." His voice was weak.

"Ahhhh. You're up." She put her tote bag on the chair and, being careful not to disturb the tubes attached to his frail body, she kissed his cheek and hugged him gently. "Yes, it's me."

"I've been waiting all day for you. Will you stay?"

"I'll stay," she assured him, adjusting his blanket. "I'll stay for as long as you want me to."

"Did you bring it?"

"Yes, I have it right here." She reached into her tote, took out the pink envelope, and placed it in Isaac's hands. It fell from his fingers. Isaac asked her to open it. "Jidaw, this is the title to your house. I don't understand."

Isaac lived on Ocean Parkway, just down the block from Rayna's family home. His property in that prime location was worth a lot of money. "Rayna, come close. I have little strength left."

Rayna moved nearer. "I can hear you."

"I made an irrevocable trust. All that I have goes to my nine children. They can split it anyway they want. But to you, I leave the house and all that is in it."

"But . . ."

"Shhh. Let me finish. I have no energy to argue with you."

With her fingers, she combed through his full head of white hair and smoothed his bushy eyebrows. "Okay, I won't interrupt."

"I want you to have my house. Our house. The house your grandmother and I lived in for over fifty years. It's yours. The title is now in your name. Look at it."

She examined the paper. "But, Jidaw . . ."

"Shhh. Your sitaw also wanted it this way. The trust was made while she was still alive and it can't be changed. Now, there's another sheet of paper inside the envelope."

Rayna reached down and took it out.

"It's the name of my lawyer and the people who will purchase the house. There's no realtor involved, so there's no commission. Just the lawyer's fees, which I have paid in advance. We worked through all the loopholes. The buyer offered three million dollars and paid one-third of it up front in earnest money. It's in an escrow account until settlement. The lawyer, who is my designated trustee, is expecting your call. The buyer wishes to close as soon as possible. It's a Syrian family who wants to live near the shul."

Isaac struggled for air, and Rayna was concerned. "You need to rest now."

"Let me finish. I don't have much time." His voice was weak. She cradled his cheeks in her palms and kissed his forehead. Her tears flowed down onto his face. With a mischievous grin, Isaac toyed, "Is it raining in here?"

"My tears," she laughed, blotting his face with a tissue. "I don't want to lose you."

"I know that, but we don't always get what we want in life."

"You'll get better and we'll live together in your house."

He took her hand. "Invest the money wisely and you can live well off the earnings and still keep the principal. Don't get caught up in the materialistic lifestyle of the Syrian community or your money will disappear very quickly."

"Jidaw, I'm really sorry I went away to school and left you . . ."

"The lawyer is a good man. Wise and ethical. He will guide you. The only lawyer I ever trusted."

"No! I won't let you go."

"Shhh, listen to me. Be prepared to face difficulties from your parents, your aunts, your uncles, your cousins. They will all be angry about . . ." A coughing spell overtook him.

Rayna lifted his head and reached for the water. She put the straw to his lips. The whooping subsided. "Jidaw, don't be upset with them."

"No, rrawhee, I'm not upset with them. I'm disappointed. Do you know that next to your grandmother, I love you second." He shut his eyes and dozed.

Her head rested next to his on the pillow and her fingers gently stroked his face. *My grandfather and my husband. The two people in this whole world who call me 'rrawhee' because they love me so much.* "Jidaw, did I ever tell you how handsome you are? I used to dream about marrying a man just like you." She took hold of his hand. Soon, Rayna felt Isaac kneading the gold band on her finger.

"What is this?"

"Nothing."

"Nothing? Rayna, I may be a dying old man, but I have not lost my mind. You have never kept things from me before. Don't start now."

Rayna was at a loss.

"I will quietly listen to what you have to tell me."

I cannot lie to my grandfather, but how do I tell him the truth? And so it was that Rayna told her grandfather all that occurred from the very first moment she met Rami.

"An adventurous love story for me to share with your sitaw up in heaven. Together, we will worry about you."

"You're not angry?"

"I can never be angry with you. Who else in the family knows?"

"Only you."

"Being married to a Muslim. This is not what I hoped for you. Your marriage will prove to be a far heavier burden around your neck than anything you have ever known. The rabbis will be punishing. They'll banish you from the community. Everything that has been your life for the past eighteen years will be no more. You'll be thrust into Rami's world, and the only way out may be through . . . through . . . through . . ."

"Through what, Jidaw? Through what?"

"Through death, Rayna. Is your love that strong? Can it withstand that kind of future?" Neither took their eyes from the other until Isaac's eyelids grew heavy and he drifted.

Quietly, Rayna rose from the bed, postured herself on the floor, maneuvered into a lotus position, and meditated. An hour passed. Isaac stirred, "Rayna. Rayna. Are you still here?"

"Yes, I'm still here." She came to him and sat on the bed.

"My poor Rayna. I'm to blame for persuading your parents to let you go away to school against their better judgment. Now, I'm deserting you when you need me most."

Rayna rested her head on her grandfather's chest and wrapped her arm around his waist.

"God has challenged you for a reason. Some day it will become clear. You know, a long time ago, I learned from your grandmother that absolute love is two sides of a single soul yearning to be one. True love comes to everyone, but only once in a lifetime. Love makes no distinctions. It is what it is. For most people, if it doesn't fit their way of life, they walk away from it. You didn't."

Reaching inside her tote, Rayna pulled out the little music box. She wound it up and held it close to Isaac's ear. "Remember? The wheat song? Whenever I was sad, you sang this to me."

"How can I ever forget the joys you brought me. Where did you find such a treasure?"

"Rami brought it back for me from Syria."

Winding it up again, she sat beside Isaac and sang to him. "Ya rra bee barrek ee barrek weezeedawn, ya rra bee barrek ah ah, ya rra bee barrek ah ah, ya rra bee barrek weezeedawn. Lalala lalalala, lalala lalalala, lalalalaaaaaa . . ." When the music stopped, Isaac slept. Rayna snuggled close. Within the warmth of her grandfather's mortal frailness, she, too, slept.

* * *

It was almost ten o'clock when Eli came to pick up his sister. "I'm sorry," he whispered, gently touching Rayna's shoulder to wake her. "There was a major problem at the Fifth Avenue store and I had no choice but to stay and work it through, especially with Dad being in Deal."

"It's okay."

"Did you have dinner?"

"No."

"We'll stop and get something to eat on our way home."

Eli walked to the other side of the bed and kissed his grandfather's forehead. "Jidaw, I have to take Rayna home now. She'll be back tomorrow around five. I'll come by in the morning."

Rayna tried slowly to detach from her grandfather. He clung to her. "I love you, Jidaw, but I have to leave." She stroked his face.

"I love you, too." Isaac spoke under his breath so that Eli could not hear, "I want to meet Rami before God takes me. When?"

"Friday. Can you hold on until Friday?"

"I'll hold on."

Discreetly, Rayna slipped the band off her finger. In the morning, at work, she would put it back on.

EIGHTEEN

If you want to shrink something, you must first allow it to expand. If you want to get rid of something, you must first allow it to flourish. If you want to take something, you must first allow it to be given.—Lao-tzu

On Friday afternoon, Rayna was submerged in the differences between negligence and malice. She read:

> *Negligence implies failure to exercise reasonable care. A magazine editor has more time to check a story than a daily newspaper editor has. A television documentary team has more time to verify details than does the producer of the nightly news. Media with an abundance of funds can afford to do more checking. Malice is reckless disregard for the truth. It is lying.*

"Hmmm." As Rayna absorbed the obvious, her cell phone rang.

"Rrawhee, I am here. The train just arrived. I will be there soon. I love you."

"Me, too." It had been days since Rayna last saw Rami. She missed him a lot.

* * *

Outside Penn Station, Rami hailed a cab. Through heavy traffic, the driver skillfully maneuvered in and out of lanes. Down Avenue of the Americas, past Greenwich Village, Soho, and Tribeca, the vehicle sometimes lurched forward, sometimes crawled, and sometimes stood still. From the rear-seat windows, Rami gazed up at the tall buildings and gaped at the surroundings. Masses of people attempted to cross at every intersection. Automobile horns blasted at the double-parked vehicles blocking lanes. Stores and restaurants lined the streets in endless succession. All of it had the familiar ring of Aleppo, only on a grander scale.

With his backpack mounted behind him, Rami paid the driver and entered the massive south tower of the World Trade Center.

* * *

"Wow!" He slowly turned, surveying the seven-story glass atrium. He reached for his cell phone. "Hi, rrawhee. I am in the lobby."

"I'll be right down." Coming off the elevator, Rayna caught sight of her husband and rushed toward him. Their hands joined and she guided Rami up to the ninety-first floor.

* * *

After introducing Rami to Marianne, the receptionist at the front desk, Rayna led him back to Kamil's office. She tapped on the half-opened door. Kamil looked up from his computer. Rayna poked her head in, "Kamil, this is my husband, Rami."

"Salaam," Kamil smiled.

"Salaam."

"Kamil, would it be okay to leave early?"

"Going to see your jidaw?"

"Yes."

"Have a good weekend. See you Monday."

"Thanks, Kamil. You and Maddy, also."

* * *

Leading Rami into her office, Rayna showed him the tutorial she was working on, then handed him Yousef's profile. "Here's something to read. Give me ten minutes to finish up."

"Who is Maddy?"

"Oh . . . Kamil's American wife. She's a schoolteacher. They're expecting their first baby in November. I met her yesterday. She came to have lunch with Kamil and . . ."

Smiling to himself as she spoke, Rami shut the door and planted a long kiss on her mouth. "I could not have stood another moment away from you."

Rayna's eyes glistened, "Tonight we stay at a first-class hotel. And tomorrow night. And Sunday night. My parents didn't want me traveling back and forth from Brooklyn to Manhattan alone at night . . . and for sure not over Shabbat. Little do they know about my easing off of their strict orthodox practices . . . and I'm not about to tell them. They also don't know you are with me. I'm not about to tell them that, either."

Looking at her hungrily, Rami kissed her again, "I cannot wait to have you alone."

"Mmm." Rayna made some notes, then shut down the computer. "I'm ready."

Rami had skimmed Yousef's profile. "This is frightening. Later, I want to spend time studying it. We have a lot to discuss."

"More than you can imagine. But first the hospital."

* * *

"Hi, Jidaw," Rayna gave her grandfather a big hug. The bed was partially raised, and Isaac sat in a semi-reclining position. "You're looking better than I've seen you all week."

Isaac's full head of snow-white hair was combed neatly. An impish glow illuminated his eyes. "I've been waiting for you to come."

Rayna grasped Rami's hand. "Jidaw, meet Rami."

Isaac squinted. "Rayna, my glasses." He waited for her to put the spectacles on his face. "Aha! My granddaughter is right. You are handsome."

"Uh-oh. What else did Rayna tell you?"

"Rayna, I want an hour alone with Rami."

"Jidaw, just what are you up to? Where did you get this sudden burst of energy?"

Weakly, Isaac motioned with his hand. "Has Rayna told you?"

"Told me what?"

"The secret."

"You sure are feisty today. I think we can take you home soon." She fluffed Isaac's pillow and straightened his blanket.

"Rayna . . . an hour alone with Rami. Please . . . for me."

Rayna looked at Rami, then back at her grandfather. "Jidaw, Rami and I will be just outside your door for a couple of minutes. We'll be right back."

* * *

"What is this all about, Rayna? What am I supposed to say to your grandfather? And the secret? You and I have a commitment. No secrets, remember?"

Rayna did not know what her grandfather had planned, and said so. She suggested to Rami that he do a lot of listening and speak cautiously.

"And the secret?"

"There's no secret. So much has happened this week. I was planning to tell you everything tonight. *Everything*! Including the three million dollars my grandfather is leaving me."

"Three million dollars!" Rami could not comprehend having so much money.

"My grandfather is waiting. Go to him."

"Where will you be for an hour? No . . . an hour is too long. Come back in half an hour."

"There's a gift shop in the lobby. I'll go there and browse, maybe buy something for him."

The couple returned to the room. "Half an hour, Jidaw. You have Rami for half an hour, then I'll be back." She kissed Isaac's forehead.

"An hour, Rayna. I want one hour with Rami."

"No, Jidaw. Half an hour." She quickly exited the room to avoid Isaac's hassling.

* * *

Seated on a chair beside the bed, Rami waited for Isaac to speak.

"I love my granddaughter very much. The first time I held her, she was only four days old. I was drawn to her angelic beauty. My wife, may she rest in peace, and I . . . we lived just down the block from Rayna. We saw her almost every day." The old man labored to stay alive. Rami grasped Isaac's hand and held it. "Water. I need water." Rami reached for the cup on the tray table and put the straw to Isaac's lips. Isaac sipped, then pushed it away. "Rami, I don't have much time. I will be gone before Rayna returns. I sent her out because I don't want her to see me go. And because you and I must talk."

"Isaac . . ."

"First listen, please. This is not how it should be, Rayna married to a Muslim. She doesn't deserve this kind of struggle in her life."

Rami said nothing.

"From the beginning, Sarah never had the patience or love for Rayna . . . not like she has had for her sons. Abe's love for Rayna runs very deep. I suspect my daughter is jealous of that. Other than me and Rayna's grandmother, the only other person Rayna has been close to is Eli. I know my daughter resents that relationship." Isaac wheezed. Rami lifted Isaac's head and fumbled for the buzzer. "No. No nurse. We need to talk more."

"Isaac . . ."

"No. Please. Be patient with me."

Rami let down Isaac's head and tried to make him more comfortable.

"Rayna's determination to go away to school has upset the whole family. And now this happens. You, a Muslim.

We're religious Jews. We marry within our own people, just as Muslims do. Have you any idea what this union is going to do to Rayna's life? Why did you force her into . . .."

"I did not force her into this marriage."

"I think you did. I know my granddaughter. She must have expressed some misgivings. Do you know that Rayna's family will disown her? She will be ostracized from our community, a community that has been a major part of her existence. You have pulled out her roots, snatched Rayna from all she knows. How will you protect her from this? What kind of love made you do such a thing? And what will be your own family's reaction?"

Remembering Rayna's advice, Rami was careful with his words. "I love Rayna, and she loves me. I loved her before I ever met her. And I *will* take care of her."

Isaac rested his head on the pillow. "Rayna's wealth. Greed is a powerful motivator."

"Do you think I married Rayna for her money? I knew nothing about any wealth. Rayna never even hinted at it. When we were married in March, I still did not know. It was only after I took her home for Passover and saw the extravagant house that I realized the family's fortune. I married Rayna because I love her. Money is not my life's blood. Rayna is."

"Rayna is so young. You're both so young. Her life with you will bring enormous hardship for her. I worry about Rayna's future . . . if your love will survive." When Rami started to respond, the old man raised his hand and stopped him. "Tell me your innermost thoughts. I want to know the in-sides of Rami. Then I will have my answer."

For some unexplained reason, Rami spoke of a recurring dream that haunted him over the years. "I was holding the hand of a beautiful young girl, someone I deeply loved. We were running from somewhere, or to somewhere. I do not know. People all around were being slaughtered . . . massacred. Suddenly, she was swept from me. Frantically, I searched for her, but she was gone. In my sleep, I would call her name, awakening myself. . . . and my parents. My nightmares became a family joke. Then, this past January, when Rayna and I made love for the first time . . . I felt peace. No more nightmares."

A profound silence fell on the teenager and the old man. They were drawn to one another. "Tell me more about you and my granddaughter."

"Rayna and I have much in common. We have the same values. We like the same foods. We have the same birth date. On August tenth, we will be nineteen . . ."

"Much too young, but . . . these are my last few moments. I must know that Rayna will be in good hands before God takes me."

"I trust Rayna implicitly. We learn from each other, and share honesty and respect. When we make love . . ." Rami caught himself.

"What happens when you and Rayna make love?"

"We feel Allah's presence all around."

"Do you think God, your Allah, will protect my grand-daughter from the struggles this marriage will bring?"

"I will protect her."

"Is my granddaughter's life in your hands or God's hands?"

"Rayna and I will not deny our love because others decide that we are different and should not be together."

"People can be cruel. That's reality. I'm worried about Rayna."

"I adore Rayna. I will be good to her, take care of her, and love her until the end of time. I give you my word."

"And al-Shahid? Yousef? Terrorism is a destructive force."

"It seems Rayna has told you everything. Is there nothing she left out?"

"I must know from you. Why do you think your Allah has dealt you these cards? Can you be smarter than your opponents? Can you play to win?"

"I must win."

"Eli is the one person who will stand by you both. Don't . . . ghaaa . . . ghaaa." Isaac convulsed.

* * *

Returning from the gift shop with a present in hand, Rayna was shaken to see her jidaw's condition. She rushed to his side and pressed the button for the nurse. Rami cradled Isaac's head, but it was too late. The old man choked out his last breath and closed his eyes.

"No, Jidaw! Don't leave me! I need you! Don't leave me, Jidaw!" Rayna threw herself over her grandfather and wailed. "Come back. Come back. I need you. You can't leave me. I need you . . ."

Drawing his wife close to his heart, Rami comforted her.

* * *

Rami had been surprised at the marked similarities between Judaic and Islamic burial rites. Isaac's body had been ritually washed. His corpse was wrapped in a plain white shroud, and he was buried forty hours later. When the wooden coffin was lowered into the ground, mourners shoveled earth on top. A seven-day grieving period called *sitting shiva* was held in Deal at the home of Sarah's sister, Livia. The bereaved family received hundreds of visitors who came to pay their respects, bring meals, join in prayers, and reminisce about Isaac.

Rami found it disturbing that such a deep division existed between Muslims and Jews. *We believe in the same God of Abraham and share similar customs and rituals. How could such intense hatred occur in a human soul? Why must religion have such a dark side? Why must it pit man against man?*

* * *

According to Isaac's instructions, the lawyer paid a visit to the family at the end of the shiva week. Gathering the siblings together, he informed them of their father's iron-clad trust. Angrily, they accused him of being in cahoots with Rayna and manipulating Isaac. The lawyer assured them that these were Isaac's wishes long before Rayna ever knew anything.

Incensed, Sarah berated her daughter and forbade her to return to Maryland. "If you want to continue your education, it will be done in New York and you will live at home." She ordered Rayna to spend the rest of the summer in Deal with the Syrian community and not to bring shame upon the family. "Your friendship with that Muslim will cease as of this moment!"

In a rare move, Abe supported his wife and spoke harshly to Rayna, "We will no longer allow your brother Eli to come to your rescue. It won't work anymore."

In tears, Rayna ran out of the house and called Rami on her cell phone.

* * *

Rami abruptly left campus, packed his things and, within hours, met Rayna at her parents' home in Brooklyn. "You do not need to stay here any longer. You are coming back with me."

"I can't . . ."

"Yes, you can. I gave my word to Isaac that I would protect you from the ravages of this world, and I intend to do just that."

"But my internship at *InterContinental Weekly*. How am I going to finish my internship? How am I going to clean out my jidaw's house?" She began to cry, pleading desperately for Rami not to go to South America. "Don't leave me here alone. Please, don't leave me here alone. I need you," she sobbed.

"Rayna, rrawhee, I am not going to leave you. We will go to your jidaw's house and stay there until we can figure out what to do next. I will not return to school for the summer." Rami crushed her hair in his hands and held her. "You need me and I need to be here for you."

"What about the Triple Frontier? And Yousef? Make him go away . . . please make him go away."

"Shhh, shhh. It will be okay. We will find a way out of this." He helped Rayna pack up her belongings, filled their two cars with her things, and they drove to Isaac's house.

NINETEEN

You cannot direct the wind, but you can adjust the sails.—Reverend Bernice A. King

The summer proved to be far more tumultuous than either Rayna or Rami had anticipated. With each chasm they leaped across, another awaited them on the other side.

* * *

After moving temporarily into Isaac's house, the couple changed the locks and recoded the security system to keep out family members who felt they had a right to access the residence. Feeling relieved now that no one could barge in on them, they began to go through all of Isaac's possessions, keeping what they wanted and giving away the rest to charity. Rami proved to be a tremendous help, and Rayna was grateful to have him near. While she was busy with her internship at the magazine, Rami sifted through years of her grandparents' accumulations.

Isaac's 1940s two-family brick home did not compare with the lavishness of Rayna's family home. However, the dwelling had been updated twice in its lifetime. The second-floor apartment was rented out. The main level consisted of two bedrooms, two bathrooms, an eat-in kitchen, and a large living room that occupied the front portion of the house. The finished basement with three bedrooms and another bathroom had once accommodated Isaac's growing family of nine children. There was no garage. Instead, a narrow driveway had space for two cars, if one were parked directly behind the other.

The buyers planned to demolish the house and rebuild on the property. Essentially, they were paying three million dollars for the small parcel of land so they could live close to the Syrian shul. "Location is to real estate as oil is to Arabs," Rayna had said. "The value of living near the synagogue on Ocean Parkway is highly prized."

* * *

Abe and Sarah persisted in hounding their daughter, but Rayna stood her ground. She refused to go to Deal, refused to end her summer internship, refused to switch to a school closer to home, and refused to disengage from Rami.

One weekday evening, Abe left the family summer home in Deal and made the one-hour trip into Brooklyn to confront his daughter and lay down the law. Rayna and Rami were having dinner when the bell rang. "I will get it." Rami walked through the living room and toward the front door. He peered into the peephole. Abe stood on the landing. Rami opened the door. Without any warning, Abe swung his fist at Rami. Quickly, Rami ducked to avoid the blow. Abe went into a spin from his own force and fell against the wall.

Hearing the commotion, Rayna rushed to investigate. The sight of Abe and Rami in such a state momentarily froze her, and she attempted to analyze the situation.

"I did not touch him. When I opened the door to greet your father, he swung his fist at me. I ducked. He fell into the wall."

Rayna threw a sharp look at her father. "Is that true?"

Abe did not answer. He only scowled at Rami.

"Dad, I think you better leave. Now!"

"Rayna, I'd like to come in."

"We're having supper, Dad. If you can control yourself, you're welcome to join us."

"I want to talk. *Alone!* Just you and me. Why is *he* here?"

"*He* has a name. It's Rami." She moved into the kitchen. Abe followed her.

"Don't try my patience, Rayna. Look at what he's doing to you. Open your eyes. He's playing with your mind." When Rayna resisted, Abe's voice grew stronger. "For God's sake, Rayna, I'm trying to save you from destroying yourself! Tell him to leave."

"No, Dad."

"What have you done to my daughter, you conniving Muslim? You've brainwashed her and . . ." Suddenly, Abe was taken aback. He leered at Rami. He scrutinized Rayna. Abe saw their wedding bands. "No! No! Dear God, tell me it isn't true." Horrified at the sight, he grabbed Rayna by the hair and affronted her. Rami jumped in to block Abe, but Rayna put up her hand to stop him. "Are you sleeping with him, Rayna? Are you married to him?"

"Yes, to both questions. In March, a reform rabbi married us in Maryland, license and all."

Abe's face went from red to white. He released Rayna and, for a second time, lunged at Rami. Not wanting to hurt Abe, Rami grabbed the man's hands, forced him down on the chair, and held him there. Abe struggled to rise and lost his balance. Rami caught him. Abe began to retch. Rayna grabbed the salad bowl from the table to catch the vomit. Rami ran cold water on a dish towel, wrung it out, and placed it on the back of Abe's neck. The two then helped Abe onto the sofa in the living room. Rami went back into the kitchen to clean up the mess. Rayna stayed with her father.

"You took this house from your grandfather. How could you . . ."

"I did not take this house from Jidaw."

"Look what you're doing to us. To me. To your mother. To yourself. To our family. You're ripping us apart. Did you ever once stop to think of the repercussions of your actions?" Abe was angry, but desperate to get his daughter back. "Rayna, we can fix this. Nobody needs to know. It will be just between you and me. We could have your marriage annulled and go back to how it used to be. You're only eighteen . . ."

"Almost nineteen."

"Whatever. You're too young. He has taken control of your mind. You no longer know yourself or what you are doing."

"No, Dad. I do know what I'm doing. It's about love, Dad. I need love."

"Are you pregnant? Is that it? We can fix it . . ."

"No, Dad, I'm not pregnant. Rami and I married for love. Love, Dad."

"Love! What about dishonor? What about shame? What about the scandal you're bringing upon our family? He's a Muslim. One day you'll regret this, but it will be too late.

Muslim men quickly grow tired of their women. It's in their nature. What will you do when he's had enough of you? After he's mistreated you? Abused you? You can't come back to us. Our door will be locked. You'll have ruined your life."

"Dad, just listen. I'm not sorry for loving Rami. He's a good human being. He's decent and kind and . . . he loves me. Doesn't that count for something?"

"He's not our religion."

"I love him."

In a huff, Abe stomped out.

Rayna ran after him, "Where are you going?"

"Why should you care where I'm going?"

"Please don't drive back to Deal tonight. Go home to Eli. Please, Dad."

Abe slammed the car door shut and drove off. Rayna went back into the house.

* * *

In the archway separating the kitchen from the living room, Rami had silently witnessed the scene. He wanted to step in and protect Rayna but restrained himself, knowing that Rayna needed to deal with Abe on her own terms. Giving Rayna a supportive hug, he urged her into the kitchen. Dinner was cold. Rayna pushed away her plate and went back to the living room.

Rami lifted the phone, "Eli, this is Rami. Your father is on his way over and . . ."

"Where are you? Where's Rayna?"

"We are at your grandfather's house."

"Why are you there? What's going on?"

"Your father and Rayna had an unpleasant encounter. Abe vomited and is in no condition to drive back to Deal tonight."

"Rami, where's Rayna? Is she alright?"

"Yes."

"Rami, I've gone to bat for you. Now level with me. I want the truth."

"Well . . . uhhh . . . ummm . . . Rayna and I are married." Rami moved the receiver away from his ear. Shock waves reverberated across the line. "We planned to tell you . . ."

"How nice. You planned to tell me. Where's my sister? I want to talk with her."

"I will get her." In the living room, he handed the phone to Rayna, "Your brother wants to speak with you." She shook her head. "Eli, Rayna is too upset right now. Give her a little time."

"Let me hear her voice. I want to know that she's okay, or I'm coming over right now."

Rami put the phone to Rayna's ear. "Just say hello to your brother. He wants to hear your voice and know that you are okay."

"Yes, Eli."

"Has Rami hurt you? If you can't talk, just say yes or no. I'll come over right now."

"I'm fine. I'm okay, Eli. Rami has not hurt me. He would never hurt me."

"Did you really marry him?"

"Yes."

"Why?"

"Love. That's why."

"Rayna, are you sure you don't want me to come over?"

"Yes, I'm sure."

"Then let's meet in the city for dinner tomorrow night. The kosher Italian restaurant that you like. Seven-thirty. Rayna, are you sure you don't want me to come over?"

"I'm really okay, Eli. Except, I'm sorry we kept this from you."

"We'll talk tomorrow. Dad just came in. I heard the garage door."

"Look after him tonight. He's not in good shape."

"Tomorrow, Rayna. I'll see you and Rami tomorrow."

"Eli, I'm sorry. I'm really sorry we didn't tell you sooner. I'm sorry you had to find out this way . . ."

"Seven-thirty, Rayna. I'll see you and Rami at the restaurant. Bye."

"Bye, Eli." Rayna hung up the phone. Rami knelt down and massaged her neck and shoulders.

"We're meeting Eli for dinner in the city at seven-thirty tomorrow. Now, I need some quiet time to meditate." She shifted into a lotus position.

Rami returned to the kitchen to finish cleaning up. When he was done, he cautiously approached Rayna and sat down beside her. Calmly, he grappled to get into the same lotus position, twisting his legs and tugging at his ankles. Yet no matter what he did, he could not quite make one leg go inside the other.

Eyeing her husband, Rayna muzzled her amusement. Reaching out, she tried to help him move his legs into position. But the more she pushed and pulled, the more she giggled, until they both rolled on the floor laughing. Playfully, Rami tickled her, then scooped Rayna into his arms and carried her off to the bedroom.

* * *

"Dad, did you eat? You don't look well. What's wrong?"

When Abe told his youngest son about Rayna and Rami,

Eli wanted to raise the issue of his father's infidelity, but, given Abe's emotional state, he held off. "Dad, you act like they've committed the worst crime in the world."

"Well, your sister . . ."

"Hold on, Dad. Just listen for a moment. Are they into alcohol or drugs? No. Are they into immoral or promiscuous sex? No. Have they indulged in any criminal behavior? No. Are they evil people? No, Dad. They don't even smoke."

"But . . ."

"So what is their sin? Because they were born into different religions, are they to be condemned for falling in love? Are you so worried about what the rabbis will say? Is your standing in the community worth so much to you that you're willing to give up your daughter?"

"Why are you always so quick to come to your sister's defense? She married a Muslim. *A Shi'ite Muslim!* And she's sleeping with him. Oh my God, Eli."

Eli waited for this opportunity. "What you did is okay, but what Rayna did is wrong?"

"What are you talking about? I never did anything to disgrace our family."

"Like hell you didn't. You had a seven-year affair with a California congresswoman who was *not* Jewish . . . and you were both married and had families. How do you justify committing adultery with a Christian while condemning your daughter for sleeping with her own husband?" With disgust, Eli looked sharply at his father. "You violated one of the ten commandments."

Beads of perspiration formed on Abe's forehead. "What are you talking about?"

"You think I didn't know about all the times you were away in Washington under the pretext of attending to business? Did you ever once stop to think what your affair would do to Mom if she had found out? Did you care? To me, your infidelity is far worse than what your daughter has done. At least Rayna isn't cheating on her husband."

Abe turned ashen. "That affair is over. And she wasn't a Muslim."

"Your secret is out, and your hypocritical double-standard sickens me."

"So what do you suggest I do?"

"I don't know. What do you think you should do?"

* * *

In the morning, Rayna called *InterContinental Weekly* and told them she would not be in. The stress was beginning to wear on her and she needed time to clear her head. Rami convinced Rayna to go out and do something fun with him before they met Eli for dinner.

They took the subway into the Financial District and walked to the Federal Reserve Bank on Liberty Street. Inside, they learned about the central banking functions, saw the bank's vault of international monetary gold, and digested a lesson on the history of money. After that, they strolled over to the West Side Highway and caught a bus going north to Midtown. Getting off at Pier 86 by the Hudson River, they entered the Intrepid Sea-Air-Space Museum and walked the flight deck of the nine-hundred-foot-long aircraft carrier.

* * *

During lunch, Rayna discreetly reached under the small table and affectionately squeezed her husband's thigh. "Thank you for cleaning up after my father last night, and for allowing me to handle him on my own. I know it was difficult for you to keep silent." She leaned over and kissed him. "I love you very much."

"And I love you very much."

* * *

After lunch, they went to the Lladro Center and bought a bride-and-groom figurine. In a shop on Orchard Street, Rami presented Rayna with a set of pink and purple sheets for their future king-size bed. At Macy's, they indulged in some serious clothes shopping. The hours passed quickly and seven-thirty soon approached. Laden with packages, the two hurried out onto the street. On Broadway, they searched for the restaurant. "There it is, across the street," Rayna pointed. Impatiently, they waited for the light to change before dashing to the other side.

* * *

"Sorry we're late . . . time got away from us."

"I just got here myself." The coldness in Eli's voice left no mistake about his displeasure with them. The waiter arrived and took their drink orders. They all requested water. Eli glared at the young couple sitting across the table.

"Thank you for seeing us," Rami said. Eli did not respond. In awkward silence, the three looked over the menu. The waiter returned with their water and a basket of bread.

Tapping his fingers on the table, Eli made his anger known. He shifted his gaze back and forth between his sister and brother-in-law. "So, let me hear the reason why you lied . . . why you deceived me."

Rayna cast her eyes downward and murmured, "I'm sorry. We didn't mean to . . ."

"Look at me when you speak, damn it. I defended you. Both of you. I befriended *your husband*. Why did you shut me out? Is it that with Rami in your life, you no longer have use for me?"

"Eli, do not blame Rayna. She wanted to tell you. We both wanted to tell you."

"Then why didn't you tell me?"

"Eli, lower your voice, please. Let's not make a scene in the restaurant. I was wrong not to tell you. Rami and I . . . we were both wrong. We're sorry."

"In March! You married in March! Three months ago! You didn't think to tell me? You didn't have the time? What? What was it?"

The waiter came over to take their orders. "Is there a problem?"

"No, there's no problem," Eli was irritated by the intrusion.

Rami put his arm around Rayna and smoothed back her hair. "Eli, Rayna loves you very much. You must believe that. Besides Isaac, you have been the one constant in her life. I have not come to take your place. I have a different role in her life."

"I'll bet you have! You sleep with her! Is that why you married my sister? Before Rayna met you, she was innocent and pure. Why couldn't you keep your hands off her?"

Rayna fidgeted nervously. Rami took her hand and held it. "Eli, give me twenty minutes with no interruptions, no facial expressions. Just listen."

"Why should I give you anything? You took my sister from me. I can have you deported back to Syria."

"Eli, listen to Rami. Please!"

"I'm listening. This better be good."

Rami spoke of the special love he and Rayna shared. He told of his own father's hatred for Jews and of Rayna's fears over losing her family. "Rayna was conflicted and scared. That is why she did not tell you." Rami accepted full responsibility for the situation. "Your grandfather was right. I pushed Rayna into this marriage. I love her so much that I could not risk losing her to outside influences."

In the end, Eli was left with no choice. He did not want to lose his sister. He loved her. Reaching inside his shirt pocket, he took out an envelope, "Dad asked me to give this to you."

Troubled, Rayna quietly read the letter.

Dear Rayna,

I also know about love. I have loved you so very much from the day you came into this world. You were my baby. My only daughter. Do you know how much I wanted a daughter? Your mother and I kept having sons. Four of them. I was determined to have my little girl. Your birth brought me so much joy. Now, your marriage has brought me so much sorrow. I want to disown you, but I can't. Your mother will not take this well. When she finds out, there will be no forgiveness. I promised to put you through school and I want to keep that promise. This check is for the coming school year. Deposit it into your account. Hold onto your grandfather's money. It is your

insurance policy for the future. And manage your
trust fund wisely. We may never speak again, but
know that I love you.

Daddy

Withdrawing a fifty-thousand-dollar check, she stared at
it for several seconds. "I can't accept this. Not after what I've
done to hurt him. Oh, Eli, I'm so sorry for the grief I have
caused everyone." Weeping, she handed the check back to
her brother.

Eli refused to take it. "Deposit it into your school account.
Don't hurt Dad any more than you already have. Last night,
Dad said that one day he'll contact you. But right now, this
is all very difficult for him and he needs time."

"Thank you, Eli. From the bottom of my heart. I don't
know what happened last night between you and Dad. What
did you say to him?"

"Rayna, we all have skeletons hidden in our closets. Dad
is no exception." He smiled. "My dear sister, your mascara
is running."

* * *

Early Friday afternoon, Rami turned onto Liberty Street
and met Rayna in front of the south tower. They were going
to Maryland to find an apartment to live in while attending
school. Marisa had insisted that they stay with them for the
weekend and offered the sofa bed in Jason's office. "The
children will be so excited to see you. Plan to arrive in time
for shabbat dinner."

Advancing toward the Holland Tunnel, Rami was grateful to escape the city before the start of rush-hour traffic.

Two hours into the trip, Rami's cell phone rang. He glanced over at Rayna and rolled his eyes before focusing back on the road. "That has got to be either Nolan or Yousef." He shrugged his shoulders, wanting to ignore the call. Rayna lifted the phone from the dashboard and handed it to Rami.

"Yes?" Instant turmoil ignited in his stomach. It was Yousef ordering him to the Triple Frontier on July fifteenth, the same day Rayna would be closing on the sale of her grandfather's house. Rami would not leave her to go through it alone. "No, Yousef. I cannot be there on July fifteenth. August fourth, Yousef, and for two weeks only. Then school starts."

Yousef threatened to kidnap Rayna, do with her what he wanted, then return damaged goods back to Rami. Rami clenched his teeth. He grasped the steering wheel so tightly that his knuckles turned white. "Do not threaten me, Yousef!" He pushed the button and ended the call, then threw the phone onto the back seat.

"A rest stop in two miles. Let's stop, Rami."

"Yousef wants me in Ciudad del Este on July fifteenth. I defied him. He threatened . . ." Rami stopped himself. He did not want to alarm Rayna.

"Don't go," she begged. "I've got a really bad feeling about this. Please don't go."

It is because of me that Rayna is in danger. I cannot allow harm to come to her. I must find a way out. I will speak with Eli. He will look after her while I am away in South America.

TWENTY

Dreams do come true if we only wish hard enough. You can have anything in life if you will sacrifice everything else for it.—James M. Barrie

Ciudad del Este, Paraguay, the contraband capital of the world—this is where Omar was working for the summer. Yousef had employed him in an electronics store crammed with confiscated goods and defective merchandise that carried forged name-brand labels. A steady flow of unwitting people flocked to buy the cut-rate, adulterated goods. In the back of the store, a concealed door leading into a warehouse rested flush against the rough, dark-paneled wall. Behind the wall, partitions separated the contraband from stockpiles of weapons and explosives. The weapons were traded for cocaine with Colombian and Brazilian drugpins.

Defying detection, handguns, automatic assault rifles, machetes, small missiles, cluster bombs, and land mines arrived periodically in the Triple Frontier via Syria. In turn, refined cocaine was shipped in sophisticated containers to ports of entry in the United States and Europe, where an abundance of willing buyers provided the business that bankrolled much of al-Shahid's worldwide activities.

Witnessing corruption and total disregard for human life, Omar recalled a sociology professor he had had during his first semester at the University of Maryland. From this teacher, he learned about 'survival of the fittest' and 'caveat emptor'. With these lessons in mind, Omar did what he had to do for his own self-preservation. He could not risk warning Rami of the danger to his life. If word were to leak back to Yousef that he had alerted Rami, then Omar's life might be marked as well. So Omar had chosen to be silent. Fear was a greater motivator than friendship.

* * *

One morning, as Omar entered the warehouse to gather some of the black-market merchandise to restock the store's shelves, he witnessed Yousef and Abdallah in fiery contention. In Arabic, Yousef was vehemently disparaging Abdallah, who was not taking it lightly. It became clear to Omar that the two men wanted Rami eliminated. Abdallah wanted to blot out Rami as soon as he arrived in the Triple Frontier. Yousef demanded restraint.

"Not until a secure replacement is found to work with Doctor Nolan. So far, Abdallah, you're incompetent. You're a failure." Brutally, he lifted a loaded handgun off the shelf and held it to Abdallah's temple. Yousef pulled back the hammer. Abdallah flinched. Viciously, Yousef snarled, "Find a replacement before Rami arrives. Am I clear enough, Abdallah?"

The diabolical power that Yousef held over others sent a terrifying chill through Omar. *No one is immune from Yousef's wrath. Not even Abdallah.*

* * *

Putting aside his apprehension over the danger that loomed ahead, Rami focused his attention on Rayna. The couple had spent an exhausting weekend in Maryland searching for an apartment. Late Sunday afternoon, Marisa and Jason advised the pair not to be foolish, "Don't throw away your money on high rent when you could do better by investing in real estate, especially since you have the funds to do so."

* * *

Convinced of the financial judiciousness, Rami and Rayna returned the following weekend and went house hunting. In the upscale corridor of Tuckerman Lane in Bethesda, Maryland, they found a large, newly-built townhouse. The location was perfect, and the house was more than they could have hoped for—three finished levels, spacious rooms, lots of sunlight, and rich appointments. The half-hour drive to the university would provide the wedge they wanted from the activities and clamor of campus life. A short distance away were two metro stations, good restaurants, lots of shopping, supermarkets, movie theaters, and Marisa and Jason's home.

Trying unsuccessfully to strike a deal with the real estate agent, Rami had insisted on speaking directly with the builder. Rayna sat back and watched her husband delve into negotiations. Rami pointed to the slump in the real estate market and emphasized the eight months that the house had been sitting vacant, at much cost to the builder. Offering to pay with a check, to forego any changes, and to settle the following week, Rami tempted the developer. What had begun as an asking price of $480,000 became a selling price of $390,000. Rami had negotiated superbly, and Rayna was delirious with joy. She wrote a check for the deposit, and the contract was sealed.

Before starting back to New York, Rayna urged her husband to go see Nolan. "Drop me off at the mall. I'll shop while I'm waiting for you."

* * *

Wild with excitement about the new house, Rayna chattered incessantly during the trip back to Brooklyn. She rattled on about where they would put Isaac's furniture, what they needed to buy, how to decorate, cooking meals in the large modern kitchen, and making love on a new king-size bed under the big skylight. The more she rambled, the deeper Rami withdrew, until Rayna's words were reduced to background drone.

Rami recognized that his life with Rayna was filled with more good than he could ever have imagined possible. His love for her was stronger than anything he had ever known before or would ever know again. Still, a struggle churned within. Sometimes the love he felt was so great, it hurt. When she had written a check for the deposit on the house, he perceived it to be his responsibility, one that he could not fulfill. Rayna's overly generous nature and insistence that her money belonged to them both made him feel inadequate. He was accepting from her more than he was giving to her. Furthermore, after observing Abe's reaction to Rayna's marriage, Rami concluded that the man loved his daughter more than he loved intolerance. This brought memories of

Ibrahim. Rami saw his father embracing intolerance more than loving his son.

Adding to the tension were Yousef's demands on him. Rami did not want to return to Ciudad del Este, nor did he want to be separated from Rayna. Yet, Yousef's threat, if he did not go, scared him. Rayna would be kidnapped. Yousef did not make idle threats. How could he tell Rayna that the only reason he would be going to South America was to protect her?

Moreover, his visit with Nolan that afternoon had only intensified the stress. Nolan had informed Rami of two Arab men who had approached him, wanting him to cut all ties with Rami. They bribed and bullied. When Nolan rejected their demands, the men launched into scare tactics, intimidation, and dire warnings.

How long can Nolan resist before his life is in real danger? Rami was determined to free himself from Yousef's domination and also to look after the professor. But how?

* * *

Overwhelmed with enthusiasm, Rayna had not noticed her husband's disengagement. After exhausting the subject of the house, she talked about Kamil giving her the name of an excellent immigration lawyer in Washington. "As soon as we're settled, we should make an appointment. We'll both rest easier once you have your green card." When Rami made no gesture of acknowledgment, Rayna thought it was because he did not understand, so she clarified, "Permanent resi . . . " All at once, she latched onto the daunting expression blanketing Rami's face. She noted the speedometer needle grazing ninety. *He did not hear one word I said.* "Rami, slow down!" When he did not react, she screamed, "Rami!" Something was amiss. Rayna wanted him to stop the car. "Sweetheart, please pull off at the next exit. I have to go to the bathroom."

In silence, he slowed the car, followed the signs off the exit, and pulled into a gas station. While he remained with the car to fuel up, Rayna went inside. When she returned, she coaxed Rami into letting her drive the rest of the way. "You look tired. Why don't you shut your eyes and rest a while. I don't mind driving." Rami did not argue.

* * *

In bed later that night, Rayna rested her head on his chest. "It's Yousef, isn't it?"

"It is many things. Yes, Yousef is a big chunk." Rami wrapped his arms snugly around her. He spoke of all the things plaguing him—all except Yousef's threat against her.

"It's not true that you take from me more than you give to me. Your love is priceless. No amount of money could buy your love. Don't you see that?" Rayna then suggested that Rami speak with Kamil. "He hates Yousef more than you do. Remember, it was Yousef who killed Kamil's father during the Hamah massacre. It was Yousef who pulled Kamil's little brother from his arms and dragged away the child."

Rami recalled the story well. He had cringed when Rayna first narrated the account, almost as if he had been there himself. "Yes, I would like to speak with Kamil."

* * *

On Monday morning, Rayna waited anxiously for Kamil to arrive, continually checking his office. Rushing toward his door for the sixth time, she did not see Kamil coming and collided head-on into him. "Whoa!" he grinned, catching her. "To what do I owe this pleasant greeting?"

She eased him into his office and shut the door. "Rami wants to meet with you today. He needs to talk . . . about Yousef."

Kamil eyed her apprehensively. "Oh?"

"Kamil, I gave you my word that you would know about Yousef . . ."

"And why now? Why today? What is the urgency?"

"Rami is very troubled. He needs someone other than me to confide in. Someone else he can trust. Like you. You're both from Syria. Same culture, same language. Please, Kamil, I'm begging you. You and Rami have a common enemy . . . Yousef."

He glanced at his calendar. "I must write my column this morning. After that, I have a luncheon appointment. Two o'clock. Tell Rami to come by my office at two o'clock." For fifteen years, Kamil had been agonizing over an opportunity to get at Yousef.

"Oh, Kamil, I could hug you."

Kamil smiled, "Next time I will not refuse."

* * *

At noon, Rami met Rayna in the concourse of the World Trade Center. They picked up veggie melts at the sandwich shop and took their lunch outside to the plaza—the open square separating the north and south towers. Overshadowing the grounds were an enormous sculpted globe and a commanding central water fountain. During the summer months, free concerts were given. On this particular day, a small orchestra played the musical score from *West Side Story*. Looking for an empty bench, Rami and Rayna found one in the shade. A mild breeze tempered the summer's heat. As they ate their lunch, the two decided to postpone the closing on Isaac's house and coordinate it with the move into their new residence.

Rayna's cell phone rang. "Hello." As she spoke, tears trickled down her cheeks. Nervously, she chewed on her lower lip.

"What is it, rrawhee? Who was that?"

Rayna shook her head and looked away, trying to regain her composure so as not to draw attention to herself. "That was my jidaw's lawyer. Two of my aunts, my mother's sisters, have brought a three-million-dollar lawsuit against me with accusations that I manipulated Isaac and stole the house from the family."

In the background, the small orchestra played "Somewhere." Rami took out a tissue from Rayna's tote and patted the droplets from her face. Stilled by the music, they sat for several minutes with their eyes locked. Breaking the trance, Rami clasped his wife's hand, "Come."

* * *

He led her up the elevators and to the enclosed observation deck on the one-hundred-seventh floor of the south tower. From there, they followed sightseers who were climbing the stairs to the roof. "Hmmm, how strange," Rayna remarked. "After the 1993 attack on the towers by Muslim terrorists, the fire marshall ordered the rooftop doors locked. I wonder why they're open today."

Outside on the roof, the world had a surreal quality. Clear skies commanded incredible three-hundred-sixty-degree views.

I wish we could stay right here. Down below, our lives are on a roller coaster. One minute the wind raises us to glorious heights and the next minute a downdraft forces us to the bottom." Sinking to the rooftop floor, Rayna allowed herself the luxury of escaping into oblivion. Rami brought her back to reality. It was almost two o'clock and he did not want to keep Kamil waiting.

* * *

Rayna sat in her office watching a video on the ease of manipulating the minds of the public. Rami was with Kamil behind a closed door. Two hours later, Kamil buzzed, "Come on into my office."

* * *

Rayna took the seat beside her husband. Looking across the desk, Kamil spoke directly to her. "I'll be on that flight with Rami when he leaves for South America. He will not be out of my sight during those two weeks. I give you my word."

Kamil's message made her tremble. Rayna tried to steady her hands in her lap. She had expected Kamil to talk Rami out of going. Now she felt betrayed. Angrily, she rose from the chair and leaned over the desk. With venom in her voice, Rayna bore down on Kamil in an unwavering, icy glare, "I trusted you. You double-crossed me. Through my husband, you may now find the revenge you have so long been looking for. It should make a great story for a reporter of your caliber. You may even be able to write a book about it. Maybe you can even kill Yousef and avenge your father's death. And your brother's death, too!" She turned to leave, hesitated, then swung back around. "If anything happens to Rami, you will carry a heavy yoke around your neck for as long as you live. I will not allow you a moment of peace."

"You have my word, Rayna. I will return Rami safely to you."

Pivoting, Rayna reached for the doorknob. Kamil jumped up and stopped her. "Sit down. Rami isn't doing this to put himself in danger or to upset you. He's struggling to keep you safe. Yousef has threatened your life. If Rami doesn't go to Ciudad del Este, Yousef will kidnap you."

Slowly, Rayna shifted her gaze to Rami, "Why didn't you tell me?"

"Because I love you and you already have enough to worry about."

Without uttering another word, Rayna left the room.

* * *

Over the next week, a tense silence filled their marriage. Rayna spoke to Rami only when necessary. In bed, she slept at the far edge with her back toward him, refusing his tender attempts at resolving their impasse.

* * *

At *InterContinental Weekly*, Rayna informed Simon that she had learned enough media law and wanted to tackle a writing assignment. She threw herself into a thorough investigation of the 1993 World Trade Center bombing.

Rami spoke with Eli about the upcoming trip to South America, asking him to look after Rayna while he was gone. He withheld the enormity of the situation, preventing Eli from learning the full threat to Rayna's safety.

* * *

In their new townhouse, between unpacked cartons and sheer exhaustion, Rayna lay quietly at the edge of the bed trying to sort through the past year, wishing to come to terms with her life in the present. Aware that she had been behaving badly toward Rami and that he did not deserve her brusque recoiling, she concluded that although she feared for his life, he in turn feared for hers. She must let go. She must allow Rami to follow his own judgment. She could warn him. She could beg him. But in the end, the decision was Rami's to make. Losing him would devastate her. *Love changes everything*, she thought. *How you live. How you die. Once you make that commitment, nothing can ever go back to how it was.*

This time, when Rami reached over and gently brought her to him, she did not resist. When his hands moved slowly over her slim frame, she responded. Facing the man she loved so completely, Rayna met his lips and surrendered. Together, they penetrated a dimension where love and death are transposable. Rami and Rayna had known an earlier life together.

TWENTY-ONE

I have seen that in any great undertaking, it is not enough for a man to depend simply upon himself.—Lone Man, Isna la-wica, Teton Sioux

Familiar with danger, Kamil was known to delve into perilous investigations to get his stories. He had endured kidnapping, torture, and incarceration. Living through the Hamah massacre of 1982 had sharpened his survival instincts. In 1989, he was caught in the middle of a violent insurrection against Indian rule in Kashmir. That same year, he was taken prisoner when Islamic fundamentalists seized power in Sudan. When Kamil went to Rwanda in 1994 to cover the massacre of the Tutsis, Hutus captured him and buried him up to his neck, then set a swarm of bees around his head. And it was just a year ago that Kamil had gone to Afghanistan to report on the Taliban. He was taken hostage and forced into an isolated cave with only vipers to keep him company.

Rami, on the other hand, was a novice to the brutalities of life.

* * *

"Fanatics represent no government and no country. They follow no rules. International law doesn't restrain them. Irrational beings stop at nothing to get what they want." Sitting in Simon's office, Rami listened to Kamil's dire counseling. "Yousef Mugniyeh is a bully of the worst kind. He is evil. Slime. This is not a scare tactic session, Rami. I want you to fully grasp the dangers ahead. Simon himself has misgivings about our going. A man like Yousef has no conscience. When you're dealing with someone so twisted, you better have all your antennas up." He handed Rami a hexagon-shaped copper coin. "You are to keep this with you at all times. I also will carry one. This allows Simon to track our whereabouts, just in case."

"The coin is linked to the GPS tracking system," Simon explained. "There are two types of satellites—those that look out into space and those that look down on earth. GPS, the Global Positioning System of satellites, looks down on our world and, with the proper tools, we can get pretty near the exact location of anyone or anything. So don't lose this coin. It may mean the difference between life and death for you."

Rami studied the piece of metal in his hand, then closed his palm over it, contemplating where to put it. *In my pocket, with the other coins.*

"Dense areas block the signal and will prevent Simon from getting a reading on your site. So, although we don't anticipate it, be sure to keep out of forests and jungles, just in case you and I were to get separated." Kamil wanted Rami to be aware of all the dangers.

A pit formed inside Rami's stomach.

* * *

On Monday, August fourth, Rayna drove Rami to JFK International Airport. As the couple walked toward the gate, Kamil spotted them. He had arrived moments earlier and was on the phone. Rayna approached him and glared into his face. Kamil hung up. "If anything happens to my husband, I swear to God I'll make your life miserable for the rest of your days."

From the beginning, Kamil had been struck with Rayna's beauty and sensuality. Grasping her passion to love and to commit so completely to another, served only to intensify his arousal for her. After losing all his family during the Hamah massacre, Kamil's emotions had shut down. Rayna ignited feelings in him that he had never known. She awakened sensations he had thought were long gone. Observing her now, he wished she were his, but knew better than to overstep that boundary. Kamil's wife, Maddy, was a schoolteacher who lived her life in a lecture mode. Their marriage was not idyllic.

Rami assured Rayna that he would call often and twice on August tenth, the day they both were to turn nineteen, and promised to bring her back a special gift. Then, dramatically, their hands separated. "Allah maak. God be with you, my love." She watched Rami start down the ramp. Kamil was next to board. Rayna grabbed his sleeve, "Salaam. Peace. Kamil, don't you dare return without Rami."

* * *

When Rami and Kamil arrived at the small airport in Foz do Iguaçu, they found Omar waiting. "As-salaam alaykum."

"Wa-alaykum as-salaam." Rami introduced Kamil. "This is a friend I met on the plane. He is here on business. I offered him a ride into Ciudad del Este."

"Yousef told me to pick up only you. Nothing was said about him." Cautious to do exactly what Yousef bid, Omar did not want to give the stranger a ride. Rami's persistence won out.

* * *

The car crept above the Paraná. All was as Rami remembered. Traffic inched along at a turtle's pace, traversing the decaying Amistad Bridge. Pedestrians scurried along the outer edge of the overpass, pushing carts filled with cigarettes and hauling backpacks bulging with black-market merchandise. They tossed their loot over the side to avoid inspection. Below, their go-betweens carried off the spoils to sell for significant profits.

As the vehicle approached Ciudad del Este, the sun was just beginning to set. "It is not safe to be out after dark. I will take your friend to a hotel," Omar announced. Stopping at a seedy-looking place, he turned around and faced Kamil, "Get out. This is as far as I can take you."

Glaring at Omar, Kamil raised his brow and shook his head, "Surely, you do not expect me to sleep in such a place. Take me to where Rami will be staying."

"No! Now get out!" When Kamil did not budge, Omar clutched the steering wheel in exasperation, and stepped hard on the gas pedal. The car lurched forward. Dodging potholes and snaking the shabby gravel alleyways, Omar drove to the outskirts of town. Maneuvering onto a narrow dirt street, he parked adjacent to an old one-story adobe bungalow. "Rami, this is where I am living for the summer. There is one vacant room with two beds. You and your friend can share it . . . for tonight. Tomorrow, he goes or we will all suffer Yousef's wrath." Omar's fear of Yousef was pronounced. "There is one bathroom out in the hall. A woman comes everyday to clean and cook. She leaves food in the kitchen. If Yousef finds out about this . . ."

"Omar, thank you for . . ."

"Forget it, Rami. You have forced this upon me. I will be at Yousef's mercy if he . . ."

"Omar, you already are at Yousef's mercy."

* * *

That night, Rami's haunting nightmare returned, the same one he had grown up with in Halab. "Raynaaa! Raynaaa!" He wakened Kamil.

Approaching Rami's bed, Kamil calmed him. "Shhh. Shhh. A bad dream. You were calling out for Rayna. It's okay now."

Unsettled, Rami was embarrassed, "I am so sorry to have wakened you."

"Don't be sorry. Even I have nightmares," Kamil smiled protectively.

An hour later, Rami was still awake. He glanced over at Kamil who was now fast asleep. Quietly, he got out of bed, reached for his jeans hanging over the chair, and put them on. Barefooted, Rami went into the kitchen. A bowl of petite bananas sat on the table. He ate one, then slipped his hand into his pocket and took out the GPS coin, twiddling it between his fingers. Soon, Rami's eyelids grew heavy and he was ready for sleep. Putting the coin back in his pocket, he returned to the bedroom. In the darkness, Rami slipped off his jeans and tossed them over the chair. Noiselessly, the coin fell and rolled under the bed. Rami did not notice.

* * *

Driving into town to meet Yousef and Abdallah the next morning, Omar hoped that he would not have to explain the stranger in their midst. His face paled; his palms turned clammy.

"What's wrong with you, Omar? You look sick." Abdallah then disregarded Omar's presence and turned his attention to Yousef. "Sami is the best we've got, boss. If he can't break Nolan, nobody can. By this time tomorrow, we should be free to dispense with Rami. Nolan and the bacteria will be yours."

With an evil eye, Yousef leered at Omar, "Where's Rami? I want him at the warehouse."

"I will go get him. He is at the house." Relieved that he was not questioned about Kamil's presence, Omar drove back to the house.

* * *

"Get your things. You are to leave now." Omar was anxious to get rid of Kamil before anyone discovered him.

Kamil nodded courteously, then glanced at Rami.

"Rami, Yousef is expecting you. Now! I will drive your friend back into town. That is as far as I can take him."

With their backpacks, Rami and Kamil climbed into the car. Omar swerved around the cratered streets until he came to a sprawling concrete building fortified by barred windows and steel doors. He pulled around to the back of the structure and parked. "Mister Kamil, I believe you came to this city on business. I suggest you go do it."

* * *

Kamil made himself invisible, observing Omar and Rami entering the building from the front. He followed, keeping a reasonable distance behind. Through a barred window, Kamil was able to see that the structure housed a store. He watched Omar and Rami walk to the back. A camouflaged door opened, just enough to allow Omar and Rami to squeeze through.

Guards approached, motioning Kamil to move on. He went into the shop. Young Arab men assisted customers. Kamil mulled around, pretending to be a shopper. He kept close vigil on the back of the store, and hoped Rami was safe behind the hidden paneled door.

* * *

"Salaam, Rami."

"Salaam, Yousef."

Yousef walked with Rami to the far end of the stockroom. "There's a man named Carlos el Negro. Until four months ago, we had a lucrative arrangement trading arms for drugs. Then the bastard accused me of cheating him. Now, el Negro refuses to do business with me or with any of my people. But he has heard much about you from others. He inquires. Sometimes too much. He knows more than I care for him to know. The man likes what he has heard of you. Young. Smart. Master negotiator. And as I, he is also taken with your beautiful wife."

The color drained from Rami's face.

"Carlos el Negro wants to meet with you. On my behalf, of course. You are to revive the alliance and negotiate for me. I want his drugs. He wants my weapons. You succeed and I will reward you handsomely."

"Yousef, I know of the attempts you have made to replace me on Doctor Nolan's project. If you have such big plans for me, then why do you want me out of the way?"

Yousef grabbed Rami tightly by the throat, "Nobody challenges me! Nobody!"

Jolted by Yousef's severe reaction, Rami felt his breath being taken from him and he gasped for air. Meanwhile, Yousef grappled to keep his own volatility in check, mindful that he needed Rami, at least for now. He released his hold. "Tomorrow morning, you leave for Manaus in northwestern Brazil. From there, you will fly to Putumayo in southern Colombia. Someone will be waiting to take you into La Paya National Forest. There you will meet Carlos el Negro."

* * *

A national forest! Rami's senses heightened. *Dense areas block the signal. Keep out of forests and jungles. Be alert in case you and I get separated.* Reflecting on Kamil's warnings, uneasy thoughts whirled through Rami's brain. *I do not know why Yousef is providing me with information. He could have sent me on this trip and said nothing. He could have kept me guessing. For sure, he would not be so forthcoming if Kamil's nearness were known. So Omar kept his mouth shut, not to protect me but to protect himself. Still, I am grateful.*

"Are you going to show me the weapons, Yousef . . . the ones to trade for the cocaine? How much leeway do I have in negotiating?"

"Leeway! You want leeway?"

"If you want me to negotiate, I must know my bargaining space. How much?"

Yousef's explosive disposition unleashed full force. He shoved Rami hard against the wall. Once again, he grabbed Rami tightly by the throat, strangling his air supply. "I give leeway to no one. I dictate the terms and you carry them out. Understood?"

In his peripheral vision, Rami caught sight of Abdallah closing in. Regaining strength, Rami swiftly drew up his knee and rammed it into Yousef's testicles. Doubled over in pain, Yousef's hold on Rami dissolved. "You slimy bastard! You are worse than a dog . . . than a pig!"

Abdallah raised his handgun and aimed it at Rami's temple. Through his pain, Yousef managed to strike the firearm from Abdallah's hand. "Not yet, Abdallah . . . not yet."

* * *

Maintaining a low profile, Kamil kept vigil over the camouflaged door, unaware of the situation behind it. Slowly, Yousef cracked the opening just enough to peer out into the shop. Kamil caught a glimpse of his father's murderer. A need for revenge engulfed him. Impulsively, he reached for the small pistol hidden inside the waist of his jeans and pondered the risk of assassinating Yousef. The door shut. Kamil withdrew his hand from the weapon. *Get hold of yourself. You gave your word to return safely with Rami. A foolish move now could cost both of us our lives.*

Kamil waited a long while before Rami emerged from behind the hidden door. He made eye contact, then walked down the street. Rami followed. When they were safely out of sight, Kamil paid a man to drive them both to a respectable hotel. "Omar will not report your absence from the house. He's too scared . . . and he couldn't care less where you sleep tonight."

* * *

Over lunch, Rami spoke of Yousef's attack on him in the warehouse. Then Rami told of the journey ahead, the meeting with Carlos el Negro in La Paya National Forest, and Yousef's expectation for a successful arms-for-drugs trade. "I am frightened, Kamil. If something should go wrong . . . I am really worried about Rayna. I cannot leave her to be alone."

"Nothing will go wrong. I'll be near all the time and Simon is tracking your every move."

"Like in the warehouse today? You had no clue what was happening. Yousef could have killed me. You were not inside to see."

"You're right. Let this be a lesson for both of us not to take anything for granted."

In their hotel room that evening, Kamil briefed Rami on the dangers inside the forest, then reached for his satellite phone, checked the signal, and dialed Simon. Reporting in, he provided the details of Rami's journey, agreed to call again when they landed in Manaus, and said that Rami wanted Rayna kept informed of everything.

* * *

On the flight to Manaus, Rami and Kamil made sure to sit together. "What do you know of Carlos el Negro?"

"Not much, Kamil."

"The estranged brother of our Syrian president runs a drug smuggling ring and employs a notorious South American to oversee the operation. Remember those facts when dealing with Carlos el Negro or you may find yourself in quicksand."

Rami's stomach flipped.

* * *

Inside the Manaus airport, while waiting for their flight to Putumayo, Kamil placed a call to Simon. Not able to hear above the airport clamor, Kamil cupped his hand over one ear and pivoted so that his back was facing Rami. When Simon expressed concern over the GPS coins, Kamil checked his pocket. "Yes, I have it right here. Why?"

"Something's not right, Kamil. I see only one of you at the Manaus airport. The other coin is tracing back to Ciudad del Este. Ask Rami to show you his coin. Then put him on the phone. Rayna wants to talk with him."

Kamil turned. Rami was gone. Slowly, Kamil's eyes scoured the area. Rami was nowhere in sight. Kamil's heart pounded. *Take it easy. Rami probably went to the restroom.* "Simon, I'll call you right back." Kamil searched the restrooms. He searched the entire airport. No sign of Rami. He inquired at the ticket counters. Still no Rami. An icy chill crawled up his spine and Kamil's flesh slithered. *What do I tell Simon? What do I tell Rayna? That I lost Rami? That I may never find him?* Perspiration bled through his pores as he made the dreaded call. "Simon . . . Rami has disappeared. He was right here with me. I turned around for one minute and when I looked back, he was gone. I've searched everywhere."

"How could you lose him, Kamil? Do you know what the repercussions of this will be for us . . . for the magazine? Find him! My computer shows his coin in Ciudad del Este and we both know he isn't there. I don't care what it takes, find Rami!"

What Kamil found most insufferable was the shrill background cry coming from Rayna.

* * *

With a loaded pistol at his back, his hands secured behind him, and a handkerchief stuffed in his mouth, Rami was whisked onto a small private plane. He sat facing his two abductors. Rami wanted to feel for the coin in his pocket, but his hands were bound.

After what seemed like hours, the aircraft set down at the primitive airport in Puerto Asis in the state of Putumayo in southern Colombia. From there, Rami was forced into a jeep, the gun now at his head. The risk of fleeing or attempting anything foolish would surely cost Rami his life. The coin he believed to be safely in his pocket provided a false sense of security. *Simon will know where I am. He will inform Kamil and send help.*

* * *

Traveling over dense terrain, Rami felt nauseated from the long, bumpy ride. In time, the jeep stopped in front of a large, austere log house that sat high off the ground and was supported by beams made from tree trunks. One of the abductors rechecked Rami for weapons, then untied his hands and freed his mouth. Subtly, Rami put his hand in his pocket. The coin was not there.

Accompanied by several bodyguards, an intimidating and grandiose black man with a bald head and a powerful build came out to greet them. Carlos el Negro stood well over six feet tall. When he smiled, a gold tooth glistened through his perfect set of white teeth. His authoritarian demeanor told of a man one would not want to displease.

Rami was cautious not to bring attention to himself. Still, he wanted to check his other pockets. Carlos el Negro invited Rami inside and motioned for him to have a seat at the table. Cold Colombiana soft drinks were served along with platanos, fried yucca, and a cold maize soup. The strange foods added to Rami's queasy stomach, but he did not dare refuse the omnipotent man. Inwardly, he prayed to Allah. *Please keep me from being sick all over this man's table.* Gradually, he swallowed down the foreign tastes. Allah answered his prayer.

"I know Yousef is eager to get his hands on more of my opiates." Carlos el Negro spoke in perfect English, a language the others present did not understand. "The sale of illegal drugs adds a great deal of money to al-Shahid's treasury. But what Yousef chooses to offer me in return is insulting. Twice he cheated me on the weapons. Twice he broke his word." Carlos el Negro paused, waiting for Rami to respond.

"I will not make excuses or defend Yousef. He wants to renew his business with you and knows not to deceive you again." Rami rationalized that if he succeeded with Carlos el Negro, then Yousef would see his worth and Rayna's safety would be secured.

"You tell Yousef that next time he strays from an agreement with me, I will take his life in exchange." Carlos el Negro motioned to one of his men, instructing the worker in Spanish. A short dialogue ensued. Rami took advantage of those brief moments to recheck his pocket. The copper coin was definitely missing. In a panic, he reached into the other pocket. Not there, either. He sunk his hands into the two openings in the back of his jeans. His fingers fumbled nervously. *It must be here.* He scanned the floor, hoping it might have fallen. *Nothing.* Rami's blood curdled and he tried to mask his alarm.

"Is something wrong?" el Negro asked.

"No." Rami smiled. *What could be wrong? Kamil is nowhere in sight. The coin is gone. I am in the middle of a jungle with a gang of murderers. Simon does not know where I am.* Collecting his composure and weighing his options, Rami proceeded as if all were well. "You each have something the other wants, so let us not waste time playing games. Look at what is really at stake. Examine the trade-offs that you and Yousef can live with."

"I can see that you and I will do well," el Negro acknowledged approvingly. The two men talked late into the evening until a deal was struck. The burly black man who could put the fear of the devil into any individual offered Rami a place to spend the night.

* * *

After breakfast, Rami and his two companions thanked Carlos el Negro for his hospitality. The three climbed into the jeep and advanced deep into the treacherous labyrinth of the national forest. The dense trees obliterated the sun, wiping out all sense of direction and time for Rami, especially so since the two men had taken his watch when he was on the plane. Instinct dictated that he must stay with the vehicle. Rami hoped Yousef would be pleased with the deal he had secured with Carlos el Negro, and he eagerly anticipated his return to Rayna. Rami had no clue about the arrangements Yousef had made with his henchmen.

* * *

"You are to lose him somewhere in the jungle. Leave him to the mercy of the animals. They will devour him and our hands will be clean of Rami's death," Yousef had ordered. Aware that the Syrian government and the supreme leader of al-Shahid had high hopes for Rami, Yousef could not risk the fallout if it were discovered that he had tampered with those expectations. Rami's death must never be traced to him.

* * *

The abductor who was driving picked up speed. Rami sat beside him. Without warning, the other man sitting in the rear whacked Rami across the back of the head with the butt of his pistol, inflicting a severe wound. Stunned and slightly dazed, Rami struggled with the man until he was shoved out onto the rough ground. Quickly, Rami pulled himself up, making a desperate attempt to go after the moving vehicle. From the open window, the assassin pointed his gun and took several shots. Rami moved back and forth, trying to dodge the bullets. The jeep swerved and then vanished.

For a while, Rami followed the tire tracks. Then, without warning, a heavy downpour washed away the little hope he had. "Kamil," he cried out, "where are you?" *Has Simon lost all trace of me? Does anyone know where I am?* Rami yearned for the shelter of Rayna's love. *Help me, Allah. I do not want to die out here alone.* The rain stopped as abruptly as it had begun.

In sweltering heat and oppressive humidity, Rami trudged through the mud in his wet clothes with no sense of where he was. He swatted sandflies and dodged armadillos. Unknowingly, he waded through crocodile-infested swamps while yapoks nipped at his feet until they bled. Soon, the pain in the back of his head spiked and the vision in his left eye blurred. Rami hoped for Kamil to miraculously appear. Desolate, he worried that night would fall and he would still be in this deadly environment with ferocious animals devouring every part of him.

Plodding through a field of mango trees, Rami picked one of the fruits and ate it. A wrenching pain seared through his head. Sighting a monkey several yards in the distance, he watched the creature dart away. Boom! A landmine exploded, blowing the primate to pieces. "Please, Allah, help me find a way out of here before dark." Thoughts of Rayna tugged at his brain. Crawling vines and plants clogged the red dirt trail, parts of which were submerged in ankle-deep water. Pushing ahead, Rami stumbled onto the banks of a languid brown river. In the distance, children frolicked and mothers bathed their infants. He thought he was hallucinating. A tarantula climbed up his shirt and struck, sending its poison through Rami's body. Immobilized, he fell to the ground, unconscious.

* * *

Rayna was frantic. Today, on their nineteenth birthday, when Rami had promised to call twice, no one knew where he was. Her stomach wrenched. She could not eat or sleep. She pleaded with God to watch over her husband and keep him safe. Sitting in Simon's office, Rayna monitored the computer screen and the telephone, desperate for a signal, a sign that Rami was alive. "He promised," she sobbed. "Kamil promised to look after Rami and bring him back safely. He gave me his word."

"Take it easy, Rayna. We'll find Rami. I'm getting a search party together . . ."

"If anything happens to Rami, I swear I'll kill Kamil."

"Rayna, we'll find Rami. I have every confidence in Kamil. I've known him for nine years. He's a good, decent man and will put Rami's life above all else, including his own."

"Can you guarantee me that?"

Just then, Simon's private line rang. He activated the speaker for Rayna to hear. "Simon, I can't talk long. Just listen before we get cut off. I'm in Putumayo . . . Puerto Asis. Was inside the forest." Kamil spoke quickly, sometimes in fractured sentences. "I begged and bribed to rent a jeep. A compass and guide also. Maps are useless. Terrain is the worst I've ever encountered. Without the guide, could not have found my way out. It's treacherous. Dangerous. Have no idea where to begin looking."

"Kamil, give me the reality."

"Doesn't look good."

Listening to Kamil on the speaker, Rayna broke down, "You promised to bring Rami home safely. You promised, Kamil. Why did you take your eyes off of him? Why did you make me a promise you weren't going to keep? Why? Why?"

"I'm doing everything I can. Do you have a better suggestion?" Kamil was frustrated.

Impulsively, Rayna made a decision. "I'm coming down there. Meanwhile, you find Omar. Omar will know where

Rami is. Omar can lead you to him. Find Omar! Go back to Ciudad del Este and get Omar! Take him with you to that God-forsaken place and find my husband! And Kamil . . . may your Allah protect you from me if anything happens to Rami."

"Kamil, I'm trying to round up some men who know the forest," Simon broke in. "I'll get them there as soon as possible. In the meantime, you heard the lady. Find Omar, whoever he is. Rayna seems to think he can lead you to Rami. Move on it. Now!"

"I'm coming down there to find Rami," Rayna screeched into the speaker. "I'm leaving on the next plane."

"Simon, whatever you do, don't let Rayna leave New York. She won't survive this environment," Kamil warned.

After hanging up, Simon placed his hands on Rayna's shoulders. "Under no circumstances will I allow you to go. I will not expose you to the enormous dangers . . ."

"But the place is not too dangerous for my husband, is it? Is it, Simon?"

"I don't want to worry about you, also. It's too dangerous. Didn't you hear Kamil? For Christ sake Rayna, we're trying to find Rami and bring him home alive. Don't add to the burden. One of you is enough." Simon's stress was beginning to show.

"What if this were your wife?"

Rayna's question provided Simon with a greater comprehension of her turbulence. He picked up the phone and made a call. Rayna waited until he hung up.

"Four of my people in South America are on their way. The continent is big and they have to fly in from distant places, so give them time."

"Time!" she wailed. "Time is something my husband doesn't have. I'm leaving. I'm going to find Rami. I want him back." She started for the door.

With his body, Simon blocked her way. "You're not going anywhere. You have no understanding of what you're doing. What if you die out there, devoured by a crocodile or a jaguar? There are pythons as big as tree trunks. That's what's in the jungle. And if we bring Rami back alive but we never find you . . . is that what you want? No, Rayna. Use your head. You're not thinking clearly. We'll find him."

An hour later, Kamil phoned again. "I've arranged for a private plane to take me back to Ciudad del Este. I'll get Omar. Tell Rayna that I will find Rami. I swear . . ." A click in the line ended the call.

* * *

In the office, Eli spent hours consoling Rayna. He took her to lunch, then watched as she picked at her food before leaving it on the plate. In the evening, Eli sat with her as she cried. He agreed with Simon that it was not wise for Rayna to travel down to that perilous part of the world. "Don't give up hope," Eli encouraged. "With all your might, pray to Hashem. Have faith in God. Have confidence in Kamil. I do. Promise to introduce me to Kamil when he and Rami return. And you, my beautiful sister, are to keep busy with your investigation into the 1993 World Trade Center bombing. You must not fall apart. Be strong for Rami when he returns. Think positive thoughts, they are contagious. Rami will feel them."

* * *

Back in Ciudad del Este, Omar witnessed the escalating rancor between Yousef and Abdallah. In Arabic, Yousef castigated his assistant. No matter whom Abdallah had sent to replace Rami, Nolan could not be broken.

Yousef was pushed into a corner. He needed Rami back in Washington with the professor. Additionally, Rami had negotiated a very fine deal with Carlos el Negro and re-established that relationship. Yousef was forced to accept that, no matter how rebellious Rami might have been, he was more valuable alive than dead. "You find Rami, Abdallah. I want him back alive!"

"You said to get rid of him, boss. I did what you ordered. By now, even Allah can't bring him back."

"Don't you dare tell me what I said! When I ask for something, nothing is impossible. I'm commanding you to find Rami. Bring him back. If he is dead, then you shall meet the same fate."

* * *

Exhausted from lack of sleep, Kamil made his way back to Ciudad del Este. Entering the store, he found Omar with a customer. Kamil signaled to him. Omar pretended not to see. Kamil signaled again. Omar ignored him. Kamil stepped up to him.

"I am busy with a customer," Omar snapped.

"You're coming with me. I need you to help find Rami."

Omar continued with the customer, discounting Kamil. Kamil lost his temper and grabbed Omar by the neck. "Look, I'm tired and I'm hungry, so don't try my patience. If you persist in ignoring me, I will slit your throat. Like Yousef, I don't make idle threats."

In fear, the customer fled the store. Omar twitched nervously. His hands shook. He nodded. Kamil released him. Omar walked to the back and pressed a hidden buzzer. Kamil followed closely behind. Abdallah cracked the door. "I need to speak with Yousef. It is urgent."

"Omar, if a customer has a complaint, handle it." Abdallah moved to shut the door. Kamil quickly shoved his foot into the open space before Abdallah could close it.

"You heard Omar. Get Yousef! It's urgent!" Defiantly, Kamil kept his foot wedged in the doorway.

"Yousef," Abdallah called out, "Omar says it's urgent."

"What do you want, Omar? Make it quick. I'm busy."

Through the crevice, Kamil came face-to-face with Yousef. *This is the monster who killed my father and snatched my brother from my arms. Killing him now would be easy. Just reach for the gun.* Then Kamil considered the consequences. *Saving Rami must take priority. Another opportunity will come.* Kamil was certain of it.

"Ummm, this is a friend of Rami's . . . ummm . . . ummm . . . well . . ."

"Say it, Omar! I don't have all day."

"He asks for my help . . . to find Rami."

"Then go with him. Take what you need. Bring back Rami. I want him alive. Your life depends on it. Do you understand?" Yousef slammed the door and bolted it.

TWENTY-TWO

Maybe the wildest dreams are merely the need-ful preludes to the truth.—Alfred Lord Tennyson

In a clearing behind palms and mango trees, a crude hut made of branches, mud, and thatch stood on stilts. On the small allotment of land, a plot of coca plants grew in the rear. Vines with triangular floppy leaves flourished next to the coca. These vines, known as yaje, are sacred and mystical to the indigenous Cofan Indians who inhabit the forest. Male shamans in the tribe prepare the yaje for ingestion by scraping the plant's bark, boiling it, and then mashing it into an oily, putrid-tasting liquid.

In a ritual that is performed once every ten days, the men drink the brew, believing it cures infirmities, grants direct communication with God, and guides the way to treat illness and root out evil. Yaje, with its ugly, bitter taste provokes repeated attacks of vomiting, diarrhea, and cold sweats. At times, the loss of normal self-control is so strong that those drinking it feel the presence of death upon them.

Rigid about the curative purpose of purgation to cleanse physical and mental impurities, the Cofan Indians maintain that yaje chastises the drinker in order to reform him and humiliates the indulger in order to teach him wisdom. Shamans insist that to get the full effect of the plant, one must ingest as much as possible for as long as possible.

* * *

A mother bathing her infant in the murky brown river guardedly watched the foreigner approach and then saw him fall. She waited for the young man to rise. When he did not, she sent her two older sons to investigate. They reported that the man appeared to be dead, but that his heart was beating. The woman instructed the boys to carry the stranger to the hut and fetch their father, a highly respected shaman in the humble Cofan community.

* * *

Inside the hut, the healer laid the stranger on the hard mud floor. He placed a folded animal skin under his head, removed his clothing, and carefully inspected his body. Recognizing the tarantula's bite, the shaman ran his fingers over it. The back of the young man's skull was swollen and hot to the touch. He traced the marking where a weapon had left its imprint. The medicine man rose. Colorful feathers hung from perforations in his nose and ears. His skin resembled dried leather. His long, gray-streaked hair was tied back with braided yarn.

After stirring his potion in a stained clay cup, the shaman knelt down beside the unconscious stranger, lifted his head, and slowly administered the foul-tasting drug. From his comatose state, the foreigner gagged, then retched. The shaman forced more of the liquid into him. Purging again, the stranger tried fighting off the Indian, but he was too weak and disoriented. The gruesome cycle had begun—choking down the putrid-tasting yaje, disgorging, discharging, and convulsing in cold sweats. For hours, the healer inflicted the foreigner with this harrowing drill. The mortal craved death, praying to Allah to release him from this perdition.

* * *

In a small private plane, Omar and Kamil landed in Puerto Asis, rented a jeep, and headed into La Paya National Forest. Omar knew the land. He had been there several times with Abdallah, and only hours before had heard the two assassins boast about the spot where they forced Rami from the jeep. Making idle chat, Omar commented on the region and indicated that three-fourths of the world's annual production of refined cocaine came from southern Colombia. "I do not understand why people find such fascination with mind-altering substances and are willing to pay such high prices for them."

Ignoring Omar's small talk, Kamil asked the reason for his visits to the region.

"Many times, Abdallah tried unsuccessfully to make peace with a prominent drug lord that Yousef had angered. I came with him five times . . . uhhhh . . . right about here. I think this is where Nabil and Ahmad said they left Rami to die." Kamil stopped the jeep and opened the door. "No! Do not get out," Omar warned. "This place is crawling with caymans waiting for a meal."

"Let's hope that Rami was not one of their feasts." Slowing the jeep to a crawl, Kamil let their two sets of eyes do the scanning as he edged the vehicle along. There was no sign of Rami, not even a remnant of his clothing. "Well, Omar, I suggest you start praying hard because we're not leaving this forest without Rami. If he's not alive, then count yourself alongside him. It's up to you."

Omar grew anxious. "There is a village nearby. A small group of Cofan Indians live there. Maybe Rami was fortunate enough to wander into it."

"Take me there."

Omar navigated Kamil around a field of mango trees and through mud and water until they reached a murky brown river. On the banks, they saw children playing and mothers bathing their infants. "Civilization!" Kamil gave out a sigh of relief and gradually brought the vehicle to a stop.

* * *

Rami's depleted body lay dormant after hours of exorcism. Flowing colors and vivid kaleidoscopic designs whirled through his delirium.

> *The time was fifteenth-century Spain. On his flute, he played sweet music. Crouched behind a large rock, a young maiden took delight in the comforting sounds. The two were forbidden to speak. He was a Jew. She was a Moor. They had met in the big library in Córdoba where he found her hidden behind tall bookshelves. Being a female, she was banned from engaging in such irreverence and had risked discovery*

and chastisement. He began to secretly bring her books. Soon, they were defying the law and sneaking off into the mountains. They read to one another, engaged in intellectual discussions, and expressed their love—a love punishable by death because they were of different faiths.

In slow motion, patterns in the kaleidoscope shifted and colors sharpened in intensity.

At a safe distance, she watched as he entered the great library to study with his teacher, Hasdai ibn Shaprut, the famous Jewish physician and chief advisor to the caliph. The old man taught him much about medicine, philosophy, and love.

The facets reformatted. Another face appeared.

An old man with a mischievous grin, bushy eyebrows, and a full head of white hair. Was it Hasdai ibn Shaprut or Isaac, her grandfather? The faces merged. He could not distinguish one from the other.

The formations spun furiously and the colors twirled into darkened hues.

The Grand Inquisitor, Tomás de Torquemada, pushed his way into the library. His men pulled books from the shelves—books of medicine, mathematics, philosophy and religion. Copies of the Quran were taken to the streets and burned. Torah scrolls, the Jewish lifeblood, were carried away. "Death and destruction to all non-Catholics." This was the edict from Queen Isabella. Jews and Moors alike had two months to leave Spain, embrace Catholicism, or face death.

The kaleidoscopic illusion mutated into delicate silhouettes with colors spinning into soft pastels.

Hasdai ibn Shaprut invited him into his home. "I am an old man, too old to flee. But you, you are young. You must go. Take the beautiful Moorish girl and all that I have taught you. Journey south across the straits into Morocco. In Ceuta, you will find refuge. Make the young maiden your wife. She will be good to you and give you many children." The teacher reached into a box and extracted some coins. "Each day, boats carry Jews and Moors across the water to safety. These coins will pay for your passage. Hold tightly to the maiden's hand. Do not let go, not until you are both safely on the other side. If your hands separate, she will be snatched from you and you will spend many lifetimes searching for her."

"How do you know about her?" he asked the teacher.

The old man smiled mischievously. "Love always has a way of making itself known. Now go with God's blessing, and remember my words."

A peacefulness set in. Fluffy white clouds lifted him to the heavens.

> *Running, running, he held her hand securely in his. They arrived at the dock. For an instant, their hands separated as he reached down in his pocket to withdraw the coins for their passage. When he looked up, she was gone. Frantically, he searched everywhere. Again and again, he shouted her name.*

"Rayna! Rayna! Rayna!"

Hearing the loud cries, the shaman edged closer. The yaje had worked its cure. The poison was gone from his body. The back of his head was now cool to the touch. The vision Rami had experienced would bring him enlightenment.

TWENTY-THREE

Wherever there is joy, there is suffering. If you want to have no suffering, then you must accept no joy.—Excerpt from an old Vietnamese poem

Kamil turned off the engine. Cautiously, he and Omar got out of the car. A woman holding tightly to the infant nursing at her breast suspiciously eyed the two men. She motioned to her sons. They came near to protect her.

In his limited Spanish, Omar attempted to communicate, aware that the woman might not understand him. "*No queremos herirles a ustedes. Solamente buscamos nuestro hermano.*"

The baby began to cry. The mother slowly backed away with her two sons at her side. Omar pulled one hundred Colombian pesos from his pocket and held out the money. "*Por usted.*" Omar smiled, "*Por favor.*"

While keeping his eyes intently on the woman, Omar translated for Kamil. "I told her we do not want to harm them. We are only looking for our brother. But these people have their own indigenous language and I am not sure she understood."

Kamil reached into his pocket and extracted a hundred pesos. "Here." He handed the money to Omar. "Add this to what you have already offered. Money is a universal language."

The woman snatched the bills, then gestured with her hand, motioning for the men to follow her. She led them to a lone hut standing high on stilts.

* * *

Kamil climbed the crumbling dried-mud steps. Omar stayed below and kept watch. The woman called out to warn her husband.

Inside, the hut was dim, musty, and sparsely furnished. A strong, foul odor overpowered Kamil's senses and he gagged. He wanted out, but instinct told him he must stay. Impulsively scanning the room, his eyes fell upon a murky corner. An indigenous Indian rose slowly, revealing a defenseless, unclad body on the floor. Kamil moved toward the listless figure. The shaman seized a hammer-like tool and threatened Kamil with it.

Pulling two hundred pesos from his pocket, Kamil used the trace of Spanish he had learned, *"Mi hermano. Mi hermano."* He hoped the man would understand. The shaman greedily plucked the money from Kamil's hand and stepped back. Kamil kneeled down and touched Rami's face. "Rami, it's Kamil. I'm going to take you out of here. Rayna is waiting for you." Rami's body seemed without life. Kamil put his ear to Rami's chest. He listened for a heartbeat. It was weak. His breathing was shallow. *Rami needs medical attention or he'll soon die.* Kamil attempted to lift him. The shaman darted swiftly, swinging the club into Kamil's back, knocking him over. The stench of vomit rushed into his nostrils. Kamil knew that if he did not get out of the place soon, he would be sick. He pulled another two hundred pesos from his pocket and held it out. Grabbing the money from Kamil's fingers, the shaman continued to block him. Reaching inside the waist of his pants, Kamil fingered the small handgun and contemplated using it. *If Carlos el Negro is a powerful kingpin in this region, then the natives must know of him.* "Carlos el Negro," Kamil projected loudly. The shaman stepped back in fear. "Carlos el Negro," Kamil reverberated as he charged down the unsound steps with Rami draped over his shoulder.

"Come on, Omar! Let's get out of here before we have the whole tribe on our heels."

* * *

Reaching the jeep, Kamil lay Rami across the back seat. Removing his own shirt, he covered Rami's nakedness. "Omar, grab that jug of water and wet Rami's mouth with a few drops every ten minutes. I'll drive. You navigate." Throwing the four-wheeler into gear, Kamil jammed his foot down on the gas pedal, knowing not to stop until they were well out of the forest.

From nowhere, a downpour descended upon them. Kamil turned on the wipers. Steam rose as the rain hit the earth. The windshield fogged. Kamil turned on the defroster, but it did not work. "Keep moving," Omar warned. "We cannot afford to get stuck here." The tires sank into mud and the wheels spun. Kamil tried rocking the vehicle. Omar turned around, dribbled a few drops of water into Rami's mouth, then dampened his friend's face. "He is still breathing."

Drenched in perspiration, Kamil's stress mounted as the tires continued to whirl. The rain stopped as abruptly as it had begun. The car lurched forward. They were on their way.

"We've got to get Rami to a hospital or he'll die." Kamil's concern was pronounced.

"Why is Rami's welfare your responsibility?"

"Something . . . he reminds me so strongly of my . . . Rami needs medical help or he'll die."

"Not here. Medical care is primitive. Cali is the closest big city. About an hour's flight."

"I can't let him die. I can't . . ."

"That makes two of us." Omar's life depended on it. Yousef had been clear about that.

Breathing a sigh of relief as they approached civilization, Kamil reached for the phone. "A signal! I got a signal!" He punched in Simon's number. "Simon, am I happy to hear your voice. You need to listen . . . just listen. We've just come out of the forest, Omar and I. Rami is with us. He's sick . . . really sick. He's dehydrated. Needs fluids in his veins or he'll die."

"Where are you?"

"I'm approaching Puerto Asis. The town is remote and medical care is neolithic. Simon, you've got to get us out of here, fast. Omar says the closest big city is Cali . . ."

"Kamil, how soon can you get over to the airport?"

"Twenty . . . thirty minutes. The roads are poor."

"A rescue team in a private plane should be landing in Puerto Asis within minutes. I'll get word to the crew to watch for you, and fly you directly to Cali. Then I'll arrange for a medical vehicle to meet you when you land. I'll make sure they take you to a decent hospital."

"Good. Thanks. Simon . . . Simon . . ." The connection faded. He glanced at Omar. "We're going to the airport. Simon says a plane is waiting to take us to Cali."

"Kamil, I will not be on that plane with you. I must return to Ciudad del Este and report back to Yousef."

"Omar, think carefully about what you say. Don't put Rami's life in more danger."

"I will be careful, as long as it does not threaten my own survival."

"Omar, you said you have come many times into this forest with Abdallah to try and make peace with a prominent drug lord. Has Yousef himself ever come into this forest?"

"No."

"Why not?"

"Snakes. He is deathly afraid of snakes."

* * *

In a hospital in Cali, attentive nurses monitored Rami. Fluids, medicines, and nourishment dripped into the patient's vein. Kamil remained at Rami's side. "Rami. It's Kamil. I'm here with you. You're in good hands with good doctors. Rayna will be here soon. She's been very worried about you. Don't let her down. Fight with every ounce of life you have in you." *Why is Rami's welfare your responsibility?* Omar's question haunted him.

* * *

The next morning, Rayna bolted into the hospital room, gave her wheeled suitcase a push to the side, and dashed over to Rami. She did not notice Kamil asleep in a chair, but her rustling awakened him. He opened his eyes and watched Rayna blink back tears as she ran her hands over the heavy stubble on Rami's face. Gently, she pressed her lips to his. "Rami, sweetheart, it's me, Rayna. You're safe now. I'm here with you. Soon you'll be well enough and we'll go home."

Kamil longed for that kind of love. He wished Maddy had just half of Rayna's sensitivity.

"I love you so much. Squeeze my hand if you love me back." She waited. Nothing. All at once, Rayna became aware of Kamil's presence. "Why can't he hear me?" she cried.

"He's going to be okay." Kamil rose from the chair and placed his hands on Rayna's shoulders, turning her toward him. "Rami's heartbeat was barely there when we brought him in. I wasn't sure he would make it. But he's young and strong. Each day you will see improvement and soon you can take him home." Kamil looked into her face. *Without a trace of makeup, she could not be more lovely*. He wanted to comfort Rayna and, for a moment, his arms encircled her. She clung to him. The feel of her small breasts pressing against his chest aroused him. Her scent intoxicated him. Kamil felt an urge to kiss her. Swiftly, she pulled away. Flustered, Kamil stepped out of the room to give Rayna the time she needed to be alone with Rami.

* * *

The doctor soon came in. He checked Rami's vital signs, then examined him. Rayna waited patiently. When he was done, he addressed her in Spanish. "Your husband was close to death when he arrived. Weak heartbeat. Severely dehydrated. Electrolytes, potassium, minerals, and blood-sugar level were all dangerously low. The intravenous is replenishing what he lost."

Rayna wanted assurance that Rami would recover completely.

"We are waiting for the test results to be sure there is no damage to his kidneys or liver. We will know later today and I will come back and talk with you again." He turned to leave, hesitated, then swung back around. "Earlier tests showed small remains of venom from a tarantula bite, but the medication will take care of that."

"Thank you for all you have done." She waited for him to leave, but he did not. "Is there something else, doctor?"

"Yes. Your husband . . . tell me about his use of drugs."

"*Drugs*? What do you mean *drugs*?"

Briefly, the doctor spoke of the vestige of yaje in Rami's blood and explained the effects of ingesting the potion.

"Never! My husband would never do that. I know him too well. And besides, it's against his religion."

"Then the drug was forced upon him."

Rayna pressed the palms of her hands against her eyes. Rami had suffered so greatly. The pain she felt for him was unbearable.

After the doctor left the room, she climbed onto the bed and, with her fingers, arranged Rami's matted curls. She wrapped her arms around him, "You're my world now. Don't make me live without you." She rested her ear against his chest listening to the beat of his heart. Rami opened his eyes, then went back to sleep.

* * *

In the late afternoon, the doctor returned with good news. "No damage to his kidneys or his liver. Once his strength returns, you can take him home. Maybe by the end of the week." The doctor left. Rayna was overjoyed.

Kamil had been gazing out the window. He had not understood a word the doctor had said. Rayna drifted toward him, "Rami is getting better. I can take him home in a few days." Kamil swiveled to face her. "Thank you, Kamil. Simon told me you are a good man. I now see it's true." Their eyes held for a long moment.

"I'm going to find something for us to eat. You need some food in your stomach or you won't be any good for Rami when he wakes up."

"Thank you, Kamil." She touched his hand.

* * *

Rayna and Kamil ate together in the hospital room while Rami slept. "There are problems between Yousef and Abdallah. Omar said they argue often. The good news is that Yousef will not bother Rami for a long time. He needs him for the project with Nolan, and is willing to wait it out. At least that's what Omar tells me."

"Kamil, I'm grateful for all you have done."

"I know you are."

"Kamil . . . I was not very nice to you. I apologize."

"No, you were right. I had it coming." He struggled with his feelings for her and the responsibility he felt for Rami.

"Go back to New York, Kamil. You have a story to write. Just mask things and make the names fictitious."

Lightly brushing the back of his fingers over Rayna's cheek, he smiled, "I know how to do that. Now, will you be okay if I go to the hotel and get some sleep?"

"Yes. We'll be fine."

TWENTY-FOUR

The best and most beautiful things in the world cannot be seen or even touched. They must be felt with the heart.—Helen Keller

After returning from Colombia, Rami and Rayna spent the next few weeks settling into their new house and starting back to school. Given their hectic schedule, Rayna at first paid little mind to the evolving change in Rami's behavior, attributing it to his mental recuperation from the harrowing ordeal he had endured on the southern continent. Still, day after day, his demeanor grew worse. By late September, Rayna found herself carrying all of the responsibilities for them both. She did the shopping, cooked the meals, washed the clothes, maintained the house, and paid the bills. She shouldered not only her own heavy load of classes but also struggled to keep Rami focused on his studies. Apathy was crushing him. When he refused to leave the house, Rayna grappled each morning to get him up and out for school. No longer was Rami the enthusiastic, attentive, loving husband she had known. His passion and backbone had vanished. Their intimacy was gone. Rami moped. His appetite dwindled and he was losing weight. He refused to see Nolan, which put another burden on Rayna. She had to keep the professor's commitment to Rami intact. Soon, Rayna found herself stretched beyond her limits.

More weeks passed. Rami was no better. Then, just before Thanksgiving, Rayna reached an impasse. Her energy was depleted. She was existing on very little sleep and not eating well. In desperation, she called Marisa. "I need to talk. Can you meet me for lunch tomorrow? I'll be on campus."

* * *

"It sounds to me like Rami is suffering from depression. Something has happened to trigger this change in him. Tell me what's going on."

Rayna would not tell her friend about Rami's trip to South America and his involvement with Yousef and al-Shahid. She would not tell Marisa about the danger and unrest besetting their lives. Rayna would not break the trust Rami placed in her. "I don't know," she answered.

"Then you need to find out. Things won't improve unless you get to the root of the problem. Rayna, you may not be able to help Rami. You may be too close to him. Have you thought about professional help? A therapist?"

"I've tried that approach. He refuses. I've tried everything."

"Do you still love Rami?"

"Of course I do."

"Then you must keep trying. Do you remember your wedding vows?" When Rayna nodded, Marisa urged, "Say them for me."

Rayna's eyes welled. "In sickness and in health. In poverty and in wealth. In sadness and in joy. I entrust to you my heart, for the rhythm of its beat will forever nourish our love. I commit to you my soul, for it is the other half of yours."

Marisa reached into her purse, then handed Rayna a small packet of tissues. "Rami comes above all else. If you have to stop everything in your life to take care of him . . . whatever it takes to help him through this, then you must do it." Marisa rested her hand on top of Rayna's. "Time and love are good healers."

* * *

Wednesday night marked the eve of a long Thanksgiving weekend. It began no differently than all other nights of the past three months—Rami feigning sleep, Rayna staying up late with chores and homework. Yet, tired as she was, Rayna was determined to break this toxic path before it destroyed them both. She wanted her husband back.

Rayna lifted the covers, crawled into bed, and snuggled up to Rami's back. "There are just three weeks left to the semester. Let's get through it. I'll help you. Then we'll take a break for however long we need. School is not my priority. You are. Nothing matters to me except for you to be well and for us to be together. I love you so much." Several minutes passed. Rayna lay quietly next to her husband.

Slowly, Rami turned to her, "I have no life without you."

"Tell me what happened in South America. Whatever it is, we'll work through it."

"I cannot."

"You cannot or you will not?"

"I will lose you. I have done something so horrible . . ."

"Rami, I love you. You will never lose me. Nothing could be that bad. Unless . . . another woman?"

"No. No one else. Only you."

"Then what is it?" She wrapped herself around him and infused his senses with her love. "I will lie here next to you and wait until you're ready to tell me. And when you're done, I will still be here. Now, if it were me in your place, what would you do? Would I lose you?"

"No. My love for you is forever. Forever does not change."

"Then why would you think you would lose me?"

Gradually, Rami began. He described Yousef's warehouse of weapons, his own abduction at gunpoint in Manaus, the trip into the forest, the weapons-for-drugs transaction with a black man named Carlos el Negro, and his experience in the jungle where he was left alone to die. "I negotiated weapons for cocaine. Weapons that will be used to kill many people. Cocaine to sell in America and Europe . . . to craze the minds of young people. I have become part of Yousef's reign of terror. I raised money, lots of money to fund his violence. I hate myself for it. But Yousef would have had me killed if I refused and that would have left you vulnerable. More than anything, I needed to protect you."

Compassionately, Rayna listened as Rami told of being hit in the head with the butt of a gun and then pushed from the jeep. "The pain in my head hurt so bad. I was scared that darkness would come. I prayed not to be ripped apart by savage beasts. Then I thought I saw some people, women and children by the water. I started toward them. What I remember next is lying in hell. My body shook from chills. My insides gushed from retching and excreting. In front of me, I saw a vision. A very long time ago, you and I were fleeing Spain . . . southern Spain. We were boarding a boat to cross the Straits . . . to Morocco. Our hands separated so that I could take the fare from my pocket. In an instant, you were gone. Frantically, I looked everywhere and fell into a timeless pit searching for you." All that Rami had kept locked inside, he now set free. "I believed I was no longer worthy of you for what I did. So instead of suffering the devastation of your rejection, I protected myself from you."

Rami's agony was her agony. He had placed an enormous burden of guilt and blame around his neck and it was choking the life from him. Rayna wished she could erase his pain and could question God's motive for so much suffering. "The most responsible thing you can do now is to ensure that the bacteria project never reaches completion and Yousef never gets his hands on the stuff. And you know what else?"

"What?"

"Indirectly, Nolan saved your life. Kamil told me. He learned it from Omar. Yousef ordered several different men to bribe Nolan, browbeat him. They even threatened to harm his daughter, and you know how much Nolan loves Anna. Still, Nolan kept his allegiance to you, pushing Yousef into a corner. Yousef did order your death. He wanted you out of the way until he realized that you were the only one Nolan would work with. Yousef needs you. Nolan is not a nerd. I was wrong about him. He's tenacious and very loyal. Nolan is the reason Yousef allowed Omar to go with Kamil to search for you in the jungle. They saved your life."

"Thank you for telling me that." Wrapped within each other, the two fell into a deep sleep.

* * *

Through the skylight, the early morning sun made itself known. Rami opened his eyes and kissed Rayna. "This summer, can we take a trip to southern Spain?"

"That's a wonderful idea. Yes, southern Spain this summer." She rested her head on his chest. "Rami . . ."

"What is it, rrawhee?"

"We have a respite, a window of safety until your mission with Nolan is done. After that, Yousef will come after both of us with a vengeance. That's what Omar told Kamil."

"Then we will take that window of safety and extend it for as long as possible. Nolan plans to stretch the research for five or six years. Longer, if he can. The best that can happen between now and then is for Yousef to die or be killed. Anything is possible." He swaddled her in his arms. "Do you know how very much I love you?"

"Yes, I do." She kissed him.

"My behavior was very difficult on you and you did not deserve it. I am sorry."

"It's okay."

Under the covers, he surrounded her.

* * *

Final exams were over and the couple welcomed the winter break. Rami spent some much-needed time with Nolan. At great length, they discussed Yousef, Abdallah, al-Shahid, South America, Yousef's henchmen, and the bacteria situation. When Rami expressed a deep gratitude to the professor for his loyalty and credited him with the reason he was still alive, Nolan responded in kindness. "You know, Rami, I would have liked to have you for my son-in-law. That's how highly

I think of you. Never have I known a nineteen-year-old to show so much maturity and integrity as you."

Rami was humbled by this man's sincerity. "If I were not madly in love with my wife, I would have been honored to marry your daughter and make you my father-in-law."

"And if Anna didn't have a serious boyfriend, I would have taken you up on it." The two laughed, then turned their attention to the bacteria in the glass enclosure. Deeply engrossed, they lost track of time. Darkness had fallen when they emerged from the lab.

Rami looked down at his watch. "It is after seven. Rayna is expecting me home. Would you like to come for dinner? She always cooks extra."

Nolan held up two stacks of papers, "These are the finals from my philosophy and chemistry classes. Well over three hundred tests to score and only two days to get all the grades turned in. I'd like a raincheck on that dinner."

"It is yours." Then Rami graciously volunteered his assistance. "Can I be of help?"

Nolan hesitated, then accepted Rami's offer. "These are from my two chem classes. Ninety-nine papers. Multiple choice. Fifty questions, two points each. Many are chemical symbols, but not all." He handed Rami the answer sheet. "All you have to do is check each student's responses against this sheet, multiply the number of correct answers by two, and mark the grade at the top. Students won't be getting their papers back to check them, so make sure you're completely accurate."

After promising to have them back in time for Nolan to record the grades and make his deadline, Rami took the exams home.

* * *

That evening, after helping Rayna clean up from dinner, Rami sat down at the kitchen table and began grading the papers. Rayna was in the study finishing her exposé of the 1993 attack on the World Trade Center.

Reaching the halfway point, Rami began to tire. *I will mark up one more paper before turning in for the night.* The page sat in front of him. As he checked each question against the answer sheet, something kept jumping out at him. Several times, his eyes drifted to the name at the top. *Jonathan Klezman. Jonathan Klezman. The Jonathan Klezman who had forced himself on Rayna and nearly raped her. The same Jonathan who almost stole Rayna's virginity. Okay, Jonathan, this is payback time.* Shuffling through the pens in the desk drawer, Rami found one that matched the ink color on Jonathan's paper. He then proceeded to change several of the answers. Rami wrote the grade at the top—*38.* He hoped it would be low enough to give Jonathan a failing grade in the course.

TWENTY-FIVE

And the blind and the seeing are not alike; nor the darkness and the light; nor the shade and the heat.—Surah 35:19-21

The third week in December, a package arrived containing six copies of the latest issue of *InterContinental Weekly*. "It's my article! Finally in print!" Rayna was overjoyed. "Kamil said Simon didn't cut one word." Elated for her, Rami snatched one of the copies, sat down at the kitchen table, and immediately became glued to the story.

On Friday, February 26, 1993, at 12:17 PM, Islamic terrorists drove a truck with 1,000 pounds of explosives into the basement parking garage of the World Trade Center. The blast left a crater 22 feet wide and five stories deep. Six people were killed. One thousand were injured. Within a month's time, the towers were repaired, cleaned, reopened and back in business.

From extensive interviewing, narratives by those who were in the building at the time, all told a familiar story. They spoke of inadequate security, lack of emergency evacuation plans, absence of backup lighting in the stairwells, and an inefficient communication system. Phones fizzled. Lights went down. Computers crashed. Elevators froze. Still, most people had no clue about the attack.

Workers remained in their offices under the illusion it was a temporary power outage. Then, slowly, through word of mouth, news of the attack trickled in. Thousands began to flee, searching for the nearest exits. Descending blackened stairwells, the people moved in orderly fashion, guided only by the individual in front. Within a short time, they found themselves confronted by a locked door or a brick wall. Doing an about face, they ascended the steps, climbing to reach a floor where they searched for another stairwell to go down. Over and over, they repeated their actions for two, three or four hours until successfully zigzagging their way down to the entrance lobby.

If the attack had been far more extensive, if tens of thousands of people had only minutes to evacuate . . .

Rayna wrote of the New York Police Department landing helicopters on the rooftop to rescue people from the upper floors. She questioned the motives of the New York Fire Department for ordering the rooftop doors permanently locked after the attack.

"Wow! This is excellent. When did you ever find time to do all those interviews . . . and that research? I will frame it and we will hang it right here." Rami pointed to a space on the wall in the family room. "How many languages will it be printed in?"

"Thirteen. Thirteen languages. And I'm far from through. This is only the beginning. It's not just about the terrorists. I'm going after the building management, FBI, CIA. They won't like me when I'm done." The phone rang. "Hello."

"*Mabrook.* Congratulations. Your first article and it's already causing a stir. Our phones are ringing non-stop and e-mails are pouring in."

"Kamil!"

Kamil laughed. "It's nice to know you still recognize my voice. Simon wants more, Rayna. We'll pay you real dollars for the next one. Will you take it to the next level?"

"Yes. I was hoping you'd ask."

"I have more good news. I have a daughter. She's three weeks old already. Sorry I didn't call you sooner. Her name is Nida, after my mother. She weighed seven pounds, six ounces at birth, and measured twenty inches long. Lots of dark hair, down to her shoulders. Olive skin and hazel eyes just like me. Oh, Rayna, she's so beautiful."

Rayna had not known Kamil to be this animated. Privately, she hoped that the baby would secure his marriage to Maddy. "How's Maddy?"

"She's fine . . . Simon promoted me to editor-in-chief. Worldwide. He's renouncing that role. Says his micro-managing is wearing him down and his wife is demanding more of his time."

"Kamil, how wonderful. I'm happy for you. I bet Maddy's excited . . ."

"No, she isn't."

"Maybe she's going through some postpartum blues."

"Maybe."

"If men had to go through childbirth, our population would come to a screeching halt."

Kamil chuckled, "You're probably right. I can't wait for you to see Nida. When will you visit? You and Rami will stay with us, in the guestroom."

"Soon. We'll come soon. I can't wait to hold your daughter. You may never get her back."

"Well, in that case, I take back my invitation."

"Uh-uh. You can't do that."

"I better have a talk with your husband. How's he doing?"

"He's fine, just as long as I keep him satisfied with Syrian food."

"Lucky man. If he ever gives you up, tell him I'm waiting in the wings."

"Let me put the lucky man on and you can tell him yourself," she laughed, handing Rami the phone.

Rami reached for a pad and pen and took some notes. After finishing his conversation with Kamil, he tore the sheet from its perforation and held it up, "Look what I have."

"What?"

"Kamil said I should make an appointment with that excellent immigration lawyer he told you about, the one here in Washington. Tomorrow I will call."

Shaking her head, Rayna raised her eyebrows.

"I know. I know. I did not listen when you suggested it."

Rayna sighed with a hint of exasperation. "I don't ever want you to go back to Syria and leave me . . ."

"Do not worry. I am not going back to Syria. Kamil said there is more clamping down, more arrests for those speaking out, and more send-offs to Palmyra."

"Palmyra? What's that?"

"A prison in Tadmur, south of Halab. Palmyra is really an archaeological site, but the prison there is known as Syria's torture chamber. People live in fear of Palmyra. Real fear! And even if Syria were paradise, I would not return. My place is here with you." He locked his arms around her waist, "When can we make a baby?"

"Uh-uh. Remember? After we finish school. Then you can have four children."

Grinning, he hugged her. "What if I want six?"

"Four. You can only make as many babies as I agree on. This is the one area of our marriage that I definitely do have all the control."

"I would not bet on that . . ."

"Four . . ."

The two continued their bantering until Rami whisked her up in his arms, allowing their playful intimacy to swell their love.

* * *

Nolan was leaving to spend Christmas with his daughter and her fiancé. "I need to see you before I go, Rami. Can you come by at two?"

"I will be there." Rami returned the phone to the nightstand and fluffed the comforter. He stepped into the bathroom where Rayna was showering. Reaching in, he washed her back. "Nolan just called. He wants to meet with me at two. What are your plans this afternoon?"

"I have an appointment at one-thirty to get my hair trimmed, then I'm going over to the mall. I have to stop at the bookstore. What time will you be home?"

"No later than six."

"Shall I pick up some fresh salmon for dinner?"

"Sounds good."

Rayna turned off the shower. Rami reached for a towel, wrapped it around her, and affectionately moved his hands over the outline of her body to dry her. She felt him grow strong against her belly and smiled, "I just showered."

"You can take another shower later."

* * *

"How did it go with Nolan today?" Rayna asked over dinner.

"Good. Except things are moving faster than I would like, so he is slowing down and taking a long holiday break . . . I like your haircut. Shorter than you normally wear it, but I like it. Makes your exotic eyes even more tempting."

"I'm glad you like it. I saw Omar at the bookstore today. He was with a friend. Says Yousef is fuming because Nolan won't talk with him and you won't return his calls. He says Yousef's been trying to reach you for days. Omar said you need to answer your cell, or at least respond to your messages."

"I hope Yousef's fuming is enough stress to give him a heart attack and he dies."

"That would be a blessing. Anyhow, I told Omar to inform Yousef that you're working with Nolan and when you have something to report, you'll contact him. Then Omar said he had something for you and asked me to walk with him to his car."

"Did you go?"

"Of course not. I waited inside the cafe at the bookstore."

Rami sighed with relief, "Good."

Rayna fixed two mugs of cinnamon-spiced tea and heated them in the microwave, then lifted an envelope from her tote and handed it to Rami. "Omar said he picked up the mail on his way out of the apartment today. That's why it was in his car."

The aerogram showed a Syrian postmark. "It is from my father." Rami took the letter opener from the drawer and slit the thin paper along the top. To himself, he read the Arabic script. When he was done, he looked up at Rayna, then lowered his eyes and read the letter again.

"Tell me what it says, Rami."

"You will not like it." Rami translated into English.

My dearest son,

What is happening? Why have we not heard from you for so long? It has been almost a year. Your mother cries with worry and your sisters want to know about their brother. What shall I tell them? When will you come home? The father of Omar says you are married to a Syrian. I am not sure to believe him. Surely you would not keep something like that from us. I beg of Allah that you are not with that Jew that you spoke of last year. There would be no greater shame you can bring upon us. No greater disgrace to Allah than merging your life with a Jew. Each day I pray to Allah that you stay true to the words of our Prophet and remember the teachings in our Quran. Jews are pigs. Evil

*subhuman infidels. Worse than the Christian non-
believers. My son, I beg you to ease my mind. Tell
me you are not married. Come home. At least
write to us. We know little of your life this past
year. Always your mother and I curse the day you
left for America. We should never have let you go.
Ramadan will soon begin. Each fast day, look into
your heart and answer to Allah for your actions.
Remember you are a Muslim. A Shi'ite. I hope
soon a reply. ———Your loving Eby*

Rayna felt sick. "Oh, God. What have we done?"

A long silence fell between them. The phone rang. They
ignored it. Tenderly, Rami took Rayna's hand and kissed it, then
held it to his cheek. "Yes, my rrawhee, look what we have done.
We married because we love each other and do not want to
live apart. Love and marriage are not the problems. Intolerance,
religion, blind hatred are the problems. The entire world is
consumed. Our families, our communities, our governments,
our countries. They are obsessed with the fear that acceptance
and tolerance might infect them. They hate what we have done
because we shove that infection in their faces like a plague.
We are getting a good lesson on how to survive intolerance.
A lesson that schools and religious leaders fail to teach us."
Ibrahim's letter had invoked Rami's ire. He stroked Rayna's
hair. "Everything happens for a reason. Our fate was sealed a
long time ago, before we were born. Do you believe that?"

Rayna shuddered. Her neck and arms erupted in red
blotches.

"For my father, he would have preferred my death in
the jungle to my happiness with you. He would praise my

weapons-for-drugs trade and curse me for loving you. I thought I knew my father. I had idolized him. To me, the man could have done no wrong, except . . .''

"Except what?"

"Nothing." Rami took the letter and tore it into shreds. "My father will not hear from me again. Not ever. You will not lose me to anyone."

* * *

On a Saturday morning, soon after New Year's, with temperatures hovering just above freezing and a drizzling rain dampening the air, Rami and Rayna left for New York City to visit Kamil and Maddy. Although traffic was light, icy patches on the road made the trip tenuous. Given the depressing weather, Rami and Rayna were grateful that Kamil had insisted they stay in the guestroom. "I won't have you dragging back and forth to a hotel," Kamil had said.

Adhering to Rayna and Rami's religious dietary laws, Maddy ordered in vegetarian gourmet Indian food for dinner. On Sunday morning, Kamil and Rami went to Zabar's and picked up bagels, lox, an array of scrumptious delicacies, and Zabar's own brand of coffee.

All weekend, Rami and Rayna delighted in Nida. She was as beautiful as Kamil had described, and looked just like her father. They took turns changing her diapers and feeding her formula from a bottle. They bathed her, played with her, and delighted in her coos and smiles. Nida was the highlight of their visit, and it was evident that the child had bewitched her father.

The joy, however, was offset by marked tension between Kamil and Maddy. Maddy was intent on hurling pointed daggers and casting cutting remarks at her husband. Embarrassed, Kamil ignored her and focused his attention on his infant daughter and his two guests.

Rayna felt sorry for Kamil and wanted to help. Rami, at first, tried to dissuade her from getting involved, but then he, too, agreed with Rayna. Easing into the subject, they quickly learned that Maddy did not want to be a stay-at-home mom, while Kamil wanted Nida to be raised by her mother, not tossed into day care or pawned off to a nanny. The two had been arguing this point since Maddy's sixth month of pregnancy and it destroyed the few thin threads they had of a marriage. When Rayna asked why they decided to have a child, Kamil hung his head.

"There was nothing to decide," Maddy retorted sharply. "Pregnancy came first. Marriage was the by-product."

"Well, should your daughter suffer the consequences of your actions?" Rami's question further inflamed Maddy.

"My daughter is *not* suffering."

Rayna came to her husband's defense. "Rami didn't mean it in a bad way. He was only . . ."

Maddy cut her off. "Look, recently I was offered a new position. The principal is leaving at the end of the school year and I was offered the job. I accepted and am not going to risk losing that career step. Why don't you ask Kamil to decline the new position Simon has offered him? Ask Kamil to stay at home with his daughter."

Not wanting the conversation to get any uglier, Rayna said, "I think it's time for us to be heading back while it's still daylight, and before the weather gets any worse. Rami and I had a lovely weekend. Thank you for your gracious hospitality and for letting us have so much time with Nida."

Maddy gave Rayna a hug, said goodbye to Rami, and took Nida in for a nap.

"Salaam." Kamil and Rami embraced on both cheeks. "Thank you for coming. Your visit has meant a lot to me." Humbly, Kamil stumbled into an apology and thanked them both for the generous gifts of toys and clothes for Nida.

"Rami and I hope you and Maddy can work this out. And Kamil . . . know that we're both here for you, even if it's just to talk."

"Thank you. You're both very kind." Kamil hugged Rayna, finding it hard to let go.

TWENTY-SIX

He who does not have a wife lives without joy, without blessing, without goodness.—Talmud Yevamot 62b

The late March winds howled and a heavy rain rippled against the skylight. Lulled by the sounds of nature, the lovers drew close. Rayna eased her hands along his erogenous zones, and smothered him all over with kisses. Rami caressed her. Their sounds of pleasure intensified. Rayna crested and he surged. A stillness settled. They snuggled comfortably.

"Growing up in Syria, I was taught . . . all of us were taught to hate Israel and the Jews. I had never known a Jew until I met you. I was fed lies . . . lots of lies." He brought her fingertips to his lips and kissed them one by one. "Religion is a deadly weapon. Using the name of Allah, or God, or whatever, people have been driven to do horrible things. I just do not understand why people are so willing to follow blindly. Without questioning, without reasoning, they willingly give over their minds. "

"It's been the history of mankind."

"Rayna, I love you. I am committed to you. Nothing and no one will ever change that."

"I love you back, more than you will ever know. When you were in South America, I was so scared that I might never see you again. Your pain was my pain. Each day I asked God to give me your agony so you wouldn't have to suffer so. I prayed to see you just one more time."

"I put you through a lot. I am so sorry."

"Don't be sorry. You were trying to survive and to protect me." She studied his face and smiled. "Just before my jidaw died, he told me that real love comes only once in a lifetime. He said not to let go, because it won't ever come that same way again."

"I liked your jidaw. I felt a connection. I wish I could have known him more."

"Mmmm, that would have been special for both of you."

The vision of a single form, Isaac and Hasdai ibn Shaprut, appeared in Rami's mind. Although the two men lived five hundred years apart, their apparition was one and the same.

* * *

It had been months since Rami last attended the mosque. Rayna encouraged him to go for juma. "You never went once during Ramadan. I think it's important for you."

"Allah is inside of me, not inside a Sunni mosque."

"Then find a Shi'ite mosque."

"You know that there are none nearby."

"Rami, go. If you still feel the same afterward, then don't go back and I will never mention it again."

* * *

On Friday, just before twelve, Rami grudgingly entered the mosque, removed his shoes, and stood in line side by side with the other men. Facing the mihrab, symbolizing the eastern direction to Mecca, Rami experienced a tug of war raging inside. Despite childhood links pulling him in, he felt his integrity being attacked. He stood, bowed, knelt, repeated 'Allahu akbar', and touched the ground with his forehead. Concluding the ritual, Rami joined the other worshippers in a seated position on the floor. Like a programmed robot, he had moved through the routine.

* * *

Soon, all eyes were directed toward the wooden platform. The imam began, "*La hawla wa la quwwata illa bi'Llah.* In God alone is power and strength." After reading from the Quran, the cleric delivered his *khutba*. "No other faith can be equal to Islam. Islam *is* the only faith. The Quran *is* the only authority. This is our jihad, the struggle that Allah has set before us." Pausing, the imam allowed the effects of his words to set in. Once confident that he had the full attention of the congregation, he proceeded to dehumanize Jews and accuse Jewish doctors of poisoning Muslim patients. "All Muslims will never be safe until we finish what Hitler started."

* * *

Beads of sweat formed on Rami's brow. His facial muscles tensed. He wanted to expose the lies and hatred. *This is not what Allah expects of us,* he craved to scream out. Looking around, Rami saw only affirming nods validating the imam. *If I do not soon flee, I will surely erupt.* Yet, Rami knew that getting up and leaving would bring harsh eyes upon him.

The consequences would not be worth his public display of defiance against those who had already given their minds over to the imam. *Hang in just a while longer. Soon it will be over. Once I tell Rayna, she will not ever again insist I come here. This is my last time.*

As soon as the imam concluded, Rami jumped to his feet, zipped up his fleece cardigan, and raced to the front door. For an instant, he stopped to slip on his footwear. A heavy hand bore down on him. Startled, Rami spun around. The imam smiled. "Rami, it's so good to see you. You have stayed away far too long. Let's talk in my office."

Rami forced a reciprocative smile. "I wish I could, but I have an appointment," he lied.

"You are refusing me? What kind of an appointment is so important that you cannot spend ten minutes with your imam?"

"Uhhh," *think fast*. "Uhhh . . . dentist's appointment. I was up all night with a toothache. Even now I am in pain. We will talk another time." Rami darted out.

"Rami," the imam called, "I hope your tooth is better and may your dentist not be a Jew."

Rami vowed never to go back in that building again.

* * *

The following Thursday, Kamil called to say he was coming to Washington on business for the week. He would arrive sometime on Sunday. Rami invited him to stay with them. Graciously, Kamil accepted.

Early the next morning, Eli called. He was coming to Washington for the week to do research at the Library of Congress for his thesis, and also to check on his father's lighting supply stores in the area. Talking with her brother, Rayna suggested that he drive down with Kamil. "We insist you both stay with us. We have two guest rooms waiting to be used."

"That's a great idea." Eli was eager to see his sister. Spending four hours alone in the car with Kamil was a bonus he had not anticipated.

"Good. Here's Kamil's private number. You two make the arrangements."

"Thanks, Rayna. You know how much I've been wanting this opportunity."

"I know you two will hit it off. Now, I want to hear about you and Alexis. When will I meet her?"

"Last night I proposed and she accepted."

"Oh, Eli, I'm so happy for you. I can't wait to meet her."

* * *

Eli had dated a lot and was considered a good catch in the Syrian community, but no one held his interest. No one measured up to Rayna. However, with Alexis it was different. He had known her only ten weeks. She was a Sephardic Jew from Athens, Greece. Against her parents' wishes, she had accepted a fellowship to study medicine at New York University. The two had met in the campus library and Eli could not take his eyes from her. That was all Rayna knew.

* * *

Early Sunday evening, a horn beeped in the driveway. Excitedly, Rayna ran to the door. Eli was the first to enter. He put his luggage down, "I've missed you."

She gave Eli a big hug, then smiled at Kamil. "I appreciate your bringing my brother."

"Eli is great company. I'm glad you suggested it."

Appearing from behind her, Rami eagerly greeted his guests.

"Mmmm, something smells delicious," Kamil sniffed.

"It's the aroma of my sister's Syrian cooking."

"Syrian food? For dinner?" Kamil was elated.

"Yes, Kamil. It's a special treat for you," Rayna grinned.

Kamil glanced at Rami, "Anytime you're ready to give her up . . ."

"No way. Forget it. I am never giving up Rayna. She is mine." Playfully, he pulled her close.

The four then went out for a walk around the neighborhood to give Eli and Kamil a chance to stretch their legs after the long trip.

* * *

Returning to the house, Rami showed Eli and Kamil to their rooms and left them to unpack. He went down to the kitchen to help Rayna set the table and cut up the salad.

Soon, Eli vaulted down the spiral staircase. "Can I get a tour of the house?"

"Eli!" Rayna gave him a discerning look, lowered the burners, and took hold of Eli's arm. "If you can behave . . . come."

Quickly appearing on the bottom step, Kamil asked, "Am I included in the tour?"

"Of course you are. Come on."

The house did not exude the lavishness of the one Rayna had grown up in, nor did it depict the meager decor of Rami's childhood dwelling. Everywhere, Isaac's belongings were in view. A clever commingling of colors and new furnishings enhanced the setting to reflect a comfortable feeling of love and warmth in the home.

"Well, it's meticulously clean. You get that from Mom . . . uh-oh . . ."

"It's okay, Eli. Children do pick up some of their parents' ways."

"Wow! What big rooms. I like your dramatic two-story entranceway. But how will you ever get up there to change those lightbulbs in that chandelier?" Looking up at the fixture, Kamil chuckled.

"Rayna already solved that problem," Rami laughed. "No one is allowed to turn it on."

"What else has my sister put limits on?"

"Eli!" Rayna reproached her brother.

Rami and Kamil drifted into the library. Rami took some very old books from the shelf. "These are from Syria. Rayna's jidaw brought these with him when he first came to America."

* * *

Alone with Rayna, Eli admired the maplewood floors and the unusual shapes of the designer windows. "You know what I like best about your home? Jidaw is here . . . in his things. The aura of his presence is profound. He hasn't left you, has he?"

Instinctively, Rayna shivered from a chill that ran down her spine. "No, Eli, I still can't let go."

Eli put his arms around her and kissed her forehead. "Jidaw began having dreams about you sometime after our sitaw died. He explained it as a visceral forewarning. A sixth sense, if you can call it that. He knew one day you would reach out for help and he would be gone. That's why he left you the house."

"It's because of Rami, isn't it?"

"Yes."

"I want to share the money and everything of Jidaw's with you. Half of it is yours . . ."

"No. No. Dad has provided very well for me. Jidaw's money is yours. He wanted you to have it. I want you to have it."

"Rrawhee," Rami called out from the kitchen. "Shall I turn off the burners?"

"Uh-oh, he's telling me someone is hungry."

* * *

Over dinner, Eli bubbled with talk about Alexis. "From the first instant I saw her, I knew she was the one for me. Her goodness and beauty . . . well, you'll see when you meet her."

"So tell us, Eli, when is the wedding?" Rayna eagerly asked.

"We're going to Athens so I can meet her family. It will be a real Greek wedding . . . and I expect everyone at this table to be there."

"A good wife is a man's fortune. My father always said that," Kamil smiled. Kamil had not wanted to marry Maddy. She liked to party and spend lots of time with her girlfriends. She disliked housework and hated to cook. Nida was tolerated in small doses. Sex between them was non-existent. Maddy cringed whenever Kamil came near. He ached for the kind of love that Rami and Eli had found.

Masking his sadness, Kamil pulled out Nida's photos and rambled on about his infant daughter, enjoying the oohs and aahs from his audience.

* * *

Over dessert, the conversation shifted back to Eli, who addressed Rayna with a devious bend in his tone. "Have you heard the latest about our two wonderful aunts and the three-million-dollar lawsuit against you?"

Rayna shook her head. "No. My lawyer has been on vacation in Italy."

"Well, my dear sister, *it's over*!"

"Thank God." Rayna let out a sigh of relief.

"Eli, your relatives are just plain vicious. Rayna has been through enough this year and . . ."

"You're right, Rami. I apologize for them."

"It is not your fault, Eli. We will be forever indebted to you for standing by us."

Deliberately, Eli cleared his throat. "I bring more good tidings . . . Jonathan. Remember him?"

"How can we forget Jonathan? What about him?" Rami's curiosity escalated.

"He flunked his chemistry class last semester and . . ."

"Oh?" Rami smirked.

"There's more . . ."

"Go on, Eli. You're going to tell us anyway." Rayna squirmed.

"Not only did he flunk chemistry, but he also got a D in calculus. Mom says his parents are furious. They tightened the umbilical cord, took away his car, pulled him out of Maryland, and harnessed the money belt. He's now living at home, going to Brooklyn College, and commuting on the subway."

"Oooooh! Shall we all applaud?" Rayna looked at Rami and clapped her hands.

Hanging onto Eli's every word, Rami felt avenged.

"Mom says Jonathan is suffering miserably. Those are her exact words."

"Good! He deserves that and more misery. It is not punishment enough for what he did to my wife."

Kamil had been quietly listening to the family dynamics. "The guy couldn't be that bad, could he?"

"Kamil, what we say here goes no further than this table."

"Rami, by now you must know I'm good at that."

"Well, Jonathan tried to rape Rayna. I thank Allah that he did not succeed."

Kamil looked at Rayna. "I didn't know. I'm so sorry."

"I was lucky . . . now why don't you all go into the library and play tawleh while I clean up."

"No, no. We are not leaving you with this mess. You cooked. We clean. You will have your chance to inspect our perfect work afterward." Following Rami's lead, Eli and Kamil whisked Rayna from the kitchen.

"I should have a say in my own kitchen."

"No micro-managing. Don't be like our mother. And tomorrow we eat out. My treat."

"And Thursday will be my treat," Kamil chimed in.

* * *

The impeccably clean kitchen passed Rayna's inspection. "You guys are good. How would you all like a permanent job?"

"I don't know. It depends on how much you pay," Kamil joked.

"Not much. You would starve . . ."

"Oh, I do not know about that, Eli. Rayna pays me pretty well. Do I look like I am starving?"

"Definitely not!" With a burst of laughter, Eli and Kamil responded in unison.

"Okay, you guys. All into the library. Go play tawleh. I have work to do."

* * *

Rami and Kamil were first to sit down at the backgammon table, the one that Rayna and her grandfather used to play on. While Eli waited his turn to play the winner, he wandered into the study where Rayna was at the computer. "What are you doing?"

"Working on another article for the magazine."

"Rayna, I'm sorry about all that has happened to you," Eli eased into an opening.

"We make our choices and then we live with them."

"Rayna, I don't want to upset you more, but . . ."

"But you will anyway. Go on, Eli. What is it now?"

"The rabbis have ruled on your case and . . ."

"Case! What case?"

"For marrying a Muslim."

"A *beit din*? A religious court is ruling on my life for marrying Rami? You know, I recall something like that happening to Salman Rushdie when fundamentalist Islamic clerics ruled against him and put out a *fatwa* on his life."

"I should never have told you."

"Well, now that you have, finish it! Tell me the rest."

"No one in the community is to have contact with you, not ever, lest you corrupt their ways. The gossip is cruel. You've been ostracized. Excommunicated."

"Like Spinoza?"

"Yes. Like Spinoza. You can't go back. There's no forgiveness. Rayna, I'm sorry to be the messenger, but at least you know where you stand."

"And Mom?"

"Mom's not coping well and rues the day she had you. You upset her orderly little world and she'll never forgive you for it. *Never*."

"And Dad?"

"Dad is struggling with his love for you, his life with Mom, and living in the Syrian community. I'm certain his salvation will be to throw himself even more into his businesses."

"And you, Eli? What's your position?"

"You'll always be my sister. That won't change."

So the rabbis have acted as judge, jury, and prosecuting attorney. I wasn't even given the opportunity to plead my case. "Eli, I have loved you from the time I can first remember. You have been my rock . . . thank you for telling me. It's good to know who my enemies are. You know, Eli, if I consume myself with living for other people's approval, I will become their prisoner."

"Has Rami been worth it?"

"Yes, Eli. He has."

* * *

Trotting into the study, Rami announced, "It is your turn, Eli. Kamil won."

"The game was very close," Kamil smiled humbly.

"Do you know that nobody can beat my sister at tawleh?"

"He is right about that. Nobody beats my wife. She had an excellent teacher . . . her jidaw."

"Kamil, I bet ten dollars on the game. You and my sister."

Delighted to accept the challenge, Kamil sat across from Rayna. The two set up the board. Kamil caught himself staring and forced his gaze away. Rayna wore a brushed cotton, lavender turtleneck. Her black stretch pants clung gently to her lower frame. To Kamil, Rayna represented the total sensuality of a woman.

"Uh-uh, I wouldn't move there if I were you," Eli intervened, making Kamil's next move for him.

Rayna rolled her eyes, "Oh, brother!"

Rami jumped in, "No, not there. Here. Move here. I know my wife's mind. She will not take your piece." Within seconds, everyone was absorbed in the playful commotion.

* * *

Over the next few evenings, Rami, Eli, and Kamil managed to scrounge up enough men for basketball games at the gym at the Jewish Community Center. Returning home, they would be full of chatter, hunger, and body odor. Rayna would send them all upstairs, "No dinner until you shower." Then, after dinner, the three men would stay up late playing backgammon and talking into the wee hours while Rayna slept.

* * *

On the last night of their visit, Kamil took them all out to the Cheesecake Factory. The four babbled incessantly and cleaned every morsel on their plates. Feeling stuffed when the waitress came to tempt them with dessert, they all agreed to share one slice of pumpkin cheesecake. "Four spoons," Rayna requested.

This was as close to intimacy as Kamil had known since losing his family. *Connection. Bonding. Trust. Four human beings on this earth and not a bit of difference who we are. Jew, Muslim, Sunni, Shi'ite.* This was the peace Kamil was searching for. "Rayna, we're waiting for your next article."

"It's ready, Kamil. I'll print out a hard copy tonight. I've already e-mailed the file to you."

The three men lifted their water glasses, "Here's to Rayna's successful career in journalism."

* * *

Later that night, Kamil lay in bed with a copy of Rayna's latest article. She wrote about the repeated attempts by the United States government to eradicate the coca plants in southern Colombia and why the project had been failing for years. She told of greedy contractors and lax government workers who were low on oversight and high on fringe benefits.

> *. . . knowingly, the American government has allowed itself to be bilked of millions. For years, government contractors have been spraying lethal chemicals from the air over the southern Colombian states of Putumayo and Caquetá. The toxins pollute the water, contaminate the air and soil, wipe out vegetation, destroy food sources, and*

cause illness and death to the region's indigenous people. Yet, the coca plants continue to thrive and the drug trade continues to flourish . . .

When Kamil was done, he read it again. Rayna had another winner. Closing his eyes, he tried to sleep but could not. His marriage to Maddy was a big mistake. *Where was my head? What was I thinking? Was I so desperate that I could not see?* Three weeks earlier, Kamil had arrived home from work sooner than expected. His dinner meeting had been cancelled and he hurried home to be with Nida. Turning the key in the front door, he entered the apartment to find Nida in her crib crying and Maddy in bed with her closest girlfriend. *In my bed! How could she?* He was grateful to Maddy's mother, a loving and kind grandmother who adored Nida. She offered to take the child during the week and help out until the messy affair was settled. Kamil knew it would be an ugly divorce. Maddy was threatening to fight for custody.

* * *

On Friday morning, Rayna dipped each slice of challah into a mixture of eggs, milk, maple syrup, cinnamon, and vanilla. The kitchen table was set, fresh cut-up melon filled a bowl, and the aroma of just-brewed coffee permeated the air. She heard the three men coming down the steps.

"Mmmm, I'm famished!" Eli checked out the French toast on the electric griddle. He broke off a piece and popped it into his mouth. "Perfect," he smiled approvingly.

Playfully, Rayna swatted his hand. "You couldn't be that famished after the big dinner you ate last night."

"Wanna bet?" He gave his sister a peck on the cheek and carried the platter to the table.

"You know, Eli, I've always noticed that playing basketball never fails to trigger a rise in your testosterone." Using that male word, Rayna noted Rami giving her a censuring glare.

"Dig in," Eli grinned as he passed the maple syrup.

When the very last crumb was eaten, Rayna reminded everyone that it was time to get going. "Rami and I have classes and you two need to hit the road. Eli has to be home in time for shabbat, before sundown."

* * *

"Basketball was great. It certainly does cause a rise in one's *testosterone*," Rami jested as he and Rayna walked Eli and Kamil out to the driveway.

"My husband has learned a new English word which I hope he doesn't overuse," Rayna bantered. Hugging Eli goodbye, she made him promise to come with Alexis next time. Turning to Kamil, she thanked him for bringing Eli, then quietly took him aside and asked. "Are things any better with you and Maddy?"

Kamil shook his head. "I wish I could say they were. One evening, not too long ago, I unexpectedly came home early from work and found Nida in her crib crying, and Maddy . . . and Maddy . . . Maddy was in bed with her closest girlfriend. In my bed . . ." His voice trailed off.

"Oh, Kamil, I'm so sorry," Rayna gave him a caring hug. "Where is Nida now? What will you do?"

"Nida is safe and happy with her grandmother, but an ugly divorce is on the horizon. Maddy wants custody."

"Please let us know how we can help. Anything at all. Rami and I are here for you. Eli, too. You'll find my brother to be a loyal friend . . . and he lives in New York."

"Thank you for these past few days." Kamil's eyes watered. He wanted to gently take Rayna's face in his hands but refrained from doing so. "My mother . . ." he stumbled. "My mother was a lot like you. Rami is a lucky man. You are his blessing."

"What a sweet thing to say, Kamil. Someday, you will find your blessing when you least expect it. Be patient. It will happen in time. I feel it in my blood."

"I can't thank you enough for everything. Rayna, I read your article last night. You have another winner."

"Really?"

"Really."

Rayna took his hand, "I'm worried about you."

"Your caring means a lot . . . I'll be okay."

* * *

In the driveway, Rami and Rayna waved goodbye to their guests. "It was a good visit."

"Yes, it was." *Rami, Eli, and Kamil . . . I will call them my Three Musketeers, for their lives will be full of adventure and forever intertwined.*

TWENTY-SEVEN

Go, eat your bread in gladness, and drink your wine in joy; for your action was long ago approved by God.—Ecclesiastes 9:7

Awakened from a deep sleep, Rami reached across the bed and lifted the receiver. "Hello." He checked the clock on the nightstand. He glanced at Rayna sleeping. "Nolan, do you know what time it is?" Rami listened to Nolan's tale. The police were at the professor's home. He needed Rami to come right away. "There is no traffic at this hour so I can be there in twenty minutes." He hung up the phone.

Rubbing her eyes, Rayna mumbled, "Rami, what is it? Who was that?"

"Someone tried to break into Nolan's lab. Drilled a big hole through the solid oak door. The motion detector triggered the alarm when the prowlers entered. I must go help him."

"Do you want me to go with you?"

"No, my rrawhee, I will be fine. The police are there now. Go back to sleep. I will call you later, and I promise to be home by six. My cell is on if you need to reach me." He leaned across the bed, "Happy first anniversary." He kissed her. "With each new day, I love you more."

"Mmmm. Love you, too."

* * *

When Rami arrived at Nolan's house, the police were in the midst of questioning Nolan. By default, Rami's presence made him part of the inquest. Nolan explained that Rami was one of his students and also a friend. One of the officers took notes.

"This was not an amateurish burglary. Not the work of youngsters looking for drug money," said the other officer. "This was the work of professionals who wanted something specific in this house. Now, Doctor Nolan, tell us what you think that may be. Surely, you have some idea."

"A professional thief?" Nolan asked innocently. "I don't keep a lot of cash around. I don't have expensive jewelry. I don't have . . ."

"There is something in this house that somebody wants. I suggest you attempt to figure it out, because I guarantee they'll be back."

After the policemen left, Rami examined the large hole in the heavy door. "Dear Allah! How could you not have heard the drilling, Nolan? And what about your neighbors?"

"Rami, I was asleep. I assume my neighbors were, too. The alarm went off and woke me."

"Whoever Yousef sent will return. We must get the bacteria out of here. Today!"

Nolan dialed his secretary, Bertha, and asked her to come as quickly as possible. Rami leafed through the Yellow

Pages, found a security service, and requested their two best guards. Nolan called the company who had installed the door and explained the urgency of replacing it. The two then delved into the real estate section of *The Washington Post*.

* * *

In a strip mall in Gaithersburg, along the congested but convenient Montgomery Village Avenue, Rami and Nolan found what they hoped would be a safe sanctuary. With a three-month deposit up front, they could gain access by early afternoon. The large room, atop a music store, had a separate entrance and was wired with a security system.

Renting a U-Haul truck, the two men transported the contents of the lab to the new location. By late afternoon, all was set up. Nolan and Rami were exhausted. "Whew! This has been one heck of a day. May I take you and Rayna out for dinner to say thank you?"

"Thanks, Nolan, but tonight Rayna and I are celebrating our first anniversary with friends."

* * *

Jeannie and Stan were young lawyers who lived next door to Rami and Rayna. The two couples had become friends and good neighbors. Their anniversaries fell within the same week and they planned to celebrate the milestone together.

At the Marrakesh restaurant in downtown Washington, the four were escorted to a round, hand-hammered brass table that sat close to the floor. Lowering themselves onto large, colorful pillows, they felt as if they had been transported to the Casbah in Morocco. As the evening unfolded, they were pampered with a three-hour extravaganza of Moroccan food, music, and belly dancing. Joy and laughter filled their space. By evening's end, they were all feeling blissfully high.

* * *

Returning home that night, Rami went straight to bed. After a full day that had begun in the early morning hours, he could not keep his eyes open another minute. Rayna flossed and brushed her teeth, washed her face, and crawled into bed. Cuddling up to her sleeping husband, she felt something jab her and she jumped up. On her pillow was a small, delicately wrapped box. Turning on the lamplight, Rayna quietly unwrapped it, removing a dainty gold bracelet-watch adorned with brilliant stones of pink and purple. The inscription on the back read: *I will love you longer than forever—Rami.*

She brushed her lips against his cheek, "May your Allah protect you and keep you safe, always." On his nightstand where Rami would see it when he woke, Rayna placed the pocket-sized GPS street pilot that she knew he wanted.

* * *

Later that week, on his way to meet Rayna for lunch at the Student Union building, Rami spotted Omar ahead. When he called out to him, Omar increased his pace. Rami picked up speed until he was alongside his old friend. Out of breath, he asked, "Did you hear me calling to you?" When Omar remained silent, Rami jerked him by the arm, forcing him to decelerate and listen. "I am sorry for all that has not gone well. Yousef's cruel exploits have extracted a toll on our friendship. I know that I am taking great risks by not succumbing to Yousef's bullying. It nearly cost me my life. You have chosen to acquiesce and play it safe. It is not a matter of right or wrong, good or bad. I respect you for your choice. Please do not judge me harshly for mine."

"Look, Rami, I am not ready to die. And my family . . . well, I have seen what Yousef and Abdallah are capable of doing."

"You know, Omar, I never properly thanked you for guiding Kamil to my rescue. You did not even have the decency to warn me of my dire situation."

"I was scared . . ."

"And now what is your excuse? I want to know about the break-in at Nolan's."

Omar fumbled, "I . . . I have to go."

"Do not turn your back, Omar. Look what has happened to you. You are changed."

Omar's eyes blinked rapidly. He extracted an oath of silence from Rami, then revealed all that he knew. "Yousef says he wants the bacteria now. He dreams of having power over all mankind . . . threatening to unleash the bacteria. Yousef says it is like having a nuclear bomb in his hands. He has made a decision not to wait for the results of Nolan's work. Abdallah and a man named Ghazi attempted the break-in."

"I owe you for this . . ."

"There is more." Omar's hands were shaking. His books fell from his grip. Nervously, he bent and picked them up. "Yousef has plans for you. He wants to take you off of Nolan's project once the bacteria is in his hands. And he intends for your life to be one of negotiating arms-for-drugs, if he decides to let you live. Carlos el Negro was impressed with you."

A cold chill slithered up Rami's spine and he shuddered.

"Once Yousef has secured the bacteria for himself, he will kill Nolan and . . . and . . . and I am late for class."

"No, Omar. I beg you to finish. Tell me the rest."

"Yousef is taken with Rayna's beauty. He wants her."

"What!"

"He does not know that she is a Jew. Rami, I am late for class. Salaam."

A yoke of guilt tightened around Rami's neck. *I knowingly put Rayna in danger by marrying her. How selfish I have been.* A tickle in his throat triggered a coughing spasm. Tears trickled down his face. He reached into his book bag and took out a bottle of water. He drank it all. The coughing subsided. *As long as Nolan and I have possession of the bacteria, we are safe,* Rami deluded himself.

* * *

By the end of the semester, Rayna's writing had won her much recognition and many awards. Her controversial articles in *InterContinental Weekly* continued to bring in a daily deluge of mail long after publication. Never had Simon or Kamil seen such a response. A dramatic rise in the magazine's circulation, and a clamoring for more of Rayna's work, set her on a course that would eventually launch her into the public eye.

Kamil and Simon asked Rayna to work full time over the summer and offered her hefty compensation. She turned them down. She and Rami had other plans. The first six weeks of the summer would be spent in school taking classes, advancing closer to an early graduation. Then they were off to a much anticipated two-week vacation in southern Spain.

TWENTY-EIGHT

All truths are easy to understand once they are discovered; the point is to discover them.—Galileo Galilei

Approaching Málaga, Rami and Rayna stayed glued to the window, taking in the aerial view of the land. After a smooth landing, they retrieved their baggage and checked through customs. Like two children beginning their first day of kindergarten, they were bursting with excitement and anxiety. They made their way to the car rental and were informed that only manual transmissions were available. When Rayna said that she had never driven anything but an automatic, Rami countered, "I can do it. I learned to drive on my father's old Mercedes."

The agent placed a form in front of him to sign and asked to see a credit card, passport, and driver's license. After reviewing the documents and noting Rami's age, the man refused to rent the car. "All foreign drivers must be at least twenty-five," he announced in Spanish. "It is our rule." From his wallet, Rami extracted some money and hinted that rules can sometimes be broken. The man smiled, handed Rami a set of keys, and warned, "Spanish drivers are skillful, fast, and crazy. Spain's roads are excellent, narrow, and winding. Be careful!"

* * *

Checking into the hotel room, they unpacked, then went out for a walk to stretch their legs and explore the locale. Nearing a small church, they politely waited while a parade of lively, well-dressed Spaniards made their way into the chapel. Catching sight of the bride, Rayna exclaimed, "Look Rami, it's a wedding! Let's go inside." She tugged at his arm.

He gave her a look of uncertainty.

"Come on. We'll be very quiet." Pulling him in, she spied two seats in the rear by the door. The Catholic wedding ceremony, Andalucían style, gave the couple their very first glimpse inside a church. Enchanted by the ceremony, they waited until the priest announced the couple to be husband and wife before retreating as inconspicuously as they had intruded.

Under a blue Mediterranean sky, they spent the rest of the day exploring the little shops and making whimsical purchases. Soon, daylight began to fade and hunger crept into their bellies. Coming upon a restaurant crowded with natives, they went inside. As they dined on fresh vegetables, baked fish, and rice, spirited flamenco dancers entertained them with rhythmic stomping and flamboyant movements. Distracted by the gaiety, they lost track of time until their body clocks reminded them of just how sleepy they were. After paying the bill, the two returned to the hotel. Tomorrow they would drive to Ronda, the birthplace of bullfighting.

* * *

Rami steered the car over the gorge, crossing the narrow bridge that linked the old city of Ronda with its commercial district on the other side of the mountain. Under the hot afternoon sun, Rami and Rayna took their seats among an energetic crowd anxious for the drama of the bullfight to begin. Rami took Rayna's hand. Rayna shook her head, "I hope I have the stomach to sit through this."

Three groups, each fighting two bulls, warmed up the audience. Cheers rang out when all the bullfighters appeared to signal that the *corrida* had begun. The *matador* taunted the bull with his *muleta*. *Picadors* on horseback goaded the animal with steel-pointed lances to weaken its shoulder muscles. *Banderilleros* stuck spikes into the bull's back, provoking him into a frenzy.

From the beginning, Rayna found the sport hard to watch. When the matador returned, gesturing with his red cape and thrusting the sword straight into the bull's heart, Rayna covered her eyes. The audience applauded wildly. The corpse was dragged away. Music played, handkerchiefs waved, and the matador was carried out in glory on the shoulders of his men.

Rayna hated the goriness of it all and could not understand how people took pleasure in an innocent animal being heartlessly provoked to its death. Rami, on the other hand, had never seen a bullfight. Rayna was annoyed with him for being so engrossed in the unfolding production. Angrily, she declared, "It was a sick spectacle. How could you have liked it?"

"But this is part of Spain, its people, its culture. You do not need to approve of . . ."

"You're right. I don't need to approve. Reminds me of Yousef, goading people just like that poor bull was goaded."

* * *

Day after day, the lovers peeled away at their itinerary. At the beach on the Costa del Sol, Rami's eyes widened at the bare-breasted women basking in the sun, walking along the water's edge, bathing in the Mediterranean, playing in the sand with their young children. "How could they? Naked for all to see." Rami was appalled. "This would never happen in Syria. Is there no shame? No decency to cover up?"

"But this is part of Spain, its people, its culture. You do not need to approve." She echoed his own words back to him. "At the bullfight, I covered my eyes. Why can't you do the same?"

Rami's agitation amplified. "It is not the same. You will not ever parade around like these shameless harlots. You are not allowed."

Rayna suppressed her amusement and took his hand. "You need to calm down, and we need to leave this beach."

* * *

On Monday, August 10, 1998, the anticipated leap from teen years to adulthood was upon them. Deliberately, Rami and Rayna saved this twentieth birthday milestone to venture into Córdoba, the city that loomed in their past.

Córdoba is a university town with churches, monuments, and museums. It is the home of both La Mezquita, the famous mosque which was once the seat of the Western Caliphate, and La Sinagoga, the only surviving medieval synagogue.

"Where to first?" Rami asked.

"First to La Mezquita, then to La Sinagoga."

* * *

Advancing through a courtyard of orange trees, they followed the path leading into the building's interior. With amazement, they canvassed the display of one thousand columns supporting an endless chain of horseshoe-shaped arches decorated in alternating stripes of red brick and white stone. While marveling at the imposing relic, a spell suddenly overcame Rayna. In a daze, she walked to the far end of the room where an octagonal chamber set into the wall housed the mihrab. "Something is not right," she fretted. "Do you see? We have to move it. The mihrab must face east toward Mecca." Deeply stirred by some mystical power, Rayna placed her hands on the chamber and tried to forcefully dislodge it.

Concerned, Rami tried to steady his wife's hands. *How could she know that the location of the mihrab is not where it should be?* "Come, Rayna. Come, rrawhee. Let us sit down." He tried coaxing her away from the mihrab, but Rayna would not budge.

As if cemented to the center of gravity, her feet stood firmly. "We must restore the mihrab to its proper place . . . over there. It belongs over there." Frantically, she tugged at the chamber. Visitors stared. An attendant started toward them. Gently, Rami edged Rayna to the wooden pews, easing her down into a seat. Rami was now painfully aware of Rayna's hypnotic state.

"When I was a little girl, my jidaw used to come here to pray, many times every day. At special times, I would come with him. He taught me what no one else would." Droplets trickled down her cheeks, "I miss him so much."

"I know you do." Rami's vision under the influence of the yaje plant was now all too real. *Rayna had been a*

Moor living here in Córdoba during the time of the Spanish Inquisition. With all my heart, I loved her then as I love her now. Rami tightened his grip around Rayna. "Come, we must go visit La Sinagoga." Back out on the street, Rayna's hypnotic trance vanished, leaving her with no memory of the occurrence.

* * *

The pair drifted down the labyrinth of narrow winding streets, passing whitewashed homes, colorful courtyards, and a myriad of shops. Turning onto the cramped Calle de los Judíos, Rami and Rayna encountered tour groups queued all the way up the street. The couple stepped into line and waited their turn. The scorching sun beat down. Rami took two bottles of water from his backpack and handed one to Rayna.

In time, the line grew shorter. As they advanced to the front, the ancient synagogue with its white stucco exterior, arched entranceway, and Hebrew inscription overhead called out to Rami. Stepping inside the archaic structure, he gazed up, surprised at his recollection of the high ceiling. Holding onto Rayna, he moved into a shallow foyer and touched the white stucco walls of the Mudejar style decoration dating from the fourteenth century. To the left, a stairway led to a balcony once reserved for the women. Straight ahead, a small sanctuary had been secured for the men. A semi-circular arch where the holy scrolls of the Torah had been housed was now nothing but an empty space. Mindful of Rayna, Rami held tightly to her hand and guided her toward the cubicle. He stretched to touch the inside but it was higher than his reach. Tears moistened his lashes. *The Torah. The sacred teachings of my people. The Catholics destroyed even this. For what? For intolerance.* Reminders of man's inhumanity to man invaded Rami's thoughts. Staring at the panel above the cubicle, he read the Hebrew scripture: *Oh, God, listen and take haste to rebuild Jerusalem.*

* * *

The tourists outside were growing impatient. Two guides inside hurried the visitors along. Holding hands, the couple left the old synagogue. The intensity of the morning had siphoned their energy.

"How were you able to read the Hebrew inscription above the ark? You don't know Hebrew," Rayna said, as they walked through the maze of streets looking for a place to eat.

"Something very strange happened. I cannot explain it, except that the words flowed from my lips. The synagogue connected me to . . ."

"Tell me. Connected you to what?"

"To a past. To a life before . . ." Rami's voice broke off. "Let us get some lunch."

They stumbled onto an old-world restaurant with a skylit patio decorated with hanging plants and colorful glazed tiles. Sitting at a small table, they looked over the limited menu, then ordered cold gazpacho soup and tortilla española. While waiting for the food to come, they reflected on the morning's haunting experiences. Rami reached across the table and drew Rayna's palm to his cheek, holding it there for several seconds. "Five hundred years ago, I lost you. The hand of Allah has intervened to reunite us. Do you believe that?"

Rayna shivered. A chill went through her. "We'll never really know."

* * *

From the brochure, Rayna read, "The Alhambra is the best preserved medieval palace in the world. The exquisite Moorish craftsmanship of the rooms, the decorative tiling in the courtyards, the intricate wooden carvings, and the majestic columns and ceilings make the Alhambra one of the seven man-made wonders on earth."

Casually, they strolled through a succession of walkways, patios, geometric pools, and fragrant plantings. All around, Arabic inscriptions set in stucco praised Allah. "Granada is a place I have always wanted to come, since I was a child . . . more even than going to Mecca." Rami looked at his watch, then lovingly put his arm around Rayna's shoulders. "We have been here five hours."

"Are you ready to go?"

"Yes."

* * *

Leaving the Alhambra behind, they drove into a little Moroccan village in Arrayanes and inquired about a place to eat. A frail, elderly man with wrinkled skin raised his cane and pointed to a café down the street. "You eat halal?" he asked in Arabic. Rami nodded. The man's smile exposed several missing teeth. Rami handed him ten pesetas.

The establishment was packed with diners. "A table for two will be a while. An hour or more," said the young Moroccan host. "If you would like to share, a table for four is available now." He tactfully glanced at the couple who had just entered directly behind them.

Rayna tugged at Rami's arm. "Let's," she whispered.

Reluctantly, Rami smiled at the strangers, "Would you be willing?"

Edmund was a towering, handsome mulatto in his early thirties, a Harry Belafonte look-alike, a successful executive in his father's aerospace company. Inga was a twenty-seven-year-old attractive blue-eyed blonde from Sweden, a stay-at-home mother with two small children. They lived in Bethesda, Maryland. This was their fourth trip to southern Spain, the place where they had first met.

Instantly, a camaraderie between the two couples took hold. Midway through the meal, they began making plans to visit Morocco. "We've been there before. If you don't know your way around, it can get pretty harrowing. Why don't we pick you up in front of your hotel at eight tomorrow?" Edmund suggested.

"We'll be waiting. Thank you," Rayna responded appreciatively.

On their last day in Spain, Rami and Rayna would venture into the dark unknown. The excursion across the Straits represented a past that once separated them. It was an odyssey they were compelled to make. Edmund and Inga were a stroke of fate.

* * *

At eight sharp, Rami and Rayna climbed into the back seat. *"Buenos días."*

"Buenos días. That's the extent of my Spanish," Inga laughed. "If you haven't had breakfast, there are fresh sweet rolls in the white bag next to you. We already had our share."

"Thank you. You're kind." Rayna lifted the bag. She handed a roll to Rami, then took one for herself.

Heading south on the hour-long drive to Gibraltar, the four found as much to talk about as they had the night before. Edmund had tried to dissuade Rami and Rayna from going to Ceuta, but Inga convinced her husband otherwise. "We always visit Tangiers. The change will be nice."

Edmund offered the few facts he had learned of Ceuta. "It's owned by Spain, but it's in Morocco. The town has a large military presence. Not much to do except expensive duty-free shopping. At the hotel desk, they told me of a good place to have lunch there, and the best ice cream, too. The restaurant may be the only worthwhile part of the visit." Edmund shook his head and rolled his eyes, still unable to grasp why the young couple wanted to go to Ceuta.

* * *

Approaching Gibraltar, Rayna sighted the gigantic chunk of jagged limestone rising up from the Mediterranean. "Look! The Rock of Gibraltar! Can we stop?"

Edmund parked the car. They climbed to the Upper Rock and watched the dolphins jumping in and out of the shimmering blue water. In the distance, the stately Rif Mountains of North Africa swelled gracefully from the earth. "Sorry, you two, but we must leave now if we want to make the next ferry across," Inga said.

* * *

The Nordic hydrofoil sat in its slip. Rami and Edmund walked off to buy the tickets. Rayna and Inga trailed behind, deep in conversation. Rayna stopped to lace up her sneaker, which had become untied. From the boat, a horn bellowed, indicating an imminent departure. "Why don't you catch up

with the men? I'll meet you at the ferry. Be sure it doesn't
leave without me." When Inga hesitated, Rayna urged, "Go
on. I'll be right there." She knelt to the ground, concentrating
on double-knotting both laces. Oblivious to the tourists
rushing toward the ferry, Rayna was not aware of two little
boys fighting. Their mother had tried to separate them, but
they dashed from her grip and knocked Rayna over.

* * *

Absorbed in dialogue with Edmund, Rami assumed that
Rayna was close behind with Inga. He stepped onto the
hydrofoil and instinctively reached for Rayna's hand. She
was not there. Panic struck. Once before, he had let go of
her hand to buy tickets for the passage. Once before, she had
vanished. Terror engulfed him. *Please Allah, do not take her
from me again.* "Rayna! Rayna! Rayna!" He ran from the boat
screaming her name.

* * *

Swarms of people hurried to reach the ferry. Rayna tried
to get up but could not. Bodies crowded her space, almost
trampling her. Scared, she cried out for Rami.

Jolting through the masses, Rami bellowed, "Rayna!
Rayna!"

Edmund and Inga joined the search. "Rami, here! We
found her!"

Spotting Edmund's head above the crowd, Rami
frantically leaped toward him. Seeing Rayna on the ground,
he dropped to his knees and wrapped his arms around her. In
those few moments of blurred twilight, Rami was petrified
that history might repeat itself. Lowering his forehead

to meet hers, he uttered, "I am not strong enough to live without you. I do not want to take this trip."

"Rami, crossing the Straits . . . isn't it closure you came here for?"

Rami searched her face. "Yes," he nodded.

* * *

Arriving in Tangiers, a barrage of unscrupulous guides bombarded the disembarking tourists, aggressively vying for their business. Rami tightened his grip on Rayna. "If the four of us stay together, we'll be okay," said Edmund, who was now clutching Inga's hand. The two women wanted to shop at the souq and immediately became engrossed in the wares at one particular booth. In Arabic, Rami negotiated a price for a piece of jewelry that Rayna liked.

The merchant, an elderly man, stopped to talk with a younger man who had just entered. In broken English, the merchant made the introduction, "My son. Very good. Very honest. He show you Tangiers." The son smiled. His white teeth glistened against his warm brown skin. Dark shoulder-length hair hung in loose ringlets framing his face.

Rami spoke to him in Arabic. "Can you drive us to Ceuta, wait for us, then bring us back?"

"Yes," the son answered.

"How much?"

When a price was agreed upon, Rami turned to Edmund, who nodded. "Tell him we'll pay one third now, the rest when we safely return. We're as honest as his father says he is."

The son looked to his father, who approved the terms presented. Rami paid for the gold bracelet and slipped it onto Rayna's wrist. Edmund bought Inga a necklace and dropped it into her purse.

* * *

Arriving in Ceuta in the early afternoon, they found the restaurant that had been recommended and invited the young Muslim to join them. Lunch was not disappointing. Rami and Rayna ordered a dish of asparagus tips with potatoes and eggs. Edmund and Inga had rice with seafood. The Moroccan guide ate a dish of eggplant with potatoes and pimentos. Feeling pleasantly full after their big meals, the five still managed to make room for an iced chocolate drink and vanilla ice cream.

* * *

After lunch, the group walked around the town, weaving through the maze of streets. They entered old mosques, churches, and synagogues. They passed shops and cafés, upscale homes and shacks. Ceuta had a different feel. It was not Spain, but it was not Morocco either. The guide made it known that in Ceuta the Muslim residents were treated as inferiors.

Rami and Rayna wondered what might have been if they had actually arrived here five hundred years earlier. Imagining different scenarios, they concluded that this place held nothing for them except a fantasy, and the realization that, if they had succeeded in a life together back then, they might never have known the love they now shared.

The journey to Spain opened up a past that Rami and Rayna needed to understand. It had transported them back in time, then just as swiftly, propelled them forward to the present, a place where they preferred to be, at least for the time being.

TWENTY-NINE

Whatever the mind thinks of, that alone it sees.
What people call fate or divine will is nothing
other than action from the past acting upon itself.
Even as motion is inherent in air, manifestation is
inherent in consciousness.—Yoga Vashistha

Rayna had agreed to send Kamil another article by
Labor Day. Gathering all her research material, she sat
down at the computer, struggling to present an objective
picture.

> *Religion is the universal obsessional neurosis of
> humanity, Sigmund Freud once wrote. Since that
> time, many scholars of religion have asserted
> that humans have an innate need to create a
> supernatural force. The conception of a deity
> can provide comfort, order, and explanation to
> an otherwise chaotic world. It can also provide
> justification for intolerance, wars, destruction,
> genocide . . .*

She summarized the world's five foremost religions—Buddhism, Christianity, Hinduism, Islam, and Judaism. Elaborating on each denomination's philosophies, she explored the roles of peace and violence, spirituality and fanaticism, tolerance and oppression. Offering quotes from several experts, Rayna was able to make a case for the genetic disposition in humans to create a higher power—a god.

* * *

"It's too controversial," Simon argued. "Rayna is not an expert. Her take on religion could stir an international backlash. Fundamentalists will look for any excuse. Terrorism is on the rise and will get worse. Our magazine may not survive an attack like this."

But Kamil argued strongly on Rayna's behalf, pointing out that she had objectively presented her material and provided enlightenment on a subject that holds universal interest. In the end, Simon acquiesced, "You're the editor-in-chief, Kamil, so I'll defer to you. I'll also hold you responsible for the consequences."

* * *

Rayna's article generated admonishment and controversy. It also drew noteworthy praise and commendations. The magazine's circulation soared. Subscribers wanted to read more from Rayna. The media critiqued her and her work. Photographers shadowed the young journalist, clicking their cameras at every opportunity. Soon, Rayna's exquisite face flashed across magazine covers. Requests for interviews

and speaking engagements poured in. Overnight, Rayna
had become a sensation. The public was captivated.

She found the attention distressing and craved her privacy.
Discussing this new wave of events with Rami, Rayna made
a decision. Hoping to deflate the unwanted recognition, she
refused to write anything more for *InterContinental Weekly*
until after graduation. School and Rami were her priorities,
and for now she wanted to keep it that way.

* * *

Early fall brought the Jewish high holidays of Rosh
Hashanah and Yom Kippur. Nearby, Rayna had found a
Sephardic synagogue with a mostly Moroccan congregation.
The familiar liturgy and Arabic melodies reminded her of
just how much she missed her Syrian roots. When Rami
had expressed a desire to attend services with her, Rayna
cautioned, "Orthodox Judaism, like Islam, requires men
and women to be separated. And like devout Muslims, who
know the rituals and prayers as well as they know how to
breathe, orthodox Jewish men are of the same merit. Your
unfamiliarity with our ways and our Hebrew liturgy will
stand out and . . ."

"I would like to try . . . please."

"Yes," she smiled. "I'll buy tickets for both of us."

* * *

In late October, after a stressful commute in heavy rain and
bumper-to-bumper Beltway traffic, Rami and Rayna returned
home to the sound of Abe's voice on the answering machine.
From the kitchen desk, they heard, "Hello, Rayna. This is Dad.
Please call me. My new cell phone number is 718-626 . . ."

The call caught Rayna by surprise. It had been a long time. She lifted the receiver, "Dad?"

"Rayna?" There was a conspicuous pause. "Is this a bad time? I could call back."

"No, Dad, it's a good time. We just walked in the door from school."

"How is school?"

"Good. We'll graduate this year and . . ."

"I've been reading your articles. You've become quite a celebrity."

"I wouldn't quite call it that. Celebrity status is not what I want from life."

"Well, anyhow, I'm very proud of you."

"That means a lot to me. Thank you."

"I'd like to see you. I miss you."

"You're welcome to visit us. Our door is always open."

"Can I see you without the . . ."

"I know. Without the Muslim. The answer is no. Rami is my husband . . ."

"How are you?"

"I'm fine. And you?"

"At home . . . well . . . no different. But business is good. How . . . how is he treating you?"

"*He* has a name. And I'm ecstatically happy with Rami, if that's what you mean. Rami treats me with more love than I ever dreamed possible. You may have regrets, but I don't."

"Well I just wanted to hear your voice and congratulate you. That's all."

"Bye, Dad." Rayna hung up the phone before she could hear her father utter, "I love you."

* * *

The third week in December marked the beginning of Ramadan. Rami had not been inside a mosque since the imam's stinging sermon on Jewish annihilation and Islamic domination. He swore to keep his distance from the ugly rhetoric and turned to Rayna for closeness during this Islamic holy month. With her love and understanding, Rami's fasting brought new meaning. His sixth sense heightened and his connection to Allah deepened.

* * *

At the end of March 1999, Rami gave his wife a beautifully handcrafted jewelry box made from ebony and curly maple. The inscription inside the lid read: *My love for you has no beginning and no end. Happy second anniversary—Rami.*

Rayna presented her husband with a custom-made replica of La Sinagoga. The Arabic inscription on the small front door read: *El'li ma andou atiq, ma yijinou jdid.* One who does not hold onto that which is ancient, will not be able to have that which is new. *My love for you is boundless. Happy second anniversary—Rayna.*

* * *

The evening following their anniversary, Rami and Rayna celebrated the first night of Passover at the home of Marisa and Jason. Seventeen Jews and one Muslim took their places around the seder table, which was made extra long by three leaves Jason had added. Young Miriam insisted on sitting between Rayna and Rami. "Is that okay?" Marisa asked.

"Absolutely." Rayna joyfully reached out to Miriam, who climbed onto her lap.

Joseph took his seat on the other side of Rami and immediately began fidgeting with Rami's watch. Rami winked and removed the timepiece from his wrist. He put it on Joseph. "You can wear it . . . for tonight."

"Another one of our children you don't need crowding you," Marisa laughed as David started toward Rami. "David, you go sit by your father. He needs your help with the service." Unhappily, the lad did as he was told.

* * *

Rami's attention kept drifting to the matzoh that filled two plexiglass holders at opposite ends of the table. *How could anyone be so twisted with lies to believe that Jews kill non-Jewish children and use their blood to bake matzoh?* Rami never did accept the senseless, inflammatory blood libel stories, but the seeds planted in him at such a vulnerable young age did occasionally surface from their dormancy. He wanted to join the others in partaking of the matzoh, but could not bring himself to consume the unleavened bread, or even have it on his plate.

* * *

Goblets brimmed with Manischewitz blackberry wine for the adults and grape juice for Rami and the children. The traditional seder plate was placed in front of Jason. A small decorative pillow rested at his left side. Beginning the service, Jason explained the purpose of each symbolic food. David proudly pointed to the items as his father spoke. "The roasted shankbone represents the sacrificial lamb. Bitter herbs remind us of our slavery in Egypt. Charoses symbolizes the mortar we used to make bricks. Salt water depicts the tears we shed. Parsley signifies springtime and rebirth." A goblet was filled for the prophet, Elijah. A piece of matzoh was put aside for the afikomen, to be hidden so the children could search for it later. The seder began. Everyone took turns reading from their Haggadah, recounting the ancient story of Passover. Two-thirds of the way through the service, a feast fit for royalty was served. The evening ended with the merriment of Passover songs intertwined with clapping and bursts of laughter.

* * *

By the end of the week, Nolan had left for Maine to spend the Easter holiday with his daughter, Anna, and her fiancé and his family. While he was gone, Nolan's house was broken into again. The alarm triggered, bringing the police to the scene. Rami was called, since it was his name that Nolan had given to the security firm. The burglars took nothing and left no clues. At a loss, the police began questioning the neighbors.

"I have everything under control," Rami told Nolan. "Your house is locked up and I reset the alarm. Nothing was taken. I also went to the lab and checked everything there. All is okay. Relax and enjoy your Easter holiday. I will see you when you get back."

* * *

The day after Nolan's return from Maine, Rami received an anxious call. "Two men in a black van have been following me. I was on my way over to the lab, but kept on going. I'm here at Lakeforest Mall and . . ."

"Nolan, where are the men now?"

"I think they're staked out by my car, waiting for me. I'm not sure. But they're not here."

"I am on my way now. Meet you in Starbucks. Get a cup of coffee while you are waiting."

* * *

"Yousef is determined to get possession while the bacteria are in the most destructive state, while they still cannot be contained. He has no intention of waiting for you to complete the work." Over a frappuccino, Rami filled Nolan in on the details. "Yousef's power lies in his ability to threaten the world. His delusions of grandeur include holding six billion people at his mercy."

"So now what, Rami? How long do we sit here?"

"All night, if we have to. Until their patience runs out. Until those barbarians either come in here for you, or they leave. But in either case, they will be back. So, our next move, as soon as it is safe to do so . . . you are not going to like this, Nolan, but we must get over to the lab and destroy the bacteria."

"What!"

"Shhh. Keep your voice down."

"All my work, Rami. We can't . . ."

"How important will your work be to you if you are dead? Think, Nolan. You are a professor of philosophy. You taught me to look at all the angles."

"So now what?"

"We will no longer pursue this undertaking, and Yousef must never find out. As long as he believes the bacteria are within his reach, we are safe. That is the key to our survival."

* * *

In spite of the enormous stress they were under, Rami and Rayna had succeeded in graduating with high honors. They anticipated their next move—New York City and Columbia University. Rami planned to pursue a degree in international law. Rayna was determined to further her journalism studies with advanced degrees.

The couple set out in search of an apartment for their three-year stay in New York. Simon, however, beat them to it with a tempting proposal. If Rayna were willing to commit to one article a month while in graduate school, she and Rami could have exclusive use of the corporate apartment on the Upper West Side of Manhattan, rent free. It overlooked Central Park and was within walking distance of the university. "Decent housing is not only hard to come by in this city, but also very expensive." Simon's argument was persuasive. In the end, after carefully reviewing the limited options, Rayna and Rami agreed to the trade.

* * *

When Edmund learned of the couple's plans, he advised Rami to hold onto the townhouse in Bethesda. "Real estate all over Washington is booming. And besides, I hope one day you'll accept my job offer and move back here. A comparable house like yours could skyrocket, costing you double or triple what you paid. You would be smart to hold onto what you have."

So Rami spoke with Rayna, and they took Edmund's advice. They kept their home.

THIRTY

The real voyage of discovery consists not in seeking new landscapes, but in having new eyes.—— Marcel Proust

By early July, the couple were off to Greece to attend the wedding of Eli and Alexis. Rayna agonized over having to face her family. Months before the nuptials, she had told Eli that maybe it would be best if she and Rami stayed away, but Eli would not hear of it. Rayna remembered well their conversation:

"Nonsense. Rise above them. Don't give Mom the satisfaction, and don't hurt Alexis and me. Our wedding would not be complete without both of you there. Besides, Alexis is quite fond of you. At times, she jokingly says that she's marrying me just to have you for a sister-in-law."

"Really?"

"Really. And, Rayna . . ."

"What, Eli?"

"I . . . I'm not going to let anyone or anything come between us. Do you understand what I'm trying to tell you?"

"Eli, I love you. You're my brother. My very special brother. But now Alexis must come first, just as Rami must always come first with me. Do you understand what I'm saying?"

"Yes."

* * *

It was a Greek wedding with all the gaiety, music, and dancing the Greeks are known for. It was also a Sephardic wedding with all the ritualistic intent and charm that once depicted ancient Judaism at its best. Sitting together, Rami, Rayna, and Kamil were all equally touched by the significance of the ceremony, and by the warmth and joviality of the people.

During the dinner reception, Rami and Rayna glanced back and forth at Kamil, both hoping to convince him to stay on and spend a few extra days sightseeing with them. Disappointed that pressing responsibilities kept Kamil from doing so, Rayna brushed her hand over his. "Then we shall enjoy this evening of celebration."

"Yes," Kamil smiled.

Bountiful platters of assorted Greek desserts were rolled in. Rayna watched Abe make his way toward her. Uncomfortably, she squirmed, reaching for Rami's hand. Politely, Abe greeted them and asked to see his daughter alone. Uncertain, Rayna looked to Rami. He nodded, "It is okay. Kamil and I will be right here. Go with your father."

Rayna's gaze wandered toward her mother, who was sitting at a distant table. A disdainful glare oozed from Sarah's eyes. Rayna recoiled.

Abe observed the silent exchange and put his hand on his daughter's shoulder. "God knows, I have tried to soften things. But all it accomplishes is to make your mother more angry. And poor Eli. Your mother has made his life miserable because he refuses to break ties with you like your other brothers have done. I'm glad Eli is married now. If he's smart, he'll keep his distance from her."

Rayna did not respond. She followed Abe's lead and walked outside with him.

* * *

"Beautiful wedding."

"Yes, Dad, it is a beautiful wedding."

"You know, of all my four sons . . . well, Eli is special."

"Yes, Dad, he is."

Abe took Rayna's hand and held on. "Can we find somewhere quiet to sit and talk?"

Together, they walked around the back of the building and found a bench under a tree. It overlooked the water. "Do you know that Athens juts out like a peninsula into the Aegean Sea? That's what makes the climate so mild."

Rayna said nothing.

"Why did you do it?" Abe took out a monogrammed handkerchief from his pocket and dabbed at the perspiration.

Rayna prodded for clarification, "Excuse me?"

"I love you so very much. I always have. From the day you were born . . . " Abe struggled through his words. "I regret that things have not worked out for you like I had planned . . . like I had hoped."

"What were you planning? What were you hoping? What, Dad? What did you have in mind for me?"

"Marrying a Shi'ite Muslim, any Muslim, was not what I had in mind for you."

"Well, Dad, it happened."

"Why? Why did you do it?" Abe asked again.

Rayna abruptly rose. "This conversation is over."

Abe took her hand and gently nudged her back. "Please, this is difficult for me. I'm trying to understand."

"If you're really ready to understand, I'll tell you." Staring at each other, an uncomfortable silence fell between them.

Abe broke the stillness. From the inside pocket of his expensive suit jacket, he withdrew an envelope and held it out. Rayna pushed it away. "I don't want your money. It's always the money, isn't it, Dad? Do you know about anything other than money?"

Abe's eyes showed his sadness. "I will never stop loving my daughter. Can't you see that?"

"Do you think that Rami is not what's best for me because he's a Muslim? If he were a Jew, a wealthy Syrian Jew, would you think better of him?"

"Rayna, do you think that's a fair question?"

"Yes, it's a fair question. You really want to know why I married Rami? Because I love him." Unsettled, she stood to leave. Once more, Abe grasped her hand, easing Rayna down to the bench, begging her to stay.

"Do you love Mom?"

Abe hesitated.

"Do you, Dad?" She watched her father's shoulders slump as he looked away. Realizing that she had touched Abe in a vulnerable spot, Rayna put her arm around him, "You don't, do you?"

"No." His response was barely audible.

"Have you ever loved Mom?"

"Once. Maybe. It's been so long, I don't even remember."

"Is there someone else?"

"There was someone else." Abe looked ashamed.

"It's okay. I'm not judging you. What happened?"

"She wasn't Jewish. I was married. She was married. I had a family. My reputation in the Syrian community . . ."

"Do you still love her?"

"Yes."

"But you walked away. You gave up love. Life is full of trade-offs, isn't it, Dad?"

"Yes."

"I never intended to marry a non-Jew. Rami never intended to marry anyone but a Shi'ite. I didn't do this to hurt you. But with Rami . . . our love is powerful. At first, I tried to fight it. But I couldn't. Fate overruled everything standing in its way."

"Does he love you as much?"

"More."

"I wish I had your courage." Tears of affection filled Abe's eyes. "You are incredibly special, and I will always love you. It doesn't matter what your mother thinks. I'm not ready to disown my daughter."

"Rami and I are a package deal."

"He's a lucky man."

"And a good man."

Abe held out the envelope. "Please take this."

Rayna accepted, knowing just what to do with it. She and Rami would soon open an orphanage and start a school for very young children who might otherwise be doomed to a life with drug-addicted, abusive parents.

* * *

Later that evening, when Rami and Rayna returned to the hotel, they found a message waiting. *Just got news. Be at American Embassy in Damascus day after tomorrow. Soon have green card. Short flight from Greece to Syria. Call as soon as you can. Will discuss details then.*

The couple had waited a long time for this. The communiqué came from Rami's lawyer, who had been working diligently to pull strings and call in favors to change Rami's immigration status to permanent resident of the United States. In their hotel room, Rami placed an overseas call to Washington. Although relieved that the ordeal would soon be over, he worried about traveling back to Syria and about leaving Rayna alone in Athens.

"It's just for two days. I'll be fine," she said. "I'll visit the Archaeology Museum, and I'll go shopping. I'll save the Acropolis for when you return. We'll tour it together."

"I cannot go and leave you here alone in this strange city. It is not safe. If something were to happen to you . . . I am not going." Rami's words seemed final.

"Go to Syria and get it over with. We've waited a long time for this." Softly, she brushed her lips to his.

"I wish I could take you with me."

"But you can't. Jews are not welcome in Syria."

"The way of the world gives me so much pain."

"I know it does."

* * *

Arriving in Damascus early in the day, Rami rented a car and drove to the American Embassy. After signing the papers put before him, Rami turned his passport over to a gentleman who told him to return the following afternoon. "All of your papers are in order. Everything is moving along smoothly. Give us twenty-four hours to process the rest of the documents."

Uneasy about leaving his passport, but having no other choice, Rami regretted coming to Syria. He looked at his watch, then checked into a nearby hotel. From the room, he called Rayna. She was out. He left a message. After stopping for lunch, he slipped behind the wheel of the rental car and drove two hours north on Highway 5 toward Aleppo. Rayna filled his mind. He fretted about leaving her alone in Athens.

* * *

Maneuvering the old, narrow streets, Rami approached the once-familiar Babal-Qinnisrine Gate. He parked the car and entered the courtyard of his old family home. He looked around. Not much had changed. His father's old Mercedes was nowhere in sight and Rami assumed that his parents were still at the souq. He knocked at the door, hoping his sisters were home from school.

Slowly, the door cracked, then flung open. "Rami! Rami!" Jawhara burst with excitement. He followed his sister into the small kitchen. Eman, the youngest, curiously examined him. She was a toddler when Rami had gone away, and she did not recognize him.

"My, how you both have grown," he spoke in Syrian. Kneeling down to Eman's level, Rami winked, "You are very pretty. Do you know the last time I saw you, you were only three, and this high?" Rami gestured with his hand. "How old are you now?"

Eman smiled. "Six." She opened her mouth wide and jiggled a loose tooth. "These two already fell out," she proudly pointed to the two empty spaces.

"Wow! That means you are getting to be grown up like your sisters." Rami placed his arms around Eman's waist. It felt good to be back home.

Jawhara set out a dish of *ka'ak*.

"Tell me, Jawhara, where are Eby and Imee? Come sit and talk with me. I want to know all about you since I left."

"Eby and Imee are at the souq, but they will be home soon."

"Where is Maha?"

"She is married."

When Rami asked more questions, the two sisters chattered incessantly, competing for his attention. Rami smiled with amusement, delighting in the sounds of their babble. Then, Jawhara accidentally let it slip, "We are not allowed to talk about you. Eby said you are dead, but . . ."

"It is okay. You must do what Eby says. But I am not dead. Here, pinch me." He pretended to be hurt. "Ouch! You see, I am not dead."

The girls giggled.

The front door opened. "Who is here?" Salha called out. Rami stood quietly as she came into the kitchen. Salha stopped suddenly. Her eyes focused on Rami. Then, with a burst of joy, she cried, "Rami! Rami! My son! My son!"

"What is all the commotion?" Ibrahim shouted as he came through the doorway carrying a bag of food.

"Ibrahim, come here. Come see."

Rami's presence in the kitchen was unexpected. Ibrahim's nostrils flared. His breathing accelerated. Glaring at his son, Ibrahim slowly put down the groceries. He stretched out his arms and eased his two daughters behind him. Then he motioned for Salha to move away from Rami.

"Tell me. Is it true?" Ibrahim demanded to know.

Rami said nothing.

"Ibrahim," Salha naively interfered, "Rami is back. He is not dead. Why did you tell us . . ."

"Sssssss." Not taking his eyes from Rami, Ibrahim made a hissing sound to quiet Salha. "Tell me, Rami, is it true?"

Rami remained silent.

"Answer me!"

Guardedly, Rami nodded.

Ibrahim erupted in wild madness. "Get out! Get out of my house! Do not ever come back here! You are not my son! I am not your father! Take your demons and your evil ways. Get your rotting Jewish filth out of my house before I strike you dead."

A cold sweat snaked across Rami's body. Swirls of blackness cut into his vision. For a moment, he thought he would collapse. He grabbed onto a chair to steady himself. Staggering, Rami backed himself out of the premises.

* * *

Reaching the car, his hands trembled as he tried to put the key in the ignition. When he stepped down on the brake, his foot shook so that it kept slipping off the pedal. For several minutes, Rami sat frozen behind the wheel, trying to make sense out of what had just happened.

The episode marked the end of Rami's past. Parents, family, home, friends, country. *Never again. I cannot ever come back.* Aching for the warmth and comfort of Rayna's love, Rami prayed to Allah to keep her safe until he returned. *The sooner I leave this place, the better.* He turned the car around and drove out the Babal-Qinnisrine Gate for the last time.

* * *

Easing herself between the sheets, Rayna propped up two pillows behind her head. From the nightstand, she lifted *The Haj* by Leon Uris, a book she had brought to read on the trip. In the hotel room, she waited. *Almost three hours late.* Rayna worried. She called to check on flight arrivals. A loud knock jolted her. "Yes, who is it?"

"Rrawhee, it is me."

Flinging the door open, she threw her arms around his neck, "I've been so worried. I was afraid something happened to you . . . did you get it?"

With his foot, Rami nudged the door shut, put his carry-on bag down, and bolted the lock. "Yes, I got it. I can now live with you in America, forever." He flooded Rayna with kisses and swooped her to the bed. "I could not have stood another moment away from you."

Being so close to Rami, she sensed his troubled state. "Something happened. What is it?"

"Right now, I need for us to love . . ."

"You went to Halab, didn't you?"

"I can never keep anything from you, can I?"

"No, you can't. Tell me everything, from the moment you left here."

Recounting his time in Syria, Rami described, at great length, the visit to his family home. Rayna brought him into the tranquility of her arms. "We have each other. We always will."

THIRTY-ONE

And the dust returns to the ground as it was, and the lifebreath returns to God who bestowed it.—Ecclesiastes 12:7

At age twenty-three, Rami and Rayna were less than a year away from completing their graduate work at Columbia University. Rayna stood by her agreement with Simon, writing a monthly column for the magazine in exchange for the corporate apartment in Manhattan. Circulation numbers at *InterContinental Weekly* continued to climb, and the growing demand for Rayna's column brought her increased recognition, awards, and honors.

She wrote about deaths and mutilations from the abundance of land mines still lingering along the landscapes in countries like Colombia and Cambodia. Her commentaries revealing the global infiltration by the Russian Mafia exposed Rayna to threats and intimidation by mobsters. Pointing to the powerful lobbyists in Washington, Rayna disclosed the omnipotent influence over Congress by the oil and drug companies, and by the health care, insurance, and financial industries. She also delved into the serious threat of water depletion and water contamination that would gravely affect the world's population in the years ahead.

After an assignment to Bhopal, India, Rayna reported on the plight of its citizens, who continue to be exposed to poisonous leaks from a defunct chemical plant. She wrote, in detail, about the noxious fumes still seeping into the air, water, and soil, sickening and killing thousands in that poverty-stricken region of India.

Rayna expounded on the world's global-warming problem and took issue with President George W. Bush for pulling America out of its commitment to the Kyoto Agreement. She mapped out the hazards of the earth's growing population, from two billion in 1945 to six billion in 2001, and offered practical solutions that went unheeded by world leaders. On another issue, she sized up the dangers yet to come from the growing acts of terrorism in the world, suggesting that no country was immune from Islamic fundamentalists, including America.

Because of Rayna's many informative, well-researched, and controversial articles, she was both loved and hated, adulated and reproached. The list of supporters and enemies seemed to change daily. Much was written about her. Tabloids speculated on Rayna's private life. The rich and famous added her to their guest lists. Requests for speaking engagements and interviews poured in. The paparazzi snapped their cameras at every opportunity, making Rayna a much-photographed personality. The public had a fascination with her, and the media were determined to satisfy their audiences.

Celebrity status became a double-edged sword. Writing about the injustices on the planet had become a passion. The infringements on her privacy had brought greater disturbances to her already unrestful life. More and more, Rayna and Rami explored alternative measures to protect their space.

* * *

Basketball became Rami's diversion. He, Eli, and Kamil played at least two evenings a week and sometimes on Sunday mornings. The men were indeed the Three Musketeers, just as Rayna had labeled them. High levels of trust, dependence, and comfort safeguarded the trio's strong bond.

Moreover, an extraordinary relationship blossomed between Rayna and Alexis. The two women shared confidences, relied on one another, and talked with or saw each other daily. Their connection was further strengthened when Eli and Alexis purchased an apartment in the same high-rise, one floor below Rami and Rayna. The four were consistently sensitive to always include Kamil in their tightly-knit family. The group of five were as close as kindred spirits could be.

However, there was one issue that separated Rami and Kamil from the rest. It was their obsessive preoccupation with assassinating Yousef. Although their goals were the same, their approaches differed. Kamil believed that it was essential to procure Omar's help in order to be successful. Rami did not trust Omar.

* * *

Awakened from a deep sleep in the wee hours of Tuesday morning, September 11, 2001, Rami lifted the receiver. "Yes . . . hello?" He was perturbed by the initial silence from the other end. "Who *is* this?"

"Rami." The voice was muffled.

"Yes? Who is this?" Annoyed, he glanced at the clock on the nightstand.

"It is Omar."

"Omar! It is four in the morning. Are you all right?"

"Just listen. If anyone knows I have contacted you, I will be a dead man."

Rami was instantly alert.

"A few hours from now, there will be major attacks on New York and Washington. Keep Rayna out of the World Trade Center. I know she works there."

"Omar?" Rami jerked upright. "Omar? Omar!" Omar was no longer on the line. Rami broke into a cold sweat. He looked at the tiny screen on the telephone for a caller ID number, but the reading displayed an unknown communication. He dialed star-six-nine for a call-back, but the recording indicated an unrecognizable international call.

Half awake, Rayna touched Rami's unclad back, feeling the dampness of his skin. "What is it?"

"Today, you will not go into the office, and we will not go to school. That was Omar. I do not know where he called from. I only know what he said. In a few hours, there will be major attacks on New York and Washington. Omar warned me to keep you out of the World Trade Center."

"What are you talking about? Do you believe him?"

"Yes, I think I do."

The lighted dial on the digital clock showed 4:05 AM. Rami kissed Rayna's forehead, then picked up his cell phone and dialed Kamil.

* * *

"If you're smart, you and Rayna will tell no one of Omar's call," Kamil warned. "Remember, Rami, you're a Muslim from Syria. If America is attacked, it will be by Islamic radicals. The American government will look for scapegoats. Be careful you're not one of them. If this is a hoax, you'll be accused of incitement and held suspect. Either way, you lose. Believe me, I know what I'm talking about. I beg of you, Rami, keep your mouth shut. Don't bring attention to yourself, or to Rayna. Let me handle this. I'll call Simon right now."

"But . . ."

"Try not to use your cell phone. And definitely do not use your house line."

"But . . ."

"Puhleeze Rami, listen to me! America has a big intelligence network. There are at least fourteen government intelligence agencies. Someone must know something. If they're not already on top of this, then the security of America is in big trouble."

* * *

Not knowing if this were a hoax or something real, Simon chose to err on the side of the latter. He instructed Kamil to contact Marianne, the receptionist. "She keeps an employee list at home, in case of emergencies. Have her call everyone. She's to be quick and to the point. If anyone begins to question, tell her to cut them short. No one is to come to work today. No one! These are my orders. Anyone disobeying will be fired on the spot. Simple as that. And Kamil, don't reveal the reason for the calls. Just tell her to do it."

"I'll get on it immediately."

"Kamil . . ."

"Yes, Simon."

"Anyone and everyone you know who will listen and has the clout to do something, call them."

After ending the call with Kamil, Simon then proceeded to call the mayor's office, the governor's office, the FBI, and the CIA. He even called the White House. With each call, he either got a recording or someone took a message. Even the direct lines he dialed were met with, "Call back later in the morning during business hours." Simon knew he was not well liked. *InterContinental Weekly's* critical reporting on the new Bush administration and how they came into power by a decision of the Supreme Court angered many in Washington circles. Orders had been given not to speak with anyone from *InterContinental Weekly*. Frustrated, Simon turned to a trusted reporter from the *Washington Post* who promised to get word to the White House.

In those early morning hours, Kamil also made several calls. No one would attach any urgency to his report. Outraged, Kamil prayed that this was all a bad dream.

* * *

Turning on the radio and television, Rami and Rayna hoped for some early morning news about the threat of an attack. Nothing. Not even a hint of it was reported. They showered, dressed, forced down a bowl of cereal, and waited, not sure of what to do next.

At seven-thirty, Rayna called her brother. She got the answering machine and left a message. She tried his cell phone and got another recording. Aware of Eli's routine, Rayna knew that he rarely woke before eight. And since his marriage, Eli had begun each day by meeting Alexis for breakfast at Mount Sinai Medical Center, where she was doing her residency. So Rayna dialed her sister-in-law. "Good morning, Alexis."

"Hi, Rayna. I'm so exhausted. I haven't had a break since eleven last night. These twelve-hour shifts are wearing me thin, and the ER has been unusually busy this morning. I can't wait to get back to the apartment and sleep all afternoon."

"You and Eli come for dinner tonight. One less thing to worry about."

"Rayna, thanks. You're the best. Can we eat around eight-thirty? Then Eli can drive me straight to the hospital."

"Eight-thirty is good. The Three Musketeers are playing basketball at six . . . Alexis, where's Eli? I've been trying to call him."

"When I spoke with him an hour ago, he had just gotten out of the shower and was on his way to a meeting at the World Trade Center. Last night, your Dad called. He wants Eli to close some big real-estate deal this morning. Rayna, I've got to go. Try Eli again later. He's probably tied up in that meeting and has his cell turned off."

Rayna tried several more times to reach Eli. She continued to get his voice recording. "Rami, I want to walk over to the World Trade Center."

"Absolutely not. Given what we know, you are not going near the place."

"I won't go inside the building."

"No."

Rayna coaxed, pestered, and cajoled until Rami un-willingly agreed. "We will go together, but you are not to be out of my sight, not for a second. Do we agree?"

"Yes."

* * *

Outside the apartment building, the morning air was already muggy. Remnants of clouds drifted out toward the Hudson River. The couple walked south on Central Park West into Midtown, cut over to the West Side Highway, and reached the World Trade Center site at 8:35. Rami and Rayna looked up at the two magnificent towers, then watched as thousands of people scurried to work, scampering through the entranceways. Staring at each other, they wanted to scream at the top of their lungs and warn everyone to go back home. Rami placed his arm firmly around Rayna's waist, restraining her from getting too near the building.

"I'm worried about Eli. I don't know where he is. I want to warn him." She reached into her tote, searching for her cell phone. "I'll call my father . . ." Suddenly, a loud noise rumbled from overhead. A low-flying jet was aimed straight toward the north tower. "Oh my God," Rayna uttered, as if in desperate prayer. "Please, God. No."

At 8:46, the plane plunged into the skyscraper at the ninety-sixth floor, igniting more than twenty thousand gallons of fuel. Flames spewed forth from the upper levels. Rami and Rayna could hardly comprehend what they were seeing. Fire trucks stormed in. Police rushed to the scene. People in the streets fled incoherently in all directions. Rami pulled Rayna away from the melee. At 8:59, the ringing of her cell phone startled them. Rayna reached into her tote and brought the phone to her ear. "Eli!"

"What's all that noise? Where are you, Rayna?"

"Where are you?" she howled.

"Dad sent me to close some big real-estate deal. I had to disappear for an hour to give the clients and their lawyers a chance to digest my proposal. Right now, I'm standing in front of your office on the ninety-first floor, but the doors are locked. Why is your office closed today? I thought we could get some breakfast and . . ."

"Eli, get out of the building! Get out now! The other tower is up in flames. A plane flew right into it. Get out of the building!" she yelled frantically. "Oh, God, Eli, get out of the building! I don't know what's happening. I don't know what's happening . . ." Rayna heard a click and then silence. "Eli!" she screeched. "Eli! Eli!"

Another low-flying aircraft swiftly approached. There was no mistake of its target. At 9:03, the jet crashed into the south tower at the eightieth floor. Blasting a hole through the adjacent side of the building, the plane wiped out many of the supporting columns and engulfed the structure in a rapidly expanding inferno.

In horror, Rami and Rayna watched the remaining columns of the south tower buckle and the top portion slump. Rami's limbs went weak. "Please, Allah. Do not take Eli . . ."

Rayna clutched at her throat and wailed, "Eli! Eli! Eli!" Crazed, she pounded her fists into her chest, "Take me, God! Take me! Please, God, not Eli. Oh, God, let Eli live." Rayna sank to the ground sobbing.

Rami lifted her up. Running, he carried Rayna away from the sight. Desperately, she clung to him. Fifty-six minutes after it was hit, the structure crumbled, floor by floor, in ten seconds.

From a distance, they witnessed more devastation. At 10:28, the floors of the north tower pancaked, progressively collapsing the edifice from within. In eight seconds, the north tower was no more.

Incinerated bodies lay in smoldering heaps. Indistinguishable mounds of debris blanketed the carnage. Black clouds of smoke billowed overhead, choking oxygen from the air. Policemen fought back the frenzied masses. Firefighters worked fearlessly to save lives and extinguish the mighty flames. The site looked like a war zone, a place in perdition. Twenty-eight hundred people were dead. Three hundred were firefighters.

Mangled by grief and confusion, Rami and Rayna roamed mindlessly through the surrounding streets. Then, precipitously, they pushed their way through the hordes of people and raced toward Mount Sinai Medical Center.

* * *

Out of breath, they jolted through the doors of the emergency wing, stressing an urgency to see Doctor Mishan.

Alexis walked toward them. The emergency room was already being inundated with the wounded. "What is it? Here, come sit. I only have a minute. We're short on staff given the crisis on our hands, and I've been told that I will be working all day."

"Alexis . . . Alexis . . ." Rami mumbled, tears streaming down his cheeks.

"What is it? What's wrong?"

The color in Rayna's face faded. Her eyeballs rolled back and her body spiraled downward. Rami caught his wife and eased her onto the vinyl sofa. Alexis grabbed at Rami's shirt. "What's wrong? Where's Eli? What's wrong, Rami?"

Rami struggled to put into words what he must say. "Eli . . . Eli . . . Alexis . . . Eli was in the south tower . . . ninety-first floor . . . "

"No! No!" Crazed, she reached into the pocket of her white medical coat for her cell phone. Nervously, she dialed Eli.

Rami gently removed the phone from her hand, turned it off, and returned it to Alexis's pocket. "Alexis, Eli was trapped. Eli is . . . he did not have a chance. His soul is now with God . . . up in heaven."

Hysterically, Alexis beat on Rami's chest, then fell to her knees sobbing. Rami lowered himself to Alexis and held her. They cried together.

THIRTY-TWO

On Rosh Hashanah it is written and on Yom Kippur it is sealed: How many shall leave this world and how many shall be born into it; who shall rest and who shall wander; who shall be at peace and who shall be tormented.——The Rabbinical Assembly in the Mahzor

"Alexis is sleeping. The doctor gave her a sedative." Rayna blotted her swollen eyes with a tissue. "I'm going downstairs to stay with Alexis tonight. I won't leave her alone." She looked at Rami. His eyes were red and puffy. "My dad is with her right now. He doesn't want to go home." Her voice cracked and she cried.

"Your father can sleep here in the guest room. He can stay with us for as long as he wants . . . as long as he needs. It will be okay." Rami touched Rayna's hand. They found comfort in the moment.

Rayna shifted her gaze toward Kamil. Her lower lip quivered. "Now there are only two musketeers."

Grief stricken, Kamil had been quietly studying the affection between Rami and Rayna. An emptiness had been gnawing away at his restless spirit for a time longer than he could remember. Kamil's eyes watered. Rayna's words had pounded in the reality of his own suffering. He would never again see Eli. Closing his eyes, Kamil felt Eli's energy. Eli had become more than a close friend. He had become a brother. It was Eli who stood by him through an acrimonious divorce from Maddy, and a contentious custody battle for Nida. It was Eli who secured a place for him in their family. It was Eli who introduced him to the exhilarating world of basketball. Eli's zest for life was contagious. *How could this happen? Why did this happen?* Kamil mourned Eli's passing as greatly as the others did.

Rayna knelt down beside him. "Kamil, Rami and I want you to be here with us tonight. I'll make up the sofa."

"Thank you." He found Rayna's presence comforting. "I'm sorry you lost your brother. I'm sorry we all lost Eli." Kamil's voice splintered and he fought to keep the sorrow from completely overtaking him. "I'll do anything, whatever I can to help Alexis through this . . . to help all of us through this."

"Thank you, Kamil. A while ago, I spoke with Alexis's mother. As soon as her parents can leave Greece, they will come and take her home. Right now, all flights into the United States are cancelled indefinitely."

* * *

"The FBI, the CIA, I don't know who else, but they'll ask questions. I lied to Simon. I told him that the anonymous call at four in the morning was on my line and that my caller ID showed an unrecognizable international communication. Simon and I will be interrogated. So will everyone at

InterContinental Weekly, including you and Rayna. Everyone will be suspect."

"But Omar's call cannot be traced. It was an . . ."

"It's not that simple, Rami. Your call to me can be traced. They'll want to know why you, or Rayna, phoned me at four in the morning. You need to have a credible explanation, one that we both can coordinate and live with."

"I will work on it, Kamil. But another time. Right now, I cannot think straight."

* * *

Immersed at Ground Zero for two weeks, Rami, Rayna, Kamil, and Abe were determined to stay close to Alexis. They were not going to let her crumble. Ironically, consoling Alexis brought all of them comfort.

Wavering between hope and despair, the grieving clan displayed Eli's photos and looked for information on each body that was pulled from the wreckage. They investigated every name as it became known. They made daily inquiries at the hospitals and the city morgue. Abe blamed himself for sending his son into that early morning meeting. Rami and Rayna faulted themselves for not trying to reach Eli earlier in the morning, while he was still at home. Kamil condemned himself for not being more persistent in trying to reach others who might have been able to prevent the tragedy. Tormented, they all beat themselves into emotional turbulence.

* * *

By late September, Alexis's parents were finally able to get a flight into New York. They came from Greece to take her home. Reluctantly, she went back with them. One month later, she returned to New York and threw herself into her residency at the hospital.

* * *

"We understand all of your staff was ordered *not* to go to work the morning of September eleventh. Why did you instruct your receptionist to make those calls? What did you know that we didn't know?" The FBI agent was intent on grilling Simon to a pulp.

"I knew a whole lot less than you did. If you had heeded the warning signs. If you had followed up on your reports and leads. If someone had taken my calls seriously. If you had done your job . . ." Strong and outspoken, Simon refused to be intimidated.

* * *

"Muslim fundamentalists would like to see you dead because of the things you write. You expose too much of their destructive side, too many of their secrets. You're a hindrance to their jihadi cause." From across the desk, the FBI agent baited Kamil.

Kamil did not respond. He only stared in defiance at the man.

"Don't play games with me. I want the truth or . . ."

"Or what? I'm giving you the truth." Kamil's anger was escalating. "Why now? Why didn't you investigate this before September eleventh?"

The agent ignored Kamil's questions. "Rayna Mishan, or her husband, phoned you around four in the morning on September eleventh. We traced it. Why would either of them call at such an hour?"

Arrogantly, Kamil shook his head and shrugged his shoulders.

"I think we've had enough for today. Be back here at nine sharp tomorrow."

* * *

Weeks of questioning persisted. The FBI traced phone lines and searched the homes of all employees at the magazine. Frustrated, they found nothing. Moreover, to the embarrassment of both the FBI and CIA, their investigations turned up several calls made by Simon and Kamil, who both had tried to alert the proper people. Their stories had proven credible.

When the FBI turned their inquiries on Rami and Rayna, questioning them separately, the two were prepared. Conditioned by Kamil's drilling, the couple had coordinated and rehearsed their stories.

Rami had answered the phone. No idea who called at four in the morning. Caller ID showed no identity. Check with the phone company; they keep records. The cell phone was lost on campus. Did not discover it missing until the following day. With the devastation of the attacks and losing Eli, did not report the cell phone missing for two days. There is a record of that, too. Kamil's number was stored in memory dial and was always the first to come up. Whoever found my cell must have dialed Kamil, purposely or accidentally. This is how you traced the number to us. That is all I can tell you.

In reality, Kamil had taken Rami's cell and destroyed it, never again to be found.

* * *

The two agencies found themselves inundated with chaos and confusion, information and misinformation, and mounting revelations of failures and incompetencies. FBI and CIA staff members scrambled to conceal evidence of their own bunglings in the wake of a congressional investigation. Simon and Kamil were no longer significant. Neither were Rami and Rayna. "Do not waste time chasing false leads," came orders from above.

* * *

At their temporary offices in Midtown Manhattan, Kamil and Rayna teamed up to channel their energies into making Eli's death not pass in vain. Together, they wrote about the great failings within the American government, exposing every flaw they could uncover. They pressed for a full inquiry into September eleventh, and stood in support of the victims' families. They also wrote extensively about the spread of Islamism, delving into topics ranging from the quest for new world dominance, inhumane logic of suicide terrorism, Wahabiism and the Quran in Saudi Arabi, the rise of Osama bin Laden, and the inferior status of Muslim women. Parading the facts on the pages of *InterContinental Weekly* brought them threats, plaudits, and greater celebrity status. Requests for interviews and speaking engagements escalated. After a time, Rayna eased off. She had to finish school and was emotionally exhausted.

* * *

The ensuing months wove stronger links between the five individuals who had been so solidly tied to Eli. Rami, Rayna, Kamil, and Abe hovered over Alexis. Rayna prepared meals and made sure that Alexis ate. Rami did her laundry. Kamil chauffeured her back and forth to the hospital, no matter what time her shifts began or ended. Abe took breakfast to her every morning and sat with her, just as Eli had done. Their presence was the saving grace in Alexis's life.

* * *

Deliberately, Kamil began nurturing a romance with Alexis. He spent more and more hours with her and paid special attention to her needs, although she asked for little. Their long talks about Eli brought comfort, laughter, tears, and healing. When Kamil detailed the gruesome butchering of his own family during the Hamah massacre, Alexis responded with tenderness and compassion. Over time, their talks expanded beyond their grief. Kamil's boundless curiosity about medicine never failed to bring a response from Alexis, although she sometimes teased him about wanting to know in one day what it took her years to learn. Her limitless desire to know more about the world always generated long recitals from Kamil.

* * *

By June 2002, Kamil was sure that he wanted to spend the rest of his life with Alexis. She had captured his heart. Alexis was intelligent and kind. She had an unassuming manner. And she doted on Nida. Her short blonde hair fell softly around her face, accentuating her large doe-shaped green eyes. Light freckles dotted her flawless complexion. Her slender frame almost reached Kamil's height. Alexis looked more Scandinavian than Mediterranean. To Kamil, Alexis was beautiful inside and out. He was hypnotized.

* * *

Early one evening in late July, after finishing dinner at a neighborhood restaurant, the two leisurely strolled back to Alexis's apartment. The sun from the long summer day still brightened the sky. Out on the street, people emerged from the subway, or disembarked from a bus. The workday had ended. The hustle and bustle of city life had softened. Kamil took Alexis's hand. When she did not pull away, he hoped it was a sign that she would accept him completely into her life, just as she once had done with Eli. "Alexis, in you, I have found the love of my life. I don't ever want to lose you."

* * *

In Judaism, if there is no body, then there cannot be a burial. Without a burial, there is no funeral.

"Rayna, I need to talk with you. You know how much I loved your brother . . . and I need you to help me." Rayna's arms reached out to Alexis. The two women hugged.

"I want to do right by Eli. His family and friends deserve to say goodbye to him. I want Eli to know how many lives he touched in his short time on earth. I want him to know that he will always have a special place inside each of us. I want a memorial service for my husband. To celebrate his memory, his goodness, his life. To say goodbye, and wish him well, wherever he may be."

"Of course, I will help you. We'll plan a very moving service."

"Rayna . . . Rayna . . . ummm . . . there's something else."

"What is it?"

Alexis stumbled, "Ummm, well . . . nothing. Nothing."

"It's something. Please tell me what it is."

"Why did you marry Rami? Why did you marry a Muslim?"

"Because my love for Rami runs so deep. I cannot put it into words. I can only feel it. Why do you ask?"

"Is it possible, in one's lifetime, to love two men with the same intensity and passion?"

"You love Kamil, don't you?"

"Are you angry?"

"No, Alexis, I'm not angry."

"I'm terrified and full of guilt. I didn't mean for it to happen. To betray Eli. To love a Muslim, knowing what it will do to my family."

"Does Kamil know?"

"Yes. He loves me as much. I think more."

"Kamil is a good man. Eli was quite fond of him, remember? He adopted Kamil, made him his brother."

"I remember," Alexis smiled.

"In the Tanakh, when a married man died, the brother of the dead man was obligated to marry his widow. Remember the story of Judah and his daughter-in-law, Tamar?"

"So I am not betraying Eli?"

"No." Rayna embraced her sister-in-law. "Let your love flow again. Start a new chapter. Destiny has brought you both together by a most unexpected circumstance."

* * *

On Wednesday, September 11, 2002, mid-week between the two holiest times on the Jewish calendar, Rosh Hashanah and Yom Kippur, a memorial service was held for Eli. It had been exactly one year. The whole country was remembering and mourning the senseless deaths of so many Americans.

Hundreds of people filled the sanctuary in the big shul on Ocean Parkway. Many eulogies were given. Abe honored his son. Alexis glorified her husband. Relatives and close friends praised the young man who had always been so full of zest and who had left an indelible mark on so many.

Rayna wanted to speak about her brother, to pay tribute to the person she loved so much, to thank him for all he was, for all he had done. But she could not. A large crowd from the Syrian community was there. The rabbis were there. All had condemned her for marrying a Muslim. *I must honor my brother's memory and the sacredness of this service. My speaking out will only serve to trigger the ire of these people and spoil the reverence for Eli.* Rayna lifted her eyes to the heavens, hoping Eli could know her thoughts. *You will always be with me, Eli. My memories will keep you alive. Rami and I will name our first son after you, and he will know you.* Sitting quietly next to her husband, she placed her hand in his, knowing how much he and Kamil wanted to speak, knowing how unwise it would have been to do so. The service went on for more than two hours. There was not a dry eye in the room.

* * *

A catered lunch in the social hall followed. Sarah purposely cornered Rayna in the ladies' room. "You have guts showing up here with that Muslim. This community doesn't want you. None of us want you. I suggest you leave now, and never come back!"

Just when Rayna thought her tears had finally dried up, they flooded her eyes once again. "Hasn't Eli's death taught you anything? Will there ever be forgiveness, Mom?"

"Forgive you? Never! And don't *ever* again refer to me as 'mom', because I'm no longer your mother. I disowned you five years ago."

* * *

In late December of that year, after the Muslim holy month of Ramadan, Kamil and Alexis were married by a reform rabbi in a quiet ceremony in Manhattan. Rami and Rayna served as their witnesses.

Taking Kamil aside, Rami's eyes watered and a lump caught in his throat. "Eli left you his greatest treasure . . . his wife."

"I will cherish Eli's gift and thank him every day for entrusting me with Alexis. My sadness is that Eli had to die for this to happen. I will always miss him."

"Not a day passes that I do not think of Eli . . . *mabrook*, Kamil. Congratulations. This is your wedding day. Let it be full of joy." Embracing, the two men searched each other's faces. A deep-seated root had begun to stir.

* * *

By late spring of 2003, Professor Nolan's nerves were frayed from strange Arab men trailing him at all hours. America was at war in Iraq. Yousef, backed by the Syrian government, was leading a major insurgency in that country.

He desperately wanted the bacteria. If he did not get what he wanted within the month, Nolan, Rami, and Rami's Jewish wife would be dead before summer was out. One by one, he would cut them into pieces.

* * *

After graduating with honors, Rami and Rayna moved back to their home in Bethesda. Rayna had just entered her fifth month of pregnancy. In early fall, she and Rami would have a son. They would name him Elijah, after her brother, Eli. Rayna planned to stay at home, write a book, and enjoy motherhood. Rami decided to accept Edmund's offer to launch an international division in the firm's legal department. His job would begin after Labor Day. The summer agenda was already formed. Rami and Kamil were going to assassinate Yousef.

* * *

When Yousef called Rami demanding that he fly into the Triple Frontier with the bacteria and formula in hand, Rami explained that it would be too risky to bring the bacteria onto a commercial flight. "Airport security in America is tighter than it has ever been. The bacteria would be confiscated," Rami said.

Yousef exploded like lava spewing forth from an erupting volcano. "Damn you, Rami! I have a war in Iraq to fight. You bring me the bacteria, or I will personally string your heads across Baghdad for the whole world to see. Yours, Nolan's, and that Jewish whore you call your wife."

"Yousef, you shall have the bacteria." Time was no longer on his side. Rami worried about Rayna and the baby.

He wanted this nightmare to end. Yousef's death was his only hope.

"You will receive instructions to fly into a border town in Texas. From there, you will cross into Mexico. A private aircraft will be waiting at a designated landing strip. You are to turn over the bacteria and the formula to the pilot. No more games, Rami. You've run out of time."

THIRTY-THREE

Never believe that a few caring people can't change the world. For, indeed, that's all who ever have.—Margaret Mead

After dinner, Rayna went into the study to write her column. Rami cleaned up the kitchen, ran a load of laundry, and sat down to read the latest issue of *InterContinental Weekly*, but he could not concentrate. Restlessly, he paced the house, then stood in the doorway of the study. "When will you be done?"

"Rami, are you okay? Come talk to me."

In the study, he knelt down at Rayna's side. His hand rested on her abdomen. "I love you. I love our son."

Rayna saved her work, then put the iMac to sleep. Swiveling around in the black leather desk chair, she faced her husband, "Let's go into the family room."

* * *

Together, on the sofa, Rami laid his head in Rayna's lap. An unsettling stillness enveloped them. She stroked his forehead and buried her fingers in his hair. Rami glanced up and smiled, "I just felt our son move."

"He's been doing that a lot today." Lowering her head, she grazed his lips. "I want to know what's going on." Rami vacillated. Concerned, Rayna urged him on. Slowly, everything that Rami had been keeping from her, he now unleashed. She listened to all that he said. "So Yousef intends to get rid of you, and Nolan, and me. But you and Kamil plan to kill him before he does. And you need Omar's help to carry it off. Do I have it right, so far?"

Rami nodded. "Kamil will not rest until he extracts vengeance for the murder of his family. And I will not rest until you and our son are safe. Kamil believes that with Omar's help, we can do it."

"And you? What do you believe? Do you think Omar will help you? Can you trust him?"

"I only know I cannot go on like this. I cannot sit back and let Yousef destroy us."

Suddenly, a bolt of lightning flashed in the large bay window. Within seconds, claps of thunder roared across the sky. Heavy rains quickly followed. Big hailstones pounded against the house. Fierce winds rattled the windowpanes. The lights flickered. Once. Twice. The house went dark. On the sofa, protected from the summer storm, they made love.

* * *

The lights flickered again, then glowed. The tempestuous uproar had moved on to new territory. Rayna scanned Rami's troubled face, "I'm really scared. The last time you went to South America, you almost didn't come back. We both know what Yousef is capable of. He has a lot of people eager to do his bidding, including Abdallah." Rayna needed to think. She needed time to work this through in her head.

The cuckoo on the fireplace mantel made itself known. It was eleven o'clock. Rayna reached for the remote on the large mahogany coffee table. She clicked on PBS.

> *Good evening and welcome to BBC News. Here are today's headlines. Across Zimbabwe, President Robert Mugabe is operating mandatory terrorist training camps for boys as young as the age of six. Israel retaliates for three suicide attacks that killed eleven and injured scores more. And a professor from the University of Maryland has been abducted and beheaded. Now the news.*

Stunned, Rami lurched upright. Rayna let out a frightful noise. Their deepest fears were coming to life.

> *Doctor Quintin Nolan, a professor of chemistry and philosophy at the University of Maryland, was abducted yesterday. He was beheaded at an undisclosed location. His remains are on display, hanging from a bridge in Baghdad. The Islamic militant group al-Shahid has claimed responsibility. The following tape comes to us from Al-Jazeera.*

The image on the screen showed a frightened Doctor Nolan in his final moments, begging for American intervention. Tied to a chair with his hands secured behind

him and a blade at his throat, Nolan whimpered. Two men
masked in hoods flanked him.

Wearing his military uniform, Yousef Mugniyeh spoke
confidently. "This American accepted money from us. He
agreed to provide us something in return. He did not live up
to his part of the bargain. He betrayed us. He betrayed our
people. He betrayed our cause. Allah has decreed an eye for
an eye. More retribution is yet to come."

English subtitles translating from the Arabic rolled
out across the bottom of the screen. Rami did not need to
read them. He understood exactly what Yousef had said. In
horror, Rayna shrieked. The phone rang. Rami grabbed it.
"Yes?"

"Rami, are you okay? Do you know about Nolan?"

"Kamil!" Rami's voice begged urgency. "I do not care
about myself, but Rayna . . . and my son . . . and Nolan. Poor
Nolan. He did not deserve this. He was only trying to do the
right thing. Such a good man. He would not harm anyone.
And his daughter. Anna was so close to him." Fractured
sentences revealed Rami's broken spirit. "What do I say to
her? I must . . . I must . . . " his voice trailed off.

"Rami, I have more bad news. Nolan told Yousef that
you destroyed the bacteria. He spilled everything, hoping to
save his head. Literally. You are his next target. Then Rayna.
Yousef is on a rampage."

Rami's heavy, irregular breathing resonated over the line.

"I just hung up with Omar. He's been trying to reach
you."

"My cell is turned off."

"I gave Omar your unlisted home number. Rami, you
must speak with him when he calls."

"You know I have my doubts about Omar."

"Listen to me, Rami. Omar said he is no longer afraid of Yousef. He loathes the man and hates living under his domination. Omar told me there's nothing more for him to lose. He wants his life back, and killing Yousef is his only hope. Omar is asking for our help. Doesn't that tell you something?"

"I will not gamble Rayna's life on Omar's words. I do not trust him."

"Omar warned you of the World Trade Center attack. Doesn't that count for something?"

"But Eli is not . . ."

"Omar had nothing to do with that attack, and you know it. He's not responsible for Eli's death. Now, do you want Yousef dead or do you want Rayna dead? Those are your options."

Weary, Rami dropped the phone, buried his head in his hands, and cried. Rayna picked up the receiver, "Kamil, I'm going to put Rami back on, but understand how very distraught he is." She placed her arm around Rami's shoulders and put the phone to his ear. "Listen to Kamil."

"Rami, Omar has a pilot's license and has convinced Yousef to let him fly the plane that will meet you in Mexico. Your orders will be to turn over the bacteria and the formula."

"Kamil, I am going to kill the evil monster. With my bare hands I will kill Yousef. I should have done it a long time ago."

"Rami, listen to me. Alexis and I will be there tomorrow. She'll arrange for a few days off to stay with Rayna while we're gone. I have an early morning interview, then we'll head out. We should be at your place by no later than three. Don't do anything foolish. Wait until we get there."

* * *

In the late afternoon of the next day, Rayna and Alexis sat at the kitchen table sharing a pot of tea while contemplating the dire situation. In the study, behind closed doors, Rami and Kamil talked with Omar on the speaker phone.

A nervous edge filtered through Omar's muffled voice. "I do not have much time. At any moment, I may have to hang up. Can you both hear me?"

"Yes, barely. But we can hear you," Kamil established.

"At noon on Saturday, I will fly a small plane into Reynosa, Mexico, and land on a dirt strip, which someone has labeled a private airport. I have been instructed to pick up a package from Rami that contains the bacteria and the formula. But since Yousef now believes that Rami does not have the bacteria, he waits to see what will be given in its place. I suggest you make it a snake. A very large, very alive snake. A real serpent. Kamil, do you remember I once told you that snakes are Yousef's downfall?"

"I remember, Omar. We will have a snake with us."

"Rami, a man named Saleem will be on the plane with me. Yousef has directed him to shoot you. Once you are out of the way, Yousef will go after Rayna. He and Abdallah intend a grisly torture for her . . . a slow, cruel death. They know Rayna is a Jew."

Rami's stomach plunged. His dark eyes blazed with deadly hatred for the man he wanted to kill. It was not for himself that he feared, but for Rayna. What Yousef planned for her drove him mad. He could not bear the prospect. "How do I know I can trust you?"

"You cannot know except for what I tell you. Time is not on our side, so decide quickly."

Rami let out a long, audible sigh. "I need to think."

"I warned you about the attack on the World Trade Center. I backed Rayna when you were both in the Triple Frontier . . . in a restaurant with Yousef . . . remember?"

"My wife is a Jew. Why would you want to protect a Jew?"

"My father used to say that Muslim leaders use Jews as pawns to condition the people. Rallying around a common enemy unites Muslims, diverts attention away from the repressive regimes they live under, and keeps the masses from rising up."

"I remember your father well. He is a wise and tolerant man . . . soft-spoken and kind to everyone."

"Rami, my father died last year. I loved him very much."

"I am so sorry, Omar. I did not know."

Quietly listening to the conversation, Kamil put his hand up, motioning for Rami to accept Omar's help. "Omar," Kamil jumped into the dialogue, "we'll work together. All three of us."

"So it will be. I will keep in touch, but I must go now."

"Wait, Omar! What do we do next?" Rami zealously pursued.

"Wait for Yousef's instructions. Be in Reynosa at noon on Saturday with the snake."

* * *

Two hours had passed before Rami and Kamil emerged from the study. Alexis set the table and put out the salad. Rayna removed the vegetable lasagna from the oven. Over dinner, Rayna picked at her food. "Poor Nolan. There's no justice. What kind of a cruel, hateful world is this? Poor Nolan," she lamented. "He never had a chance. Like Eli never had a chance." Teary-eyed, she looked up at her sister-in-law. "I'm sorry, Alexis."

"It's okay."

"Who's next?" Rayna snapped. "Me? Rami? What about you, Kamil? Maybe Alexis. Maybe my son." Fright cast a dark shadow over her already wistful state. She turned to Rami, "When did you say you're leaving? Early Friday? The day after tomorrow? These may be our final hours together."

"Rayna, rrawhee, this stress is not good for the baby."

"Is this our destiny? My son . . . without his father?"

"You can control your destiny," Kamil proposed.

"Don't tell me about controlling destiny, Kamil," Rayna barked. "Tell me about my brother. Was Eli able to control his destiny? And what about Nolan? And your family? Your father? Your mother? Your brothers and sisters? Every one of them dead. So tell me, Kamil. Tell me how to control destiny. Tell me how! It's a random world. Random! Be careful you're not in the wrong place at the wrong time, because *random* will get you." Pressing the palms of her hands against her eyes, Rayna forced back the tears.

Rami turned his chair and blanketed his arms around his wife. "Rayna, this agitation is not good for you, and it is not good for the baby."

"Rayna is right," Alexis interrupted. "Life is full of randomness. But if Yousef plans to kill, we would be insane to sit back, to hope, and to wait for random's intervention. We would be insane to believe that random's meddlesome trail of demons will refrain from leaving a mark on us. Where, Rayna, tell me where would humanity be if some brave people did not take risks to make this world a better, safer place." Deliberate with her speech, Alexis hoped to catch Rayna's attention. "I have already lost one husband. I loved your brother. He'll always have a place within me. I don't want to lose another husband. I love Kamil as much as you love Rami. The risk is big, but the alternative is worse." Aware that all three at the table were intently listening to her, Alexis paused, then continued. "Kamil, Rami, and Omar each want Yousef dead. Each for his own reason. My husband will not rest until Yousef is no longer a menace on this earth. And Rami would be confined to a self-imposed hell if something happened to you and he had not done all he could to save you. And let's not forget Omar, who is slowly being strangled by invisible chains." Alexis rested her hand on Rayna's. "You and I have a responsibility to provide our husbands with strong wings and strong roots. Wings to set them free to do what they must, and roots to welcome them home when they return. I have faith that Kamil and Rami will return. We both must believe that."

Rayna closed her wet eyes. Rami massaged her shoulders.

Kamil took Alexis's hand and interlaced his fingers with hers. "I could never put into words how very much I love you. I can only feel it," he whispered.

Alexis remembered Rayna describing her love for Rami in much the same way.

THIRTY-FOUR

By day the sun will not strike you, nor the moon by night. The Lord will guard you from all harm. He will guard your life. The Lord will guard your going and coming now and forever.—Psalm 121:6-8

Late Friday afternoon, July fourth, as Americans prepared for Independence Day celebrations, Rami and Kamil arrived in the border town of McAllen, Texas. Money belts were strapped inside their waistbands. Kamil had said, "Pay cash for everything. We must not leave any trails." They rented a car, drove several miles outside of town to an exotic pet shop, and purchased a boa constrictor. After securing the serpent in a glass tank with a locked-down screen lid, they set it inside a corrugated box. The two then ate dinner at a local restaurant, checked into a nearby motel, and phoned their wives.

Concerned about not hearing from Omar, Rami began to speculate on the causes. Kamil's satellite phone sounded. Lifting his eyebrows, Kamil smiled, "Go ahead, answer it."

"Yes?"

"Rami . . ."

"Omar, we were getting worried that . . ."

"I do not have much time, so let us make this quick. Is Kamil with you?"

"Yes, he is right here."

"Where are you both?"

"McAllen, Texas."

"Good. Do you have the snake?"

"A boa constrictor."

"Excellent. At noon tomorrow, I will arrive in Reynosa. You have the directions to the landing strip?"

"Yes."

"Yousef is back from Iraq, but only for a few days. We will need to move quickly. Saleem will be on the plane with me. He is ruthless and intends to kill you. Abdallah wanted the honor for himself, but Yousef put him in charge here in the Triple Frontier while he is in Iraq, so . . ." Click. The connection was lost.

Rami hung up and handed the phone back to Kamil. "Omar will be in Reynosa at noon tomorrow. Someone named Saleem will be with him, ready to kill me. Yousef's orders. Abdallah wanted the honors, but . . ." Rami shrugged nervously. "Yousef is back from Iraq. He is in the Triple Frontier, but only for a few days. Omar said we must move quickly."

"With Omar's help, we survived the jungles of Putumayo. And with Omar's help, we will survive this, too."

* * *

Early Saturday morning, as Rami and Kamil were rising in McAllen, Texas, Rayna and Alexis slumbered in Bethesda, Maryland. Not being able to sleep, the two women had stayed up most of the night talking and playing Scrabble. It was not until their eyelids grew heavy that Rayna and Alexis had finally gone to bed.

The ringing of the phone wakened Rayna. Quickly, she reached for it. "Hello."

"Good morning. Did I wake you?"

"Kamil! Where are you? Where's Rami? Are you both okay?" Impulsively, Rayna rallied from a deep sleep.

"We're getting ready to leave for Mexico. We found a man to drive us. He's charging an arm and a leg but . . ."

"What about Omar?"

"Everything is set. He'll meet us at noon."

"Please, Kamil, look out for Rami."

"You know I will. Where's Alexis?"

"She's in the guest room, probably fast asleep. We were up all night worrying about both of you. I'll get her, but first I want to speak with Rami."

"Make it quick, we don't have much time. And we want to grab some breakfast before we get on the road. This may be a long day."

"Hi, rrawhee."

"Rami, please be careful. I don't want anything to happen to you."

"I am okay. You take care of our son until I get back."

"I love you."

"Rayna . . ."

"What sweetheart?"

"I am not there to protect you, so promise to stay in the house until we return."

"I'll be fine . . ."

"No, Rayna. Promise. Stay in the house and keep the security system on. Call the police if you notice anything suspicious."

"Alexis is with me. You and Kamil are the ones who need to be careful."

"Rayna!"

"Yes, Rami. Okay." Holding the cordless phone, Rayna knocked on the guestroom door. "Guess who's on the line?"

Alexis gave out an elated yelp, "Kamil!" She tugged the phone from Rayna's hand.

* * *

Allowing themselves ample time, Rami and Kamil waited in front of the hotel. The Texan they had hired to drive them across the border pulled up in his dark green RAV4. "Good timing," Kamil uttered under his breath. "I admit, I had my doubts about this guy even showing up."

"He seems so . . . so . . ."

"Not overly bright," Kamil finished Rami's sentence. "But he's here. Come on, let's get this snake into the car before he questions what it is."

Carefully, they placed the corrugated box in the back of the vehicle while the man sat at the wheel waiting. Kamil and Rami climbed into the rear seat behind the driver.

"Howdy," greeted the man. He turned up the fan on the air conditioning and instructed Rami and Kamil to keep the doors and windows locked. "Mighty risky trip. *Bandidos* or *la policía*. Take ya pick. They're both known to rob us Americans . . . even kill us. Happens all the time. Mexico's a dangerous place. Laws don' mean a whole helluva lot. That's why I hafta charge so much for the trip."

Rami and Kamil glanced at each other, rolled their eyes, and shook their heads.

"Nevah been to this airport ya tellin' me 'bout. Ya sure ya know where it's at? If I gotta take ya back, gotta charge ya 'nothah five hunerd. Only faeh, ya know. With a wife and three young'uns, gotta make a livin'." When the man paused, Rami and Kamil hoped he had stopped. His peculiar accent and incessant talking were grinding on their nerves. "You ain't said nothin' 'bout me takin' ya back, but I could if ya need me to."

Once across the border, the driver reached into the glove compartment, taking out a primitive map. Rami's patience was wearing thin. "That map is not necessary. We have the directions." When the man ignored him and made several wrong turns into dead-end streets, Rami snatched the map off the front seat and crumpled it into a ball.

"Hey, why d'ya do that?"

Rami ignored the man's question.

A small plane rose in the sky. Kamil forcibly took charge of the navigation. "Follow the path of where that plane just took off." Slowly maneuvering the bumpy dirt road, the driver complained about the rough terrain ruining his tires and dirtying his car. "Keep driving," Kamil charged, "and go left at the split ahead of you."

"But my car . . ."

"You agreed to get us to a certain landing strip in Reynosa. We paid you five hundred dollars. Now, take us there or return the money," Rami challenged.

The man kept on driving. Soon, a meager landing strip came into view. "That's it! Pull in over there and wait," Kamil instructed.

The driver pulled the car over to the side and turned off the ignition. "Ya di'in' say nothin' 'bout me waitin'. That'll cost extra."

Rami threw the man a harsh look.

"How long do I hafta wait?"

"Until we tell you to leave."

"Two hunerd if ya wa'me to wait. Two hunerd bucks for every twenee minutes. Real dangerous heah, ya know. Gotta get back. Wife an' kids 'spectin' me . . ."

"You just wait!" Rami put two one-hundred-dollar bills in the man's hand. "If it is longer than twenty minutes, you will wait longer. Two hundred dollars for every twenty minutes. And if we return to Texas with you, that means another five hundred more. Not bad for a day's work," Rami said, further tempting the man, "And there is a big tip for you, if you do your job right."

The man beamed greedily. "Sure am grateful to ya. I'll stay right heah an' wait."

"Good! You do that!" Rami did not like the leverage the driver was taking but knew that he and the vehicle were their only means of escape, if it became necessary. He glanced at his watch, then looked at Kamil, "Eleven-fifty-five . . . five more minutes."

* * *

"Rami, help me lift this box." They set the boa constrictor down on the outer edge of the paltry runway, then confirmed that their handguns were in place. They waited. Five minutes. Ten minutes. Twenty minutes. The intense noon sun beat down fiercely. Temperatures hovered at one hundred ten degrees. Reaching into their backpacks,

Rami and Kamil took out bottled water. The liquid was warm, almost to the point of being hot. They drank anyway. Kamil looked at his watch, "Twelve-thirty." The two grew more restless.

The driver hit the horn hard, "Ya wa'me to wait longah? 'Nothah twenee minutes, 'nothah two hunerd," he called out.

With his nerves frayed, Rami lost his temper and stomped toward the vehicle. Following close behind, Kamil held up ten fingers and motioned to the driver. "In ten minutes, we'll bring you another two hundred dollars."

The man shook his head and turned the key in the ignition.

"No!" bellowed Rami, throwing money into the open window. "You wait until we tell you to leave. Another thousand dollars is riding on it for you. If you leave before we tell you . . ."

Kamil drew his gun. "My aim is good. *Real good.* Even from a distance."

"Yes, suh. Yes, suh. Right heah. I'll wait right heah."

* * *

The sound of engines loomed above. Rami and Kamil looked up. A small plane was descending. The Cessna twin touched down on the rough terrain, bouncing along before coming to a stop. Clouds of dust blanketed the air. Rami and Kamil covered their faces.

The cabin door flew open. Standing in the hatch was a round-bellied man with a plump face and a bald head. He let down the steps. From above, he shouted in Arabic, "Which one of you is Rami?" Rami broke out in a profuse sweat. He was an easy target for Saleem. His eyes darted to Kamil for assurance.

"I have you covered," Kamil said. "Don't let him see you waver."

Stepping forward, Rami looked up. "I am Rami, and who are you?"

"It doesn't matter who I am. Who is that with you?"

"Where is Omar? I agreed to meet Omar. I have a package for him," Rami shouted over the noise of the engine.

Kamil kept his hand concealed on the gun.

"Who is that with you?" the man asked again.

"A friend."

"You were told to come alone." He pointed a thirty-eight revolver directly at Rami. "Ask your friend to turn slowly and walk away. He is not to look back, or I will kill both of you."

"I knew not to trust Omar."

"Take it easy, Rami. Smile. Nod your head. Don't get on that plane without me. Put your hand on your gun. Don't hesitate to use it." Slowly, without turning, Kamil began backing away, his keen eyes not leaving the scene. Intuitively, he raised his weapon. Two shots rang out. Blood spurted from Saleem's shattered face. As the man tumbled to the ground, red fluid oozed across the back of his shirt.

Appearing in the aircraft hatch, Omar threw down a large, black canvas sack. "Hurry! Make sure Saleem is dead and get his gun. Put his body in this and bring him up. We will get rid of the corpse in some remote area. It is too risky to leave him here."

Kamil climbed the steps, hauling the sack with Saleem's dead body over his shoulder. Rami followed with the serpent.

Omar latched the cabin door, sat in the cockpit, threw the engines into full throttle, and rolled the plane across the strip, stirring up dust before soaring into the cloudless sky. "Which one of you fired that second shot?" Omar asked with a subtle grin.

"I did," Kamil answered. "But if you hadn't first fired from the back . . ."

"Ouch!" Omar grimaced. "Then Saleem might have gotten Rami."

* * *

The driver from McAllen was the only witness. "Holy shit! My thousan' dollahs gone." He swerved the car around and took off without looking back. "Lord Jesus, take me home, 'cuz I ain't seen nothin'. I nevah came to this place, and this nevah happened."

THIRTY-FIVE

A wise man quickly evaluates each step and moves with confidence. A fool follows his basic instincts although they often lead him astray.— Baltasar Gracián

For two days, Rayna and Alexis had been confined inside the house. On Friday, they prepared Syrian dishes and baked Syrian pastries. They left aside portions for themselves, stored the balance in Pyrex containers, and stacked the food neatly in the freezer. In the evening, Rayna and Alexis played Scrabble, then stayed up all night talking and worrying.

On Saturday, they lathered their faces with green mud, popped in a video and watched the humorous antics of Diane Keaton and Jack Nicholson in *Something's Gotta Give*, and began the first patches of their joint quilt-making effort. At midnight, Rayna and Alexis got ready for bed. For a second night, they stayed up until dawn, talking and worrying while they added more patches to their quilt. Until their men were home and out of danger, they would remain unsettled.

* * *

Late Sunday morning, Rayna made French toast. The two woman read the paper, showered, and dressed. Alexis pulled out the Scrabble. "No. No more, Alexis. I don't know about you, but I'm going crazy worrying about Rami and Kamil. I'm going to crawl out of my skin if I don't get out of this house for a while."

"No, Rayna. We're not going anywhere. I gave my word to Kamil and to Rami that we would stay put until they return."

"Alexis, we need a break . . . both of us. Just for a few hours . . . to the mall. We'll shop, have dinner, see a movie. It'll do us both good."

When Alexis resisted, Rayna said she would go herself. No matter how much Alexis tried, she could not change Rayna's mind. "You leave me no choice, Rayna. Even a major earthquake couldn't change your mind. I either go with you or let you go yourself. Either way, I'm breaking Kamil's trust in me . . . and Rami's, too. I don't like this."

Rayna hesitated, then went up to her bedroom and changed into a pink top and purple slacks that had a drawstring waist she could release as her pregnancy progressed. She picked up her tote and slung it over her shoulder. "Ready?"

Exasperated, Alexis donned black slacks and a multi-colored tie-dyed tee. She tried to call Kamil to let him know of their outing. She could not get through. Picking up her small purse, she let it dangle from her fingertips. "Yes, I'm ready." She looked at Rayna. "I want to try Kamil one more time before we leave. Maybe I can get through." Alexis still could not get a connection.

"You'll try again later when we get back." Rayna double-checked that all in the house was closed up. She then activated the alarm. Backing out of the driveway, neither noticed the black sedan lagging inconspicuously behind.

* * *

Inside the air-conditioned mall, they dodged the people and walked briskly for an hour, determined to fit in some much-needed exercise. A leisurely shopping spree followed. Alexis bought sandals, two pants outfits, and a shirt for Kamil. Rayna purchased underwear, maternity clothes, and a stuffed otter for the baby. "I once told Rami that in my next life, I want to come back as an otter. They eat, sleep, play, and make love," Rayna laughed.

"In my next life, I'll join you," Alexis responded with amusement.

Sticking closely together, they carried their new purchases to the car, locked them in the trunk, and returned to the mall, unaware of the two men observing them. "With this place so crowded, we were lucky to get such a great parking space," Rayna commented.

* * *

After sharing an appetizer of vegetable lettuce wraps and a meal of salmon, broccoli, and rice at the Chinese restaurant, Rayna and Alexis took the escalator up to the movie theaters. They scanned the list of films on the marquis and decided on *Bend It Like Beckham.* "Good timing," Alexis remarked as they settled into their seats during the previews.

An hour into the cinema, Rayna needed to use the restroom. "The baby is pressing on my bladder. I'll be right back."

"I'm going with you . . ."

"Alexis, I'm grateful to have you here with me, really, but let's not carry this too far. You stay so you can fill me in on what I miss. I'll be five minutes."

"No, Rayna, you're not going alone. I have strict orders from Kamil and Rami to watch over you."

"Alexis, would you like to hold my hand while I pee?" She smiled, trying to soften her sarcasm. "I'll be right back." Rayna picked up her tote and eased her way out of the row.

* * *

"That's her." The two men were waiting patiently for the right moment. Yousef had been resolute with his orders. Rayna was to be taken alone—no witnesses and no one else hurt.

Moviegoers were inside the theaters. The lobby was empty except for some teenagers working the deserted concession stand. Fully absorbed in clowning around and flirting with the opposite sex, the youths never looked in the direction of the two men.

"Dark hair, gorgeous. Pink and purple clothing. Yousef described her well. Let's move . . ."

"Not so quick. Yousef never said she was pregnant. Look at her. Let her go to the bathroom. We don't want an accident on our hands."

* * *

Rayna entered the barren restroom, emptied her bladder, washed her hands, and checked her hair in the mirror. Five minutes later, oblivious to what was awaiting her, she stepped out the door, intending to return to the cinema and to Alexis. In her peripheral vision, she sighted a rugged-looking Arab. Tilting her head in his direction, Rayna sensed his dark eyes upon her. Fear struck. Intuitively, she knew to flee, but it was too late. An arm grabbed her around the neck and restrained her. A hand shoved a chloroform-soaked cloth over her mouth and nose. Rayna struggled, but quickly surrendered to the anesthetic. The two men whisked her out a rear exit.

* * *

After what seemed like much too long a time, Alexis's anxiety intensified. In the darkness of the theater, she gathered her purse and promptly left. Approaching the door to the ladies' room, she caught sight of Rayna's purple and pink tote on the floor. Alexis picked it up. She went into the restroom and called out. Silence. She checked each stall. No one. Panic seized her. Frantically, she questioned the teenagers at the concession stand. Nothing. Wildly, Alexis ran through the mall shouting Rayna's name, searching every inch of the upper level, the main level, the lower level. In the parking lot, she saw the car still there, in the same spot. It was Sunday evening, the stores were closed and the mall was relatively deserted. To any straggler who would listen, she described her sister-in-law with impeccable detail. Her hands shook, her voice quivered. Alexis pleaded for help. Sympathetic strangers tracked down a security guard and led him to Alexis. The police were called in. A wider search began. Trembling, Alexis took out her cell phone, hoping to reach Kamil, horrified by what she would have to tell him.

* * *

When Kamil chronicled Alexis's account of Rayna's disappearance, Rami's blood curdled. Excruciating waves of terror flooded his consciousness. Desperation seized every part of his body. He felt as if he were plunging into the depths of a dark ocean. An infinite craving to be forever with Rayna overpowered him. He must return home to find her.

* * *

The county police chief ordered an extensive search for the well-known journalist. By early the next morning, all major television programming, radio stations, and newspapers headlined Rayna's disappearance. A nationwide hunt was underway.

* * *

In Ciudad del Este, plans needed to be altered. Rayna's kidnapping changed everything. With flight schedules, connections, and layovers, it would take almost two days to get home, so Omar volunteered to fly Rami directly back to Washington in the morning. Kamil would join them, not wanting to abandon Rami in his distress. Carrying out their plot would have to wait.

"Where is he?" Rami nervously paced the floor of the hotel room. "Omar should have been here two hours ago. Two hours ago! We should never have trusted him. Where is Rayna? Where is my wife? What has happened to her?" he cried in anguish.

Kamil's heart ached for the man he now considered to be his family. Putting his arms around Rami, Kamil held him. "Take it easy, my brother. The police and the FBI are looking all over the country for Rayna. They'll find her."

Several taps on the door almost stopped Rami's heart. It was Omar. Unrestrained, Rami jumped all over him with physical and verbal attacks. Kamil quickly moved to calm Rami. Patiently, Omar waited for his friend to quiet down so he could tell him about Rayna.

"Rami, you must listen to what Omar has to say. Your hysterics will not help us to find Rayna."

A beleaguered-looking Omar sat down and peered at Rami. "I have seen your wife. She is here in Ciudad del Este, brought in just hours ago. That is why I am late getting here. Yousef and Abdallah have her shackled in chains. Rayna's life is dangling because Yousef says you double-crossed him. They plan to behead her like they did Nolan."

"Noooo. Noooo." Rami sobbed. "Noooo."

"Rami, Yousef believes Saleem shot you dead. He now regrets that order. Yousef is obsessed with getting his hands on the bacteria, and is now hanging onto a false notion that Nolan lied. Rayna will slowly be tortured until she provides information that satisfies Yousef. Since you are supposedly dead, Yousef is desperate. He sees Rayna as his last hope."

Crazed, Rami grabbed Omar's shirt and pulled at it. "I want to see Rayna. Take me to her. I need to be with her . . ."

Gently, Kamil sat Rami down. "Be grateful Rayna is still alive. That means we have a chance to save her. Omar and I need your help to do that. Your falling apart serves no useful purpose. It will not help Rayna."

"I know it is hard, Rami, but you must get hold of yourself. There is no time to waste on emotions. The three of us must work together quickly, and not lose sight of what we have to do. The slightest slip will be our downfall. The tiniest mistake will cost Rayna her life." Omar made his point.

"Rami, are you with us? Do you understand what Omar just said? We're going to rescue Rayna."

Rami nodded. Omar withdrew a piece of paper from his pocket and unfolded it. On one side, he drew a map of the vicinity, indicating where they now were. He marked the building where Rayna was being held, and the route to the city's small airport. On the other side, Omar sketched the exterior and interior of the building, including the room that imprisoned Rayna.

* * *

For the first time, Omar was in a position of total control. Rayna's survival depended on him. Yousef's death depended on him. Abdallah's death depended on him. Their own lives depended on him. Being in charge empowered Omar, and he liked the feeling. "From my experiences with Yousef and Abdallah, this strategy is our only hope. We must follow it to the last detail, concentrating and thinking very clearly every second. We cannot afford a misjudgment or a wrong move. Everything depends on our working together, each doing his part. Emotional anguish will ruin the equation." Omar aimed his words more toward Rami than Kamil. Getting Rami in line was his main concern.

"We're with you," Kamil confirmed.

As Omar drafted the plan, Kamil said that he wanted to be the one to kill Yousef. Rami insisted that he should be the one to save Rayna. In the end, it was Omar's decision that held.

"Rami, you need to stay focused. We will not be able to rescue Rayna while Yousef and Abdallah are alive. They must be dealt with first. When we have them out of the way, then we can save Rayna. If you attempt to reverse the order, you will never get Rayna out alive, and you will get us all killed. Are you listening to me, Rami?"

"Yes, Omar. I am listening. I will do anything. Whatever it takes. I will not let you down. I will not let Rayna down."

Omar gave Rami an encouraging hug, then looked up at Kamil. A thin smile of relief crossed his lips. Deliberately, Omar did not go into details about Rayna's current state. He had already told Rami enough. Omar would not tell Rami that Rayna's arms were spread like an eagle, shackled in irons that were anchored into a stone wall by rappelling hooks. He would not tell Rami that Rayna's ankles were securely roped together. He would not tell Rami that blood dripped down from the insides of her legs into a puddle of clear liquid from her water bag breaking. Rayna hung like Jesus on the cross above a sanguine pool that had formed on the cement floor below. Omar would not tell Rami any of this. Rami would know soon enough.

Following Omar and Rami out the door, Kamil lifted the corrugated box, carried it out to the car, and set it in the trunk. He turned off his satellite phone. Nothing must distract him.

* * *

In front of a one-story stone and concrete structure, Omar brought the car to a halt. Rami and Kamil ducked their heads.

Omar exited the vehicle and approached the two guards standing watch. Brandishing Glock automatics, they greeted him. Omar had become a familiar face in the Triple Frontier's Muslim community. "Yousef is expecting me," he smiled affably, proceeding to make friendly small talk. "There is a problem with this door . . . with the lock. Yousef wants it fixed right away." Purposely, Omar jiggled the heavy brass latch. Both guards turned to look, exposing their backs to the street. Omar had succeeded in diverting their attention.

With silencers, Kamil and Rami fired several shots. The guards lay dead. Their weapons were retrieved and their bodies dragged behind the building and hidden among tall bushes.

Omar pushed down on the heavy brass latch and opened the door. Rami lifted the box from the trunk and followed Omar into the building. Kamil remained out front keeping vigil, ready to shoot anything and anyone looking suspicious.

* * *

Cautiously, Rami and Omar walked down the dim, narrow corridor. They passed the room where Rayna was kept hostage. Omar pointed to the locked door and nodded.

Rami's teeth clenched as he tried hard to keep focused. Slipping into the only obscure alcove in the long hallway, Rami quietly set down the corrugated box, closed his eyes, and silently prayed. *Please, Allah, give me the strength to do what I must. I do not want to live in this world without Rayna.*

* * *

Omar banged on the heavy wooden door, identified himself, punched in four digits on the keypad, and entered the dismal space. Flaunting a pistol, Abdallah stepped aside.

"Where is Saleem?" Yousef spouted.

"I do not know." Omar eyed Rayna hanging like a piece of meat. A blinding light glared in her face. She turned her head toward Omar and opened her eyes. Two dark sockets pleaded with him. Then Rayna's eyelids shut. Her lips moved, mumbling something over and over. Omar inched closer, but he did not understand the words.

"*Shema Yisrael, Adonoi Elohaynu, Adonoi Echod.*" Hear, O Israel, the Lord our God, the Lord is One. In Hebrew, Rayna was reciting the central prayer of the Jewish faith, the single sentence affirming God's wholeness, the final words just before death.

"Omar, where in the hell is Saleem? Why isn't the prick here when I need him? He did return from Mexico with you?" Yousef's volatility was on the rise.

Still eyeing Rayna, Omar nodded. "I already told you he did."

"Then where is he? Did Saleem shoot Rami?"

"Yes, he did what you ordered . . . what you wanted."

With her eyes still closed, Rayna's body jerked, then slumped.

The room was musty and dingy. It had no windows. The only furniture was a metal desk and two chairs. Yousef grabbed something off the desk and shoved it into Omar's hand. "A tape of the Jewish whore," he snickered. "Get it to Al-Jazeera. The Arab satellite network will show the world that no one will save a slimy Jew. Muslims everywhere will praise the beheading of this Jewish whore who seduced one of our own men. Until she speaks and tells us what she knows about the bacteria, Abdallah will cut off her fingers, one by one."

Abdallah let out an eerie, contemptuous snort. Omar put the tape in his pocket. "Yousef, I have something for you."

"Not now, Omar. First the tape to Al-Jazeera. Later we talk. Now, go!"

Omar did not move. "What if I told you that I have the bacteria . . . and the formula? What if I told you that nothing was destroyed and Doctor Nolan had lied?"

"Omar, if this is a joke . . ."

"I would not jest about something so serious."

Yousef looked at Abdallah, then, with skepticism, back at Omar. "You have the bacteria?"

"Yes, Yousef, I have the bacteria."

"Where? Show it to me. Now!" Yousef's mouth curled up sardonically.

"Be careful, boss," Abdallah warned.

"After Saleem carried out your orders, I had him retrieve a large carton that Rami brought with him. It sat on the ground when Rami fell dead on the landing strip. The bacteria is enclosed in a glass tank. A manila envelope with the formula is taped securely to the back." Omar smiled, "Yousef, the power to rule has just become yours."

"Be careful, boss," Abdallah warned again.

"Have I ever given you reason to doubt me, Yousef?"

"No, Omar, you haven't." Surrendering to temptation, Yousef drooled at the prospect of supremacy, at the thought of controlling the world, at the pleasures of unimaginable riches. He took the bait. "Omar, you're a genius. I will reward you greatly for this." He turned to Abdallah, "You stay here with the Jewish harlot. Do not harm her, yet. Not until I return. I'm going out with Omar." Indulging in thoughts of ascendancy to a diadem, Yousef eagerly followed Omar, pulling the door shut behind him. A false sense of infallibility lured him.

* * *

Out in the corridor, Omar coughed twice, signaling to Rami. Silently lifting the lid off the tank, Rami firmly grasped the serpent in two places—just below its head and right at its tail. Moving swiftly, he approached Yousef from the rear, catching the man unprepared.

Fumbling for his gun, but not quickly enough, Yousef swung around. The sight of the boa constrictor froze him in terror. Rami shoved the snake's head into Yousef's face. Omar pushed Yousef to the ground and surged back. Rami released the snake and jumped away. Swiftly, Omar drew his gun, firing the silencer into Yousef. Sensing danger, the constrictor rapidly coiled itself around Yousef, choking the breath from him. Omar fired more shots. The boa constrictor wriggled erratically, then lay motionless. Sprawled in his own blood, Yousef expired. Rami quickly retreated to the alcove and waited.

* * *

Abdallah opened the door to investigate the commotion. Omar pretended to be in distress. "Abdallah! Abdallah!" he screamed. "A snake. It was in the hallway when we came out. It attacked Yousef, strangling him. I shot the creature trying to save Yousef. Help me! Yousef needs a doctor."

Abdallah glared at Omar, then down at Yousef.

"Hurry, Abdallah! We need to get Yousef to a doctor or he will die."

Abdallah vacillated, "What about the Jewish whore inside?"

Rami flinched.

"We will lock the door. No one can get to her . . . now help me, Abdallah!"

Looking up and down the empty hallway and seeing nothing, Abdallah tucked the gun into his waistband and bent over to inspect Yousef's motionless body. From behind, Omar pointed his gun and fired four shots into Abdallah. Blood spurted. Abdallah fell over and choked out his final breath. Omar coughed once, indicating all was clear.

Rami bolted toward the door. Omar quickly unlocked it and hurried in to turn off the blinding light shining in Rayna's face. "Raynaaa!" Rami shrieked, dashing to her side. Swiftly, he scrambled to unchain her. Just as urgently, Omar moved in to help.

"Rrawhee, my love. I am here with you now. I have come to take you home. No one will hurt you anymore." Rami carried Rayna's blood-soaked, listless body to the car.

* * *

"We need to get out of here." Omar's foot hit the accelerator. He sped toward the small airport, grateful it was in the opposite direction of the slow-moving Amistad Bridge. "I see you had your own encounters," he said to Kamil, who sat beside him.

"I took out two men. They were about to enter the building. One of them did not give up easily."

"You did well, Kamil. I almost tripped over their bodies rushing to the car. Would you like to know who they were?"

"Significant players in Yousef's court?"

Omar nodded. "They were the two who kidnapped Rayna from the mall and brought her here."

"Whew! We got them all, didn't we?"

"It sure looks that way. No witnesses. Even Saleem is gone."

Kamil turned around to check on the young couple in the back seat. Rami was cuddling Rayna. Tears trickled down his cheeks, "Hurry. Rayna needs a doctor. She is hot with fever."

Leaning in toward Omar, Kamil spoke softly, "Rayna's in bad shape. How soon can you get her to a hospital?"

"Not here. We must get out of the Triple Frontier before Yousef's people find us. We did not go through this to wind up dead by someone else's hands. And beside, the medical care here is quite bad. Rayna will surely die if we leave her to doctors in this place. I am going to take a chance and get us all out of here. East to Brazil. It is Rayna's only hope. There is an excellent hospital in São Paulo, probably the best in all of South America. Patients are the rich and famous. It is less than a two-hour flight."

Rayna's limp frame shivered spastically. Rami covered her with his body, trying to keep her warm. "Rayna, my rrawhee, hold on. We are taking you to a good hospital."

* * *

Omar raised the aircraft into the sky.

"Two hours?" Kamil asked uneasily, shaking his head in despair. "I pray she makes it."

"In the compartment behind you is bottled water. In the overhead are blankets and pillows."

Kamil took the provisions to Rami, who was removing Rayna's blood-soaked clothes. Her skin was burning. Her body convulsed. "Would you like me to stay and help?" Kamil asked, sensitive to Rami's need for privacy while he undressed Rayna and wrapped her in dry blankets.

"Thank you, but I want to do this."

Kamil put his hand on Rami's shoulder, "I'll be up front with Omar if you need me for anything. I'll come back and check in a little while."

Rami clutched Rayna to his chest. Lifting the water, he carefully drizzled some into her mouth. He patted droplets of the liquid onto her burning face and kissed her lips. "Rayna, I am here. Never again will I leave you alone. Squeeze my hand if you feel me with you. Squeeze my hand, Rayna. Please squeeze my hand." She lay spiritless. Her breathing was shallow. "Yousef is dead. Abdallah is dead. No one can hurt us anymore. You will get better. I know you will get better. Just do not leave me. I cannot make it without you. I love you, Rayna. I love you."

* * *

"Kamil, I need your help," Omar called out to him while concentrating on the skies. "I am headed toward one of the best medical centers in all of South America. We must alert them to Rayna's condition so they will be ready for her when we arrive. The hospital has a small runway. It's for their affluent patients. I want to set the plane down on the hospital grounds. Someone will need to guide me in. Use your satellite phone and see what you can do." Omar provided as much information as he knew, but he had no phone number. "I cannot risk asking for help over the plane's communication system. You understand?"

"Yes, I understand." Kamil dialed Alexis.

* * *

"Kamil, we've been sick with worry. Abe is here with me. He's falling apart . . ."

"Alexis, don't talk. Just listen. I need your help. Yousef and Abdallah are dead. So are the two men who kidnapped Rayna. Rami and I are with Omar. He's flying us to São Paulo in a private plane. Rayna is with us. She's in very bad shape. Here's what I need you to do . . ."

* * *

An hour later, Alexis called back. "Everything is set. There's a small, private landing strip by the hospital. It's used a lot. They will guide you in. A medical emergency vehicle will be waiting. Here's the number you need to contact. They are expecting your call."

"You're the one person I can always depend on. I'll be in touch as soon as I know more."

"Kamil . . . how bad is she?"

"Close to death. Prepare Abe . . . I love you. I miss you."

"Me, too. How's Rami holding up?"

"Not good. But he's fully there for Rayna."

THIRTY-SIX

There is no god beside Me. I deal death and give life; I wounded and I will heal. None can deliver from My hand.—Deuteronomy 32:39

The plane touched down. Rami nestled Rayna's listless form against him and carried her out to the waiting medical vehicle. Kamil and Omar stood at the cabin door. "Well, my friend, here is where we part company. It feels good to be rid of Yousef. I can now breathe without choking."

"Rami and I owe you our lives, Omar. We can never repay you for all you did."

"Oh, but you have. I needed you and Rami as much as you both needed me. Alone, it would have been impossible."

"What will you do now?"

"I must first return to the Triple Frontier and clear my name. Then I will return to Syria. My family needs me. It has been a year since my father's death." Omar placed his hand on Kamil's shoulder. "I will be fine. I am a free man now. Nobody owns me." Feeling more confident than he could ever remember, Omar grinned, "I am a pilot, a good one. I can always get a job . . . and it is time for me to find a wife." The two men embraced and bid goodbye. Kamil started to deplane. "Wait, Kamil." Omar held out a tape. "Yousef asked me to get this off to Al-Jazeera."

"Of Rayna?"

"Yes. Of Rayna. I trust you to destroy it."

Kamil took the tape and shook his head in revulsion. "No one will ever see it. Not even me."

"I have something else." Omar gathered Rayna's blood-soaked clothes. He stuffed them inside a large plastic bag. "If you will get rid of this, too, I will clean up all traces of blood in the aircraft and in the car. Not a hint of evidence will remain."

"My part will be done when I walk off this plane. Thank you."

"And I thank you." Omar smiled.

"Whenever you pass through New York, I expect you to stay with us. It will give Alexis much joy to know you."

"You are most kind. One day I may surprise you. Say goodbye to Rami for me. Tell him I will never find another friend like him. I pray to Allah for Rayna's recovery."

"I will give Rami your message. Salaam." Kamil stepped down and walked toward the hospital.

* * *

To clear his name in the Muslim community, and to avoid becoming a prime suspect and a hunted man, Omar had to return to the Triple Frontier. Going back and feigning shock at the massacre would divert attention away from himself. Omar was sure he could pull it off. Murder investigations in Ciudad del Este were primitive and corrupt. *Besides,*

Omar reasoned, *I am well-liked and have made many friends, neither of which is true for Saleem. I can easily point a finger at the dead man. No one would suspect the truth, that we killed Saleem back in Reynosa. Saleem's sudden disappearance will shed enough suspicion on him, and initiate a futile manhunt in the belief that Saleem is still alive somewhere out there.* Omar breathed a sigh of reprieve. *One more knot to tie and my freedom is absolute.*

* * *

Kamil made his way through the hospital's interior, searching for Rami. He found him slouched over with his head in his hands. Kamil compassionately touched Rami's arm and sat with him in silence. In time, the doctor's presence broke the quietude.

"Mr. Mahmoud?"

"Yes?" Rami jumped to his feet, desperately searching for a glimmer of hope.

Speaking in almost flawless English, the doctor delivered the grim news. "I must prepare you. Your wife has lost a lot of blood and her pressure is dangerously low. We are working to bring down the fever. Toxins have invaded her bloodstream, and she has gone into what we call septic shock, which is . . . her chances are slim."

Rami begged, "Do not let Rayna die. Please . . . please." He broke down and cried.

The doctor looked away, not wanting to give Rami more bad news. "We are doing all we can. The baby did not make it. I am sorry."

With tears streaming down his face, Rami pleaded, "Rayna cannot die. She is all I have . . . she is all I have."

"Your wife is in the best hands. A team of us are doing everything possible to save her. Now I must get back and help." Politely, he turned and left.

Losing his unborn son tore a piece out of Rami's heart. Losing Rayna would finish him.

* * *

All of Kamil's words could not comfort Rami. Only his presence mattered. So Kamil held Rami and let him cry. Haunting images of the Hamah massacre flashed before him. Terrifying wails from his three-year-old brother being yanked from his arms pounded in his ears. Holding Rami now, Kamil felt the same intensity, the same familiarity. *Don't let go. This time, Kamil, don't let go.* "Rayna will get well. She's strong and tenacious. You must believe that." Kamil offered hope, but he himself was worried about Rayna's survival.

"I did this to her. I exposed Rayna to Yousef. If it were not for me, Yousef would never have known Rayna . . . Rayna would not be . . ."

"Rami, this is no more your fault than it is Rayna's. But Rayna did insist on leaving the house when you asked her not to."

"No!" Rami sat upright. "If Rayna had stayed in the house, Yousef's men would have found their way in, endangering Alexis as well."

"I'm so sorry, Rami. I was not placing blame on Rayna. I was just . . ."

"I need to be alone." Rami edged away from Kamil and closed his eyes.

Kamil backed off, giving Rami his space. Stepping outside the complex, Kamil called Alexis.

* * *

"It's my fault," she cried. "I should never have let Rayna out of my sight. Oh God, if Rayna dies . . . I did this to her. I did this . . ."

"No. You didn't do this to her. Yousef was determined. His men would've gotten to Rayna no matter where she was."

"What am I supposed to tell Abe? He's inconsolable."

"Tell Abe that Rayna's a fighter, and with our prayers, she will recover."

"Abe and I have a direct flight into São Paulo. We're leaving Kennedy tonight and should arrive early tomorrow. We'll get a taxi straight to the hospital."

"It will be good to have you here . . . Alexis, does Rayna's mother know?"

"Yes, Sarah knows, and she's still the same Sarah. Abe said she won't ever forgive Rayna for marrying Rami, or me for betraying her son by marrying you."

"How sad for her. I love you. You know that, don't you?"

"Yes, I know. I love you back. Kamil . . . I want Rayna to get better. God, I want her well again."

"She will . . ."

"I have to go. Patients are waiting, and Abe is coming to pick me up in two hours. See you tomorrow."

"Wait! Alexis, did you speak with Simon?"

"Yes. He's already alerted the police to call off the search. He told them that Rayna was kidnapped, a ransom had been paid, and she's safe. When she's up to it, she'll make a statement. But for now, Rayna needs her privacy and is in seclusion. And, for her protection, no charges will be brought against the kidnappers."

"Good. Simon handled it well. But then again, he always does."

"Bye. Love you."

* * *

Kamil's stomach growled. He could not remember the last time he and Rami had eaten. Inside the hospital, he found a coffee shop, and returned with food for both of them. Rami's eyes were shut. Kamil sat beside him and gently nudged his arm. "You must eat something."

"I am not hungry."

"Yes you are. You must get some food in you to be strong for Rayna. She will need your strength to help her recover."

Rami pushed away the food. Kamil persisted. Another hour passed. A nurse came out. "Mr. Mahmoud?"

"Yes?"

She spoke English with a heavy Brazilian accent. "Your wife's condition is steady. We are monitoring her closely. Be patient. It will be a while." She turned and left without giving Rami a chance to speak.

An excruciatingly long five hours passed. Kamil concentrated his energy on consoling Rami. He was extra cautious with his words, sensitive not to add to Rami's suffering.

In time, the doctor returned. "Your wife is a fighter. The next seventy-two hours are critical. If she makes it through, then her chances for a full recovery are excellent. We are in the process of moving Rayna to a private room. Nurses will observe her around the clock, and I will be on call and checking in. Intravenous tubes are keeping her alive. She is heavily sedated. Someone will come and get you once your wife is settled in. You can hold her hand and talk with her, but she probably won't know you are there. Be patient."

* * *

Sitting by Rayna's bedside, Rami held her hand and tenderly stroked her face. He focused on her every breath and heartbeat. Seven years of memories flooded his mind: The first moment he saw her. Their deep-seated conversations. Their long walks. The beginning of their intimacy. Their bantering and laughter. Their marriage. The belated honeymoon to the Triple Frontier. The months she cared for him after his ordeal in the jungles of Colombia. The trip to Spain. Their grief over losing Eli. Rayna's determination to keep them both on track to finish school.

Their love was everlasting. Their trust, indestructible. Their commitment, timeless. Rayna was the essence of Rami's being. Without her, he would not go on living. "Rayna, rrawhee, I am here. I have your hand." She stirred. "You will get well. Our lives will be better and safer. I swear this to you. Yousef is dead. Abdallah is dead. Those who did this to you are all dead. No one can harm us anymore." Rami bent over and softly kissed Rayna's face. "We have come too far to throw it all away now. Once, I told you that I am not strong enough to live without you. I am telling you again. I am not strong enough to live without you. You must get better. Fight, Rayna. Fight." Rami's tears flowed. "I love you so much."

* * *

By late morning, Abe and Alexis arrived. Kamil hugged his wife. Abe rushed to Rayna's side. "Rayna, it's me. It's Daddy." She did not respond. "Oh God. Oh God," he sobbed, clutching his daughter's hand. Rayna's body fluttered and she gave out a frightful sound.

Kamil scrambled to guide Abe from the room. "Any kind of agitation is not good for her. I know how hard this must be for you, especially after losing Eli."

"No. You don't know! How could you?"

"Shhhh." Kamil steadied Abe while attempting to keep his own irritation in check. "Don't you dare preach to me about loss. My entire family was killed. My parents. My brothers. My sisters. In front of me, savages beheaded my father. Syrians. Muslims. My own people did this. My three-year-old brother was torn from my arms. I have lived with my loss since I was sixteen."

The information seemed to catch Abe off guard. "I'm sorry. I didn't know."

"Well, now you do."

"Of all my sons . . . well, Eli was special. His death was my fault. I should never have asked him to go to that meeting in the World Trade Center. May God forgive me for what I have done. I killed my son. And now, Rayna. If I lose her, my life is no longer worth living. Do you know that I am only now beginning to understand what Rayna has always known. Life is not about lots of money. Life is about something much deeper."

Kamil's heart softened.

"I love my daughter. She's from my blood. She's my seed. I wish I had never let her leave home . . . never allowed her to go away to school. What was I supposed to do? When I found out about Rami, she was already married to him. He did this to her. He . . ."

"Abe, don't go there. Stop now. Don't say something you may regret later. Learn from what Rayna has tried to teach you. Life is about something much deeper. Isn't that what you just said?"

"I'm sorry about your tragedy. Losing one child or a whole family leaves an open wound . . . forever."

"Yes, it does."

* * *

For three days, Rami did not leave Rayna's side. He watched the peaks and valleys on the screen, observed her vital signs, tracked the medications and nourishment dripping into her veins, and prayed with Abe. Alexis monitored Rayna's care. Kamil provided a balance that kept everyone from falling apart.

The seventy-two-hour safety margin approached. Rayna opened her eyes. Hope erupted in the room, then quickly faded when her eyelids went down. Rami looked up at the monitor just as the last peak flattened. A horizontal line signaled Rayna's demise. Short, rapid beeps emitted from the machine.

Rami wailed, "No, Rayna! Noooooo! Come back! Come back! The other half of my soul is with you. Do not take it from me. I want you to bring it back. Bring it back . . . bring it back . . ."

Alexis dashed to the bedside. Nurses quickly moved in and called for help. In split seconds, emergency life-saving efforts were set in motion. The flat line peaked. Then another peak. Then a stronger one. Miraculously, Rayna's heartbeat fell back into rhythm. It would be another forty-eight hours before she regained consciousness.

* * *

Opening her eyes, she searched for Rami. Her gaze fell upon him. "I came back to you. My jidaw and Eli, they kept calling, but I told them you were waiting." Rayna closed her eyes and slept. Two more days passed before Rayna was fully out of danger.

* * *

Abe sat holding his daughter's hand while she slept. Kamil and Alexis prepared to leave for home. Rami stepped out into the lounge to express his gratitude and say goodbye. "In the bottom desk drawer in the study, there is a purple file folder with Rayna's passport. Please have it couriered as soon as possible. In another few days, when I take Rayna home, I do not want any attention brought upon her."

"We can do better than that." Alexis reached into one of her shopping bags. "This morning, Kamil and I went browsing in the Muslim quarter." She pulled out a long flowing black garment and a matching black headscarf. "No one will recognize her."

Rami looked at Kamil and shook his head, not quite certain. Keeping Rayna's identity hidden from the press, the police, and the public was crucial. If her whereabouts and rescue were discovered by those loyal to Yousef, it would throw Rayna's life back into crisis. Yet, given the Islamic attack on American soil, Rami was not sure that flaunting Muslim attire was wise. How best could he protect Rayna from the invasive scrutiny? Rami vacillated before coming to a decision. "Yes, we will do it, except . . . well . . . Abe. He is not leaving this hospital until his daughter is ready to walk out with him. How do I explain to Abe about Rayna's clothes?"

Kamil's laughter reverberated. "I'm sure you'll figure it out."

"Abe is a lot softer than he comes across. He's not hard and unforgiving like Sarah. Inside, Abe is mush. Good mush," Alexis smiled.

"Thank you, Alexis. I needed that reminder. And thank you both for everything. Rayna and I owe you so much. We really do love you both."

"We'll figure out a way to collect payment," Kamil laughed, then handed Rami the satellite phone. "Keep this with you. I expect you to stay in touch, daily. That's an order." He embraced Rami. "Salaam. Peace be with you. Now, I'm going home to see my daughter. Nida's grandmother could use a break."

"Give Nida many hugs from us." Rami turned to Alexis, "You are a most special lady. All of us are very lucky to have you in our lives." He hugged Alexis, genuinely appreciative of her kindness and caring.

Rami walked with the couple to the hospital's main entrance where a car was waiting. He waved goodbye. "Remember Rayna's passport."

"It's at the top of my list, after my daughter."

THIRTY-SEVEN

We are the sum of all the moments of our lives. All that is ours is in them.—Thomas Wolfe

At the house in Bethesda, Kamil proceeded into the study. He sat in the black-leather chair and reached down into the bottom drawer of the desk. Skimming through the files, he located two purple folders. Retrieving both, he browsed through the first. What Kamil found overwhelmed him. With their own money, Rami and Rayna had started an orphanage. They had taken in infants and very young children who were barely surviving in environments where guns, drugs, alcohol, hunger, and sexual and physical abuse dominated their lives. Eighteen youngsters from a mixture of backgrounds were being fed, clothed, educated, and loved. Tiny human beings were given a chance at life. *Why have I not known about this wonderful undertaking of theirs?* Returning the folder back to its place, Kamil proceeded to open the second folder. In it, he found Rayna's passport. He tucked it into his briefcase.

Much later that day, when he was back in his office in Manhattan, Kamil called the courier service that he so often relied on. Rayna's passport would arrive safely in São Paulo, and be in Rami's hands within thirty-six hours.

* * *

Reluctantly, Abe tore himself away from his daughter. Over the loudspeaker, a voice had announced the boarding of his flight to New York. He started toward the line of people at the gate, then reversed himself. "Bye, baby. I love you." One more time, he hugged Rayna, feeling the uncomfortableness of her Muslim attire. Abe grinned and shifted his gaze toward Rami. "I like you, and I see how much you love Rayna. But life would be so much easier if you were Jewish. Any chance?"

Rami shrugged his shoulders and smiled.

"Take good care of my daughter."

"You know I will . . . and Abe, our home is always open to you. You do not need an excuse to visit."

"I intend to take you up on that offer . . . often." He reached out to Rami. The two men exchanged a farewell hug, then Abe joined the dwindling line of boarding passengers.

* * *

Rami curled his arm around Rayna's waist. Noting her weakness, he gave her his support as they walked to their gate. In half an hour, the flight to Washington would begin boarding. *Forgive me, Allah, for what I have done to Rayna. Thank you for this second chance.*

* * *

It felt good to be home. After the long flight, Rayna wanted a shower and to rest. Rami helped her bathe, then bundled her in a bath towel, blew her hair dry, and got her into comfortable clothes. Lifting Rayna to the bed, Rami massaged her back until she fell asleep.

He tiptoed down the steps. In the kitchen, he looked inside the refrigerator. *Rayna will need to eat when she wakes up, and I am not going to the store and leaving her here alone.* He opened the freezer door. *If I know my wife, there must be something in here that is easy to prepare.* Instantly, Rami spotted the Pyrex containers with the Syrian food, all neatly stacked and labeled. He selected some of the frozen fare and set it out on the countertop to defrost. *When Rayna wakes up, I will only have to heat it in the microwave.*

The doorbell rang. It was Jeannie from next door. She and Stan had just gotten home from work and had seen the light on in the kitchen. She handed Rami a plastic bag full of mail. "We had no idea when you would be back, so I took the liberty. Didn't think it was a good idea for your mail to pile up outside. I'm sure there's a bunch more waiting in your post office box. Would you like us to pick it up for you? Stan and I are going out for a bite to eat. We'll be near the post office."

"Thank you. Yes. How kind of you. That would be helpful." He handed Jeannie the key.

"How's Rayna? It was all over the news . . ."

Through his fatigue, Rami generated a limp smile. He was in no mood to discuss the details with anyone, and he needed privacy. "Rayna is sleeping. When she feels up to it, I am sure you both will talk. I do appreciate your getting our mail."

"Is there anything we can do? Can I bring back some dinner . . ."

"We are fine. I took something out of the freezer. Thank you for offering."

"Call if you need anything. I'll bring the rest of your mail later." She dallied. "I'm so sorry, Rami. It must have been a horrendous ordeal for both of you."

"It was," he politely acknowledged, edging Jeannie to the door and seeing her out.

Returning to the kitchen, Rami dumped the bag of mail out on the table. Just as he was beginning to go through it, he heard a sound from Rayna and bolted up the stairs.

In the baby's room, Rayna sat in the rocker, clutching the stuffed otter. "It's so unfair," she cried. "Our son . . . not even a chance to be born. We never got to see him, to know him."

"Let us pray that our son is in a better place than we are." Rami kissed her, then lifted Rayna to his lap. Together, on the rocker, they cleaved to each other and mourned the loss of their unborn child.

* * *

Later, Rami carried Rayna down the steps and settled her on the sofa. "Would you like something to eat?"

"I need to rest a while longer."

Rami gently stroked her shoulders and neck. When she dozed again, he covered her with a light blanket, then went back in the kitchen to finish sorting the bundle of mail. A letter from Syria caught his attention. He opened it. Inside was a note from Omar.

> *Rami—I am back in Halab. All is well. Your mother asked me to forward the enclosed letter. She misses you very much.—Omar*

Rami knew Omar could not risk writing more than a few superficial words. Mail going to America was often inspected. *How wrong I have been about Omar. Three times now, he looked after Rayna. If it were not for Omar, Yousef would still be alive, and Rayna would be . . . no, I cannot think about that. I will find a way to make it up to Omar.*

Checking again on Rayna, he found her sleeping peacefully. Rami went back to the mail. Carefully slitting the thin envelope, he instantly recognized his mother's elegant Arabic script. Salha's handwriting always had an artistic flair. Silently reading her message, Rami was shaken beyond comprehension. He was not Rami Mahmoud. He was someone else. He was not Shi'ite. He was Sunni. A numbness set in. Rami sat motionless for a long time. Then, slowly, he picked up the letter and read it again.

> *My dearest son.*
>
> *Your father died three months ago. An attack of the heart came on suddenly and took him quickly. I am struggling. Zakieh and Abu help me in the souq. Your sisters also help when they can. It is my only means of support. Things are difficult without your father. I depended on him for so much. I write to you now because I am compelled to tell you the truth which I was forbidden to do when your father was alive. Ibrahim and I had been married five years. We were childless and you know how important children are to our way of life. Family and friends told your father to divorce me and find another wife who could give him sons. But*

*he would not do so. May Allah bless his memory.
It was on a Friday in late February 1982. I will
always remember that day. Your father was at the
mosque for noon prayers. The mullah announced
that a child was found wandering alone in the
streets. He asked for someone to claim the little
boy. Your father brought you home. You were
disoriented and cried for your mother. Inside the
pocket of your red jacket a note was pinned. I have
included it so you will know for sure. I saved it all
these years. I kept it hidden from your father.*

    *Ibrahim went to Hamah to look for your
family. He was told they were all killed during
the uprising. So with a blessing from Allah we
had a son. We loved you so much. You were our
joy. Shortly afterward I became pregnant with
your sister Ayisha. Then three more daughters
came. But you were our only son. Now you
must know who you really are. It is all on the
scrap of paper. In my heart you will always
be my son. In my heart I will always be your
mother. In my heart I love you.————Salha*

Rami promised himself to help Salha and to send her
money. She had been a good mother. He held the tattered
piece of paper in his hands. Over and over, he uttered the
message written in Arabic.

    *Hello. My name is Rami Adjmi. I am three years
old. I was born 10 August 1978. I am Sunni and
live in Hamah. Whoever finds me please return*

me to my parents Nida and Jawad Adjmi or to my oldest brother Kamil Adjmi.

Nida, he reflected. *Kamil's daughter, Nida, is named after his mother. My mother. Kamil is my blood brother.* All the repressed memories gushed to the surface. Vivid images of his home and family came alive. Terrified, he had clung tightly to Kamil. *"Hold me, Kamil. Hold me."* He relived the scene of his father's head falling to the ground. *"Ebeeeeee!"*

Kamil had been running with him, clutching him protectively, searching frantically for shelter, and then . . . and then . . . forcibly, Rami was snatched from Kamil. *"Kameeeeeel! Kameeeeeel! Do not let them take me away! No, Kamil! Noooooo . . ."* Sobbing, Rami's little hands stretched out to his big brother.

Kamil screamed to him, trying to grab on, trying to reach the toddler. *"I'm here, Rami. I'm coming . . . I'm coming for you."* Yet, no matter how desperate the brothers were to cling to one another, they could not stop the power pulling them apart. Alone and frightened, Rami wandered the streets, crying and hungry. Now, he remembered it all.

Rami picked up the phone and dialed Kamil.

BIBLIOGRAPHY
By Chapters

1. Surah 47:36. (2002) *The Qur'an Translation* by M.H. Shakir. Elmhurst, New York: Tahrike Tarsile Qur'an, Inc.
2. Solomon: The Song of Songs 7:11. (1985) *Tanakh, The Holy Scriptures: The New JPS Translation According To The Traditional Hebrew Text.* Philadelphia, PA: The Jewish Publication Society
3. Quintasket, Christine, Mourning Dove. (1994) *Native American Wisdom: Photographs by Edward S. Curtis.* Philadelphia, PA: Running Press Book Publishers
4. Tagore, Rabindranath. (2003) *A Simple Buddhist Guide To Romantic Happiness* by Taro Gold. St. Catharines, ON: Andrews and McMeel Publishers
5. von Schiller, Friedrich; 1759-1805; German poet, philosopher and historian. *ThinkExist.com*
6. Schneerson, the Rebbe Menachem Mendel. (1997 & 2002) *Bringing Heaven Down To Earth: condensed & compiled by Tzvi Freeman.* 100 Years Special Edition. Toronto, ON: Class One Press
7. A Samurai saying. Author unknown
8. Ecclesiastes 3:1. (1985) *Tanakh, The Holy Scriptures: The New JPS Translation According To The Traditional Hebrew Text.* Philadelphia, PA: The Jewish Publication Society
9. Wiesel, Elie; born 1928. American writer, philosopher, humanitarian, political activist, Holocaust survivor, and 1986 Nobel Peace Prize winner
10. Lao-tzu. (1988) *Tao Te Ching: A New English Version* by Stephen Mitchell. New York: Harper Collins Publishers
11. Indian marriage blessing. *The Secret* by Lee Bogle, artist. Boulder, CO: *Leanin' Tree* greeting cards
12. Roosevelt, Eleanor. (2003) *The Flying Camel* edited by Loolwa Khazzoom. New York: Seal Press, An Imprint of Avalon Publishing Group Incorporated
13. Einstein, Albert; 1879-1955; German born, American physicist, Nobel prize in physics 1921, developed theories of relativity. *ThinkExist.com*

14. Schneerson, the Rebbe Menachem Mendel. (1997 & 2002) *Bringing Heaven Down To Earth: condensed & compiled by Tzvi Freeman.* 100 Years Special Edition. Toronto, ON: Class One Press

15. Surah 36:40. (2002) *The Qur'an Translation* by M.H. Shakir. Elmhurst, New York: Tahrike Tarsile Qur'an, Inc.

16. Freud, Sigmund. (2003) *The Question Of God: C.S. Lewis & Sigmund Freud Debate God, Love, Sex, And The Meaning Of Life* by Armand Nicholi. New York: Simon & Schuster Adult Publishing Group

17. Gracían, Baltasar. (1992) *The Wisdom of Baltasar Gracian,* adapted and edited by J. Leonard Kaye. New York: Pocket Books, A Division of Simon & Schuster Inc.

18. Lao-tzu. (1988) *Tao Te Ching: A New English Version* by Stephen Mitchell. New York: Harper Collins Publishers

19. King, Reverend Bernice A. *Occasion Gallerie from Blue Mountain Arts.* Boulder, CO*: Blue Mountain Arts* greeting cards

20. Barrie, James M. (2003) *Only In Dreams, A Book of Quotes* edited by Simon Pettet. New York: Barnes & Noble

21. Isna la-wica, Lone Man. (1994) *Native American Wisdom: Photographs by Edward S. Curtis.* Philadelphia, PA: Running Press Book Publishers

22. Tennyson, Alfred Lord. (2003) *Only In Dreams, A Book of Quotes* edited by Simon Pettet. New York: Barnes & Noble

23. Excerpt from a Vietnamese poem. (1998) *the heart of the Buddha's teaching* by Thich Nhat Hanh. Berkeley, CA: Parallax Press

24. Keller, Helen. (2006) *Jokes and Quotes For Speeches.* London, UK: Cassell Illustrated, a division of Octopus Publishing Group, Ltd.

25. Surah 35:19-21. (2002) *The Qur'an Translation* by M.H. Shakir. Elmhurst, New York: Tahrike Tarsile Qur'an, Inc.

26. Talmud Yevamot 62b. (2003) *The Israelis* by Donna Rosenthal. New York: Free Press, a division of Simon & Schuster, Inc.

27. Ecclesiastes 9:7. (1985) *Tanakh, The Holy Scriptures: The New JPS Translation According To The Traditional Hebrew Text.* Philadelphia, PA: The Jewish Publication Society

28. Galilei, Galileo; 1564-1642; Italian philosopher, astronomer, mathematician. *ThinkExist.com*

29. Vashistha, Yoga. (2005) *The Book of Secrets: Unlocking the Hidden Dimensions of Your Life* by Deepak Chopra. New York:

Harmony Books, a member of the Crown Publishing Group, a division of Random House, Inc.

30. Proust, Marcel. (2002) *Practical Intuition* by Angela Martin. New York: Barnes & Noble, Inc., by arrangement with Lansdowne Publishing

31. Ecclesiastes 12:7. (1985) *Tanakh, The Holy Scriptures: The New JPS Translation According To The Traditional Hebrew Text.* Philadelphia, PA: The Jewish Publication Society

32. The Rabbinical Assembly. (1972; Second Edition 1978) *Mahzor for Rosh Hashanah and Yom Kippur* edited by Rabbi Jules Harlow. New York: The Rabbinical Assembly

33. Mead, Margaret; 1901-1978; American born anthropologist, scientist, author; focused on gender roles in primitive cultures and in American society. *ThinkExist.com*

34. Psalm 121:6-8. (1985) *Tanakh, The Holy Scriptures: The New JPS Translation According To The Traditional Hebrew Text.* Philadelphia, PA: The Jewish Publication Society

35. Gracían, Baltasar. (1992) *The Wisdom of Baltasar Gracían,* adapted and edited by J. Leonard Kaye. New York: Pocket Books, a division of Simon & Schuster Inc.

36. Deuteronomy 32:39. (1985) *Tanakh, The Holy Scriptures: The New JPS Translation According To The Traditional Hebrew Text.* Philadelphia, PA: The Jewish Publication Society

37. Wolfe, Thomas. (1995) *Look Homeward, Angel* with an introduction by Maxwell E. Perkins. New York: Scribner Paperback Fiction, a division of Simon & Schuster Inc.